Student Workbook

Today's Math

Daily Practice

Mixed Review

Test Prep

Editorial Offices: Glenview, Illinois • Parsippany, New Jersey • New York, New York
Sales Offices: Needham, Massachusetts • Duluth, Georgia • Glenview, Illinois
Coppell, Texas • Ontario, California • Mesa, Arizona

Created by Pearson Scott Foresman to supplement **Investigations in Number, Data, and Space®**
These materials do not necessarily reflect the opinions or perspective of TERC or the authors of the *Investigations* curriculum.

ISBN: 0-328-12656-X

7 8 9 10 V004 13 12 11 10 09 08 07 06

Contents

Introduction

Why This Book?

School policies vary widely on issues of homework. Some teachers are free to assign homework as they see fit, while others are required to assign work every night, every other night, or according to some other schedule depending on the age of their students.

In order to accommodate the wide range of school and district policies, enough homework is embedded in the *Investigations* curriculum that a teacher can assign homework about every other night. Furthermore, Practice Pages, Extensions, Classroom Routines (in grades K–2), Ten-Minute Math activities (in grades 3–5), and *Investigations* Games can be used to provide or create additional homework assignments.

Recently, teachers have expressed a need for an additional resource: grade-specific books that will meet three needs:

- Relate to the math content of each day's session
- Provide daily practice in number sense and operations
- Help prepare students for standardized testing

This book meets these needs.

- It provides engaging and meaningful practice that will further develop children's understanding of the basic concepts and skills that are currently being taught.
- It gives parents and other caregivers a better sense of what children are doing in math class and over the course of the school year. Most parents understand that "the basics" now encompass all areas of mathematics, not only arithmetic. And many parents are willing, and indeed eager, to help however they can. Therefore, on all student pages there are **Family Connection** notes that give parents the information they need.
- The **Mixed Review and Test Prep** sections help develop computational fluency while preparing students for the language and format of standardized tests. (These sections review concepts and skills that were taught in the previous grade.)

Family Connection

Dear Family,

Pearson Scott Foresman is pleased to introduce a new component in your child's mathematics program: Today's Math workbooks.

Sometimes your child will complete a page in class and bring it home to show you. Other times, your child might be assigned a page to complete at home (perhaps with your assistance, as time allows).

Features of Today's Math

1. The **main activity** relates to the math content of that day's math lesson (or, in some cases, to previous lessons within the current unit).
2. **Mixed Review and Test Prep** exercises prepare your child for standardized testing. Each test-prep item **(a)** helps your child review and maintain basic number skills and concepts learned previously; and **(b)** helps prepare him or her to deal with, and indeed feel comfortable with, the language and format of standardized tests.
3. The **Family Connection** notes will give you **(a)** a "snapshot" of what your child is doing in math class; **(b)** the background you need in order to help your child; **(c)** opportunities to engage in "math conversations" with your child; and **(d)** suggestions for activities you might do together with your child.

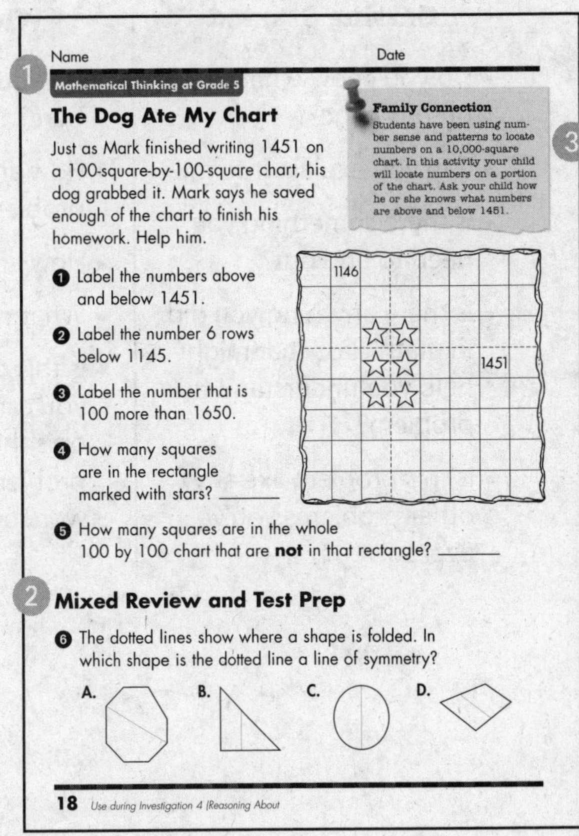

Name Date

1 Mathematical Thinking at Grade 5

The Dog Ate My Chart

Just as Mark finished writing 1451 on a 100-square-by-100-square chart, his dog grabbed it. Mark says he saved enough of the chart to finish his homework. Help him.

3 **Family Connection**
Students have been using number sense and patterns to locate numbers on a 10,000-square chart. In this activity your child will locate numbers on a portion of the chart. Ask your child how he or she knows what numbers are above and below 1451.

1. Label the numbers above and below 1451.
2. Label the number 6 rows below 1145.
3. Label the number that is 100 more than 1650.
4. How many squares are in the rectangle marked with stars? ______
5. How many squares are in the whole 100 by 100 chart that are **not** in that rectangle? ______

2 **Mixed Review and Test Prep**

6. The dotted lines show where a shape is folded. In which shape is the dotted line a line of symmetry?

A. B. C. D.

18 *Use during Investigation 4 (Reasoning About*

When Working with Your Child

Try using some of the sample questions from the chart below. They can help you start an ongoing math conversation with your child, and they will encourage your child to explain his or her mathematical thinking. It is vitally important that children learn to verbalize their thinking, voice their questions and concerns, and learn to think of themselves as effective and thoughtful problem solvers. Knowing that their parents and teachers value their thinking is very important to children.

We hope that you will enjoy working on Today's Math with your child. As always, your participation and support are greatly valued and very much appreciated.

Having Math Conversations with Your Child

SAMPLE QUESTIONS

Getting Started	While Working	Wrapping Up
• Do you know what to do on this page?	• Do you see any patterns here?	• Why did you decide to solve the problem this way?
• Can you explain it to me?	• How are these two problems alike?	• Is there another way to solve this kind of problem?
• Is there something you need to find out?	• How are they different?	• How do you know that your answer makes sense?
• Is there anything you did in math class that might help you understand this problem?	• What would happen if …?	• What kinds of math problems are easy for you?
• Is this problem like any other problems you've ever solved?	• Is this the kind of problem you can do in your head, or is this the kind of problem you need to work out on paper?	• What kinds of problems are hard for you?

Name Date

Mathematical Thinking at Grade 5

Across and Down

How many tiles across and how many tiles down is each of the rectangles? Write the numbers.

Family Connection

Students have been using tiles to build rectangles. They learned that the length and width of a rectangle name factors of the number of tiles. Have your child point out the factors shown by the rectangles on this page.

1. ____

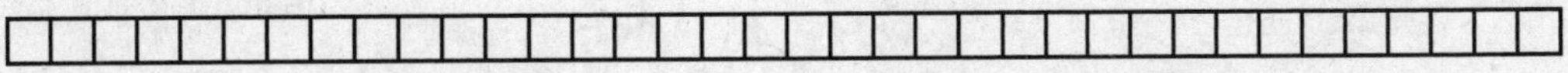

2. ____ ____

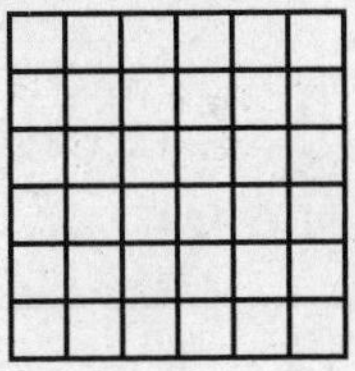

3. ____ ____

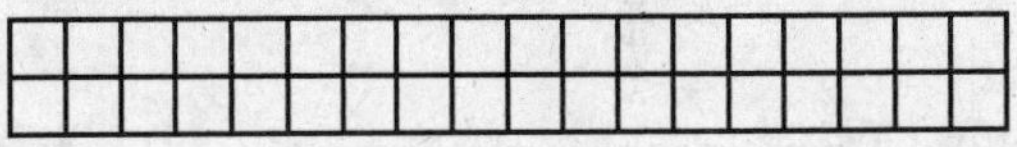

4. ____ ____

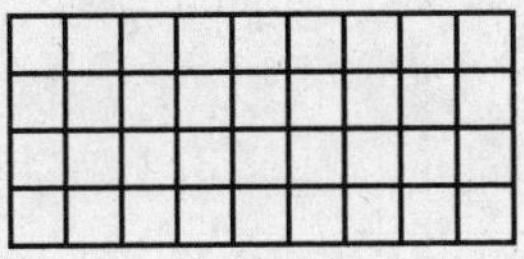

5. ____ ____

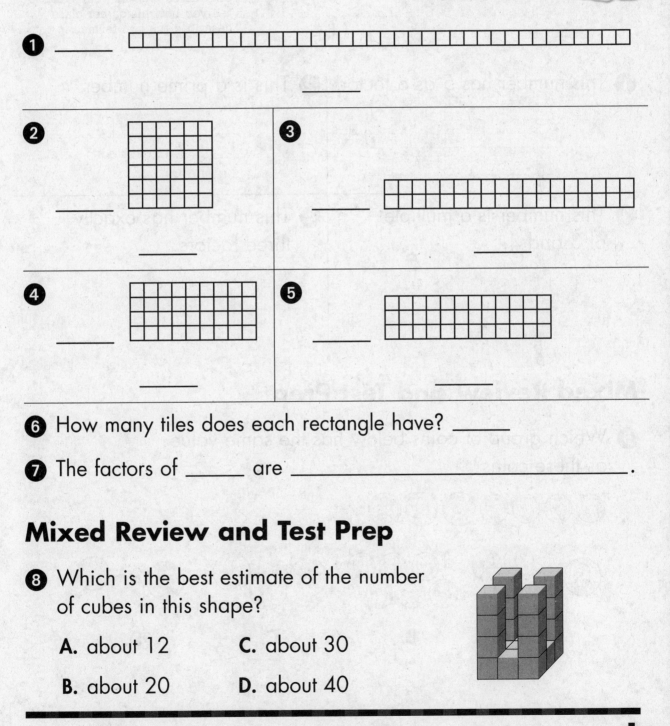

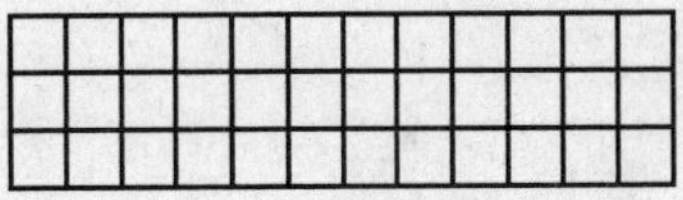

6. How many tiles does each rectangle have? ____

7. The factors of ____ are ________________.

Mixed Review and Test Prep

8. Which is the best estimate of the number of cubes in this shape?

A. about 12 **C.** about 30

B. about 20 **D.** about 40

Name Date

Mathematical Thinking at Grade 5

Think of a Number

Read the clue. Think of a number that fits. Draw and label one or more rectangles to show you are right.

Family Connection

Students are making a chart of math terms. They began by thinking up ways to explain factors and multiples. One way is by example. The factors of 12 are 1, 2, 3, 4, 6, and 12. The multiples of 12 are 12, 24, 36, 48, and so on. Ask your child to tell you how his or her class described the two terms.

1. This number has 5 as a factor.

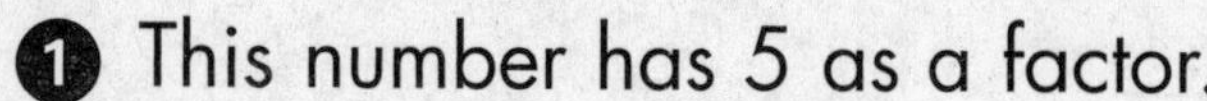

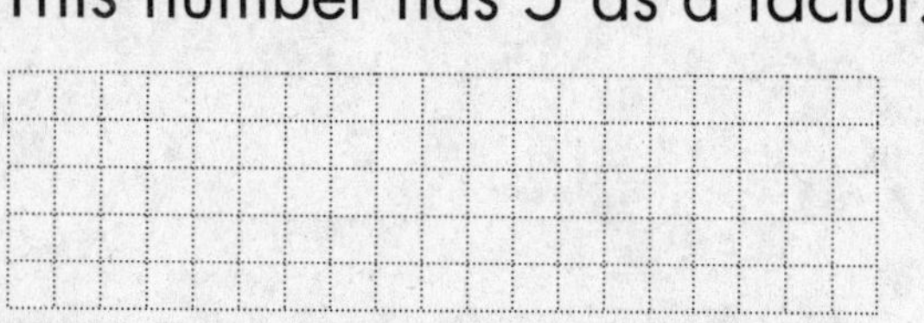

2. This is a prime number.

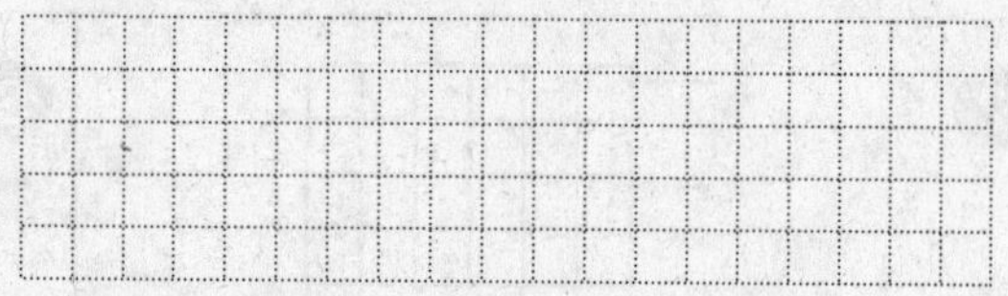

3. This number is a multiple of 3 and 4.

4. This number has exactly three factors.

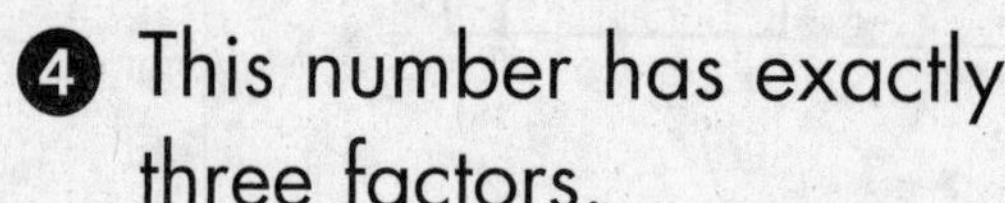

Mixed Review and Test Prep

5. Which group of coins below has the same value as these coins?

A.

B.

C.

D.

Name Date

Mathematical Thinking at Grade 5

You're So Square

Family Connection

Students have been using their tiles to learn about some special kinds of numbers. A number that can be made into a square is a square number. If the only rectangle a number can make is one tile wide, it is a prime number.

1 Draw the square that comes next. Then complete the table.

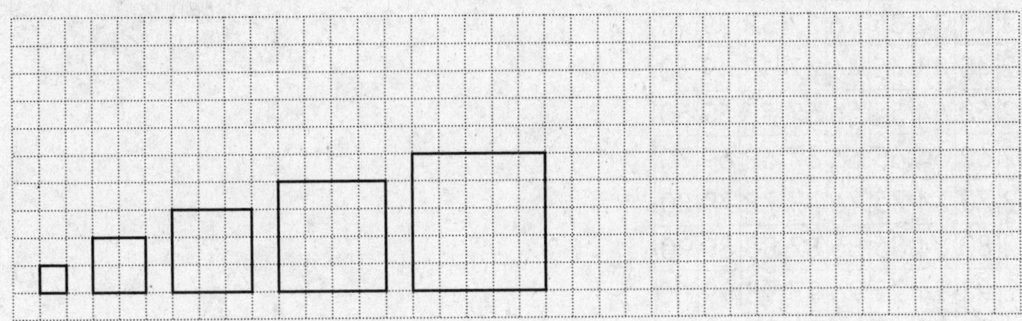

Square Number	1	4				
Factor Pairs	1×1	2×2				

Write the numbers.

2 $3^2 =$ 9

3 $6^2 =$ ____

4 $2^2 =$ ____

5 $10^2 =$ ____

6 $5^2 =$ ____

7 $4^2 =$ ____

Mixed Review and Test Prep

8 What do these rectangles show?

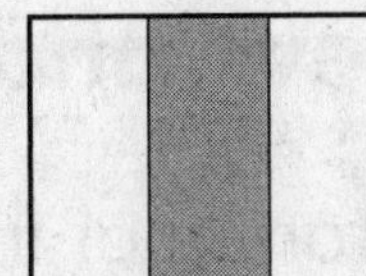
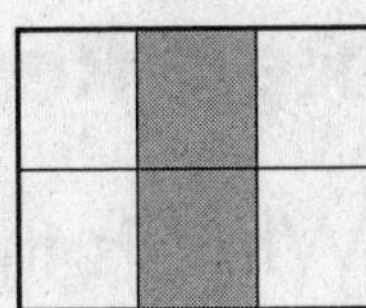

A. $\frac{1}{2} = \frac{2}{4}$

B. $\frac{1}{3} = \frac{1}{6}$

C. $\frac{1}{3} = \frac{2}{6}$

D. $\frac{1}{3} = \frac{2}{4}$

Name Date

Chart It

Family Connection

Students have been following clues to solve "What's the Number?" puzzles. One tool for recording clues is a number chart like the one shown here. Have your child show you how it can be used to solve this puzzle.

Mark the chart to help you solve the puzzle.

1	2	3	4	5	6	7	8	9	10
11	12	13	14	15	16	17	18	19	20
21	22	23	24	25	26	27	28	29	30
31	32	33	34	35	36	37	38	39	40
41	42	43	44	45	46	47	48	49	50
51	52	53	54	55	56	57	58	59	60
61	62	63	64	65	66	67	68	69	70
71	72	73	74	75	76	77	78	79	80
81	82	83	84	85	86	87	88	89	90
91	92	93	94	95	96	97	98	99	100

1. I am less than 100.
2. I am a multiple of 9.
   What numbers fit both this clue and the first clue?
   ____
3. I am a multiple of 6.
   What numbers fit the first three clues?
   ____
4. I am a square number.
   Which numbers fit all four clues? ______

Mixed Review and Test Prep

5. What is the range of these heights?

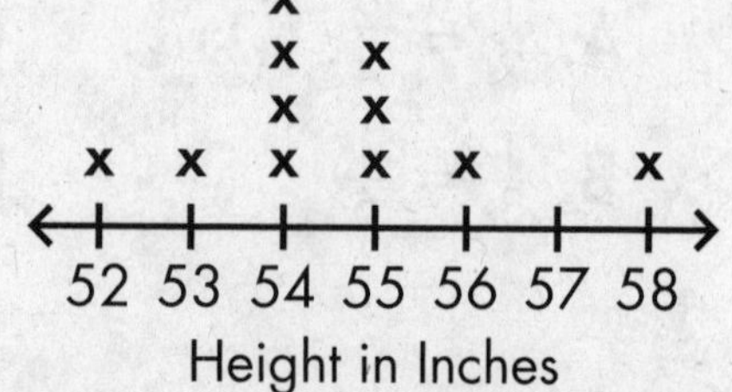

A. 52 inches **C.** 52 to 58 inches

B. 54 inches **D.** 54 to 55 inches

 Use during Investigation 1 (Exploring Numbers and Number Relationships), Sessions 4, 5, and 6.

Name Date

Mathematical Thinking at Grade 5

One Little Lie

One of the statements about each number is false. Circle the false statement.

Family Connection

Students are continuing to solve "What's the Number?" puzzles. These puzzles help them focus on the characteristics of numbers and encourage them to use mathematical reasoning. Ask your child how he or she decides whether the statements on this page are true or false.

1. 56
   I am a multiple of 7.
   I am odd.
   One of my factors is 28.
   The sum of my digits is 11.

2. 100
   I am a factor of 1000.
   I am a square number.
   I am a multiple of 10.
   I am a multiple of 15.

3. 225
   I am a square number.
   I am a multiple of 5.
   I am a multiple of 10.
   25 is one of my factors.

4. 51
   I am odd.
   I am a prime number.
   I am a factor of 153.
   I am a multiple of 3.

Mixed Review and Test Prep

5. Which conclusion can you draw from the graph?

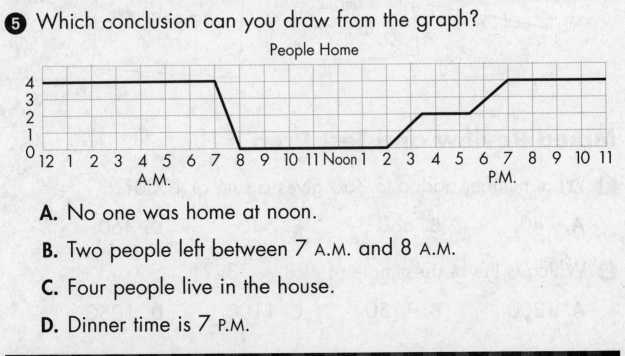

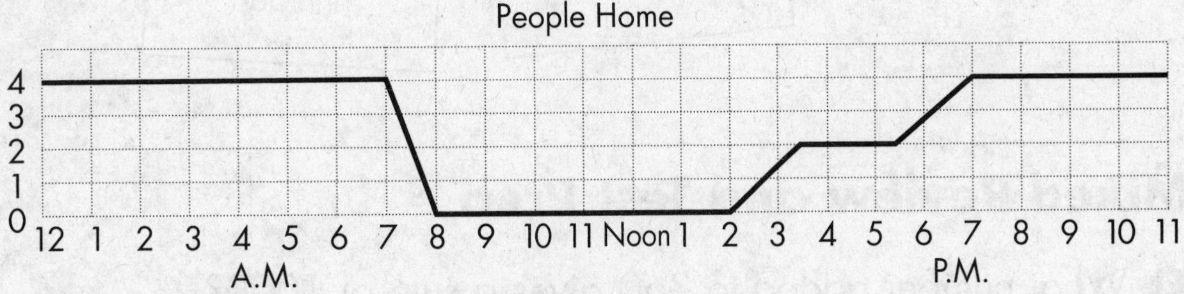

A. No one was home at noon.

B. Two people left between 7 A.M. and 8 A.M.

C. Four people live in the house.

D. Dinner time is 7 P.M.

Name Date

Mathematical Thinking at Grade 5

What a Mess

Family Connection

In class, students made their own "What's the Number?" puzzles. Examples of the types of clues they may have used are shown on this page. Ask your child to write a similar puzzle for you to solve.

1. Brian wrote puzzle clues for three different numbers. Then he dropped the cards. Draw lines to match each number to its three clues.

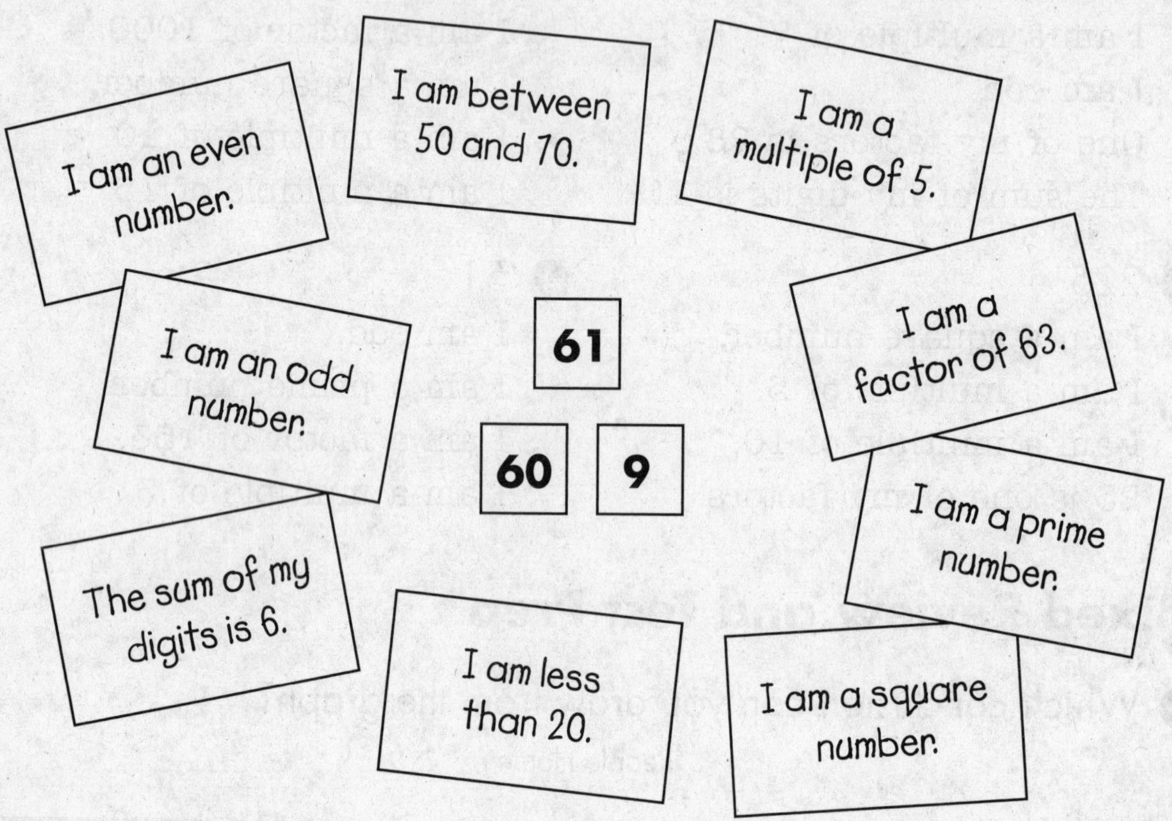
I am an even number.
I am between 50 and 70.
I am a multiple of 5.
I am an odd number.
61
I am a factor of 63.
60
9
I am a prime number.
The sum of my digits is 6.
I am less than 20.
I am a square number.

Mixed Review and Test Prep

2. What number added to 360 gives a sum of 1000?

A. 740 **B.** 660 **C.** 640 **D.** 460

3. Which is the best estimate of 428 + 732?

A. 1200 **B.** 1150 **C.** 1100 **D.** 1050

Name Date

Mathematical Thinking at Grade 5

Hockey Card Orders

Harold's Hockey Card Store sells trading cards in boxes of 20, 25, 50, and 100. Complete the table and use it to answer the questions.

Family Connection

Students have been skip counting to multiply by hundreds (100, 200, 300, ...) and by numbers that divide evenly into hundreds, such as 5, 10, and 25. Have your child demonstrate how to use skip counting to complete this table.

1. How many boxes of 25 would Harold need to fill an order for 150 cards? ______

2. Name two different ways to fill an order for 150 cards.

____

____

3. What is the smallest card order that can be filled using any size box?

______

Number of Cards				
Number of Boxes	20	25	50	100
1				
2				
3				
4				
5				
6				
7				

4. Bonita ordered 300 hockey cards. She received 6 boxes of cards. How many cards were in each box? ______

Mixed Review and Test Prep

5. Which cube building uses the most cubes?

A. 

B. 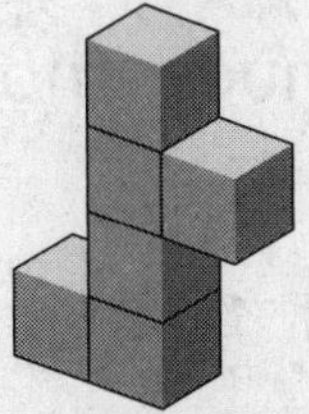

C. 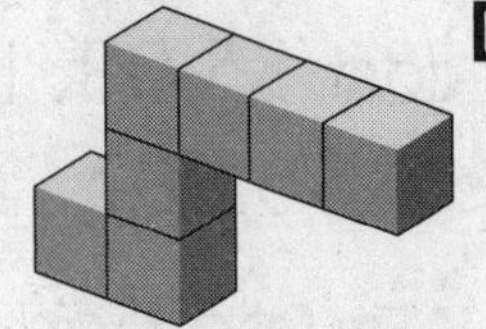

D. 

Name Date

Mathematical Thinking at Grade 5

One Coin Only

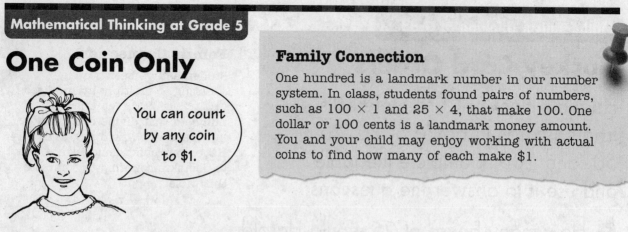

You can count by any coin to $1.

Family Connection

One hundred is a landmark number in our number system. In class, students found pairs of numbers, such as 100 × 1 and 25 × 4, that make 100. One dollar or 100 cents is a landmark money amount. You and your child may enjoy working with actual coins to find how many of each make $1.

1 How many of each coin are needed to make a dollar? Figure it out and then complete the table.

One [dollar bill] Equals	100 Cents Equal	Factor Pairs
_____ [penny]	_____ × 1 cent	
_____ [nickel]	_____ × 5 cents	
_____ [dime]	_____ × 10 cents	
_____ [quarter]	_____ × 25 cents	
_____ [half dollar]	_____ × 50 cents	

2 How do factor pairs for one dollar compare to factor pairs for 100?

____

Mixed Review and Test Prep

3 Cindy's lunch cost $5.08. How much change did she get from $6.00?

A. $0.88 **B.** $0.92 **C.** $1.08 **D.** $1.92

Name Date

Mathematical Thinking at Grade 5

Angela's Pairing Pentagon

I can find factor pairs for 300 by just multiplying by 3. My Pairing Pentagon matches the pairs for me.

Family Connection

Students are finding factor pairs for multiples of 100, such as 200, 300, and 400. Angela's Pairing Pentagon uses pairs of numbers that can be multiplied to make 100 to find pairs of numbers that can be multiplied to make 300. **Questions you might ask your child:** "How many factor pairs are there for 100?" "How many are there for 300?"

1. Multiply each number by 3. Write the answer above the number.

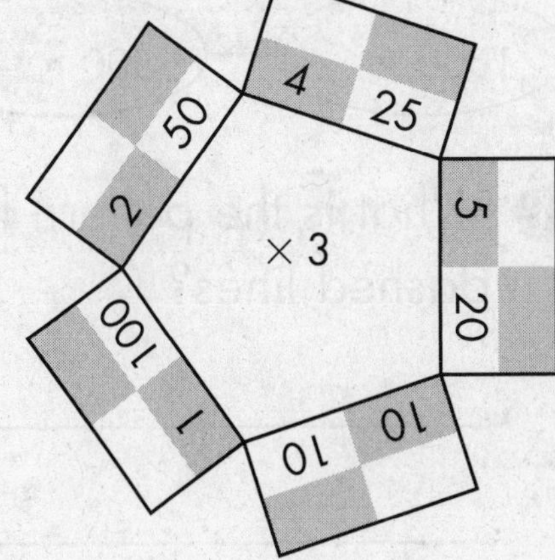

2. How can you tell which two numbers in each box go together?

____

____

3. What are the factor pairs for 300?

____

____

Mixed Review and Test Prep

4. How can 52 chairs be arranged so that each row has the same number of chairs?

A. in 3 rows of 15 chairs each

B. in 4 rows of 13 chairs each

C. in 5 rows of 11 chairs each

D. in 6 rows of 9 chairs each

Name Date

Mathematical Thinking at Grade 5

1000 Pairs

Find the missing number in each factor pair for 1000.

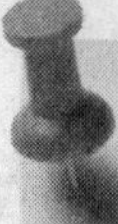

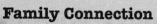

Family Connection

One thousand is another landmark in our number system. In class, students found pairs of numbers that can be multiplied to make 1000. This chart highlights patterns among the factor pairs. Have your child point the patterns out to you.

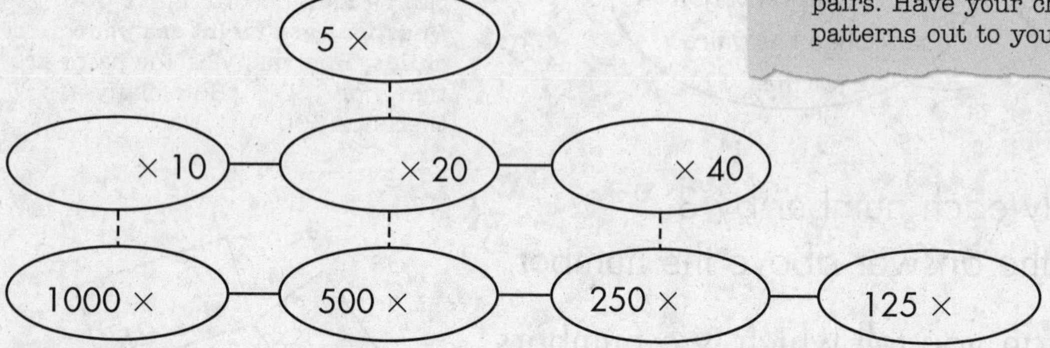

1 What is the pattern for factor pairs connected by dashed lines?

____

____

2 What is the pattern for factor pairs connected by solid lines?

____

____

Mixed Review and Test Prep

3 There are 4 rows of cars in a package. There are 5 cars in each row. How many cars are in the package?

A. 9 **B.** 15 **C.** 16 **D.** 20

Name Date

Mathematical Thinking at Grade 5

Close Up

Family Connection

Students are learning about number patterns on 1000-square rectangular grids. Ask your child what dimension rectangle he or she worked with in class and what counting patterns were used to number it.

This is a section of a rectangle that is 50 squares wide and 20 squares long.

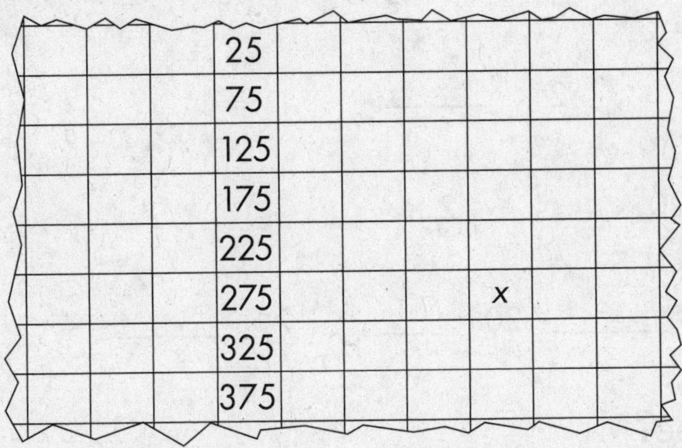

25
75
125
175
225
275
x
325
375

1. Find 31 and 172 on the grid.

2. What number is x? ______

3. Is 384 located in this section of the rectangle? If so, write 384 in the correct square. If not, explain why not.

______

Mixed Review and Test Prep

4. Which square is **NOT** divided into eighths?

A. 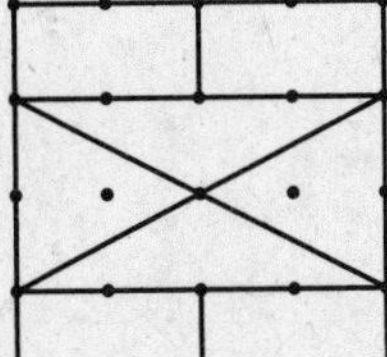

B. 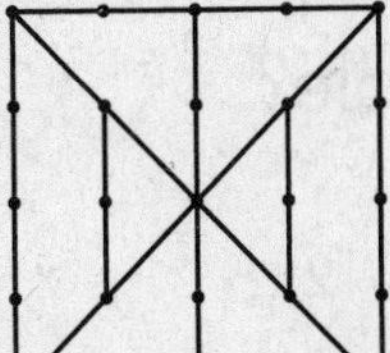

C. 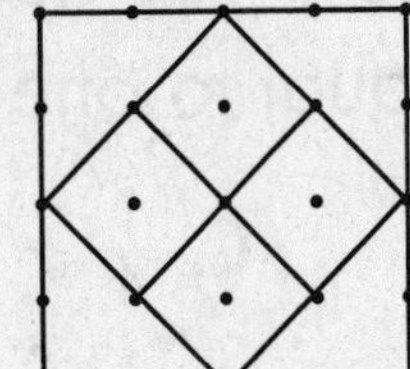

D. 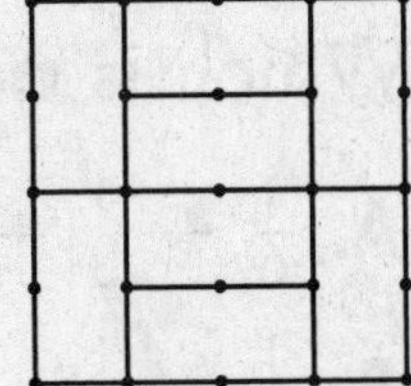

Name Date

Mathematical Thinking at Grade 5

Building on Ten

Family Connection

Students are building on their experience with smaller numbers to learn about larger numbers. They have been looking for numbers to count by so they land exactly on 100, 1000, and 10,000. Your child may choose to count to find the missing numbers in this pattern.

❶ Find the missing number in each pair.

Factor Pair of **10** $2 \times$ ______

Factor Pairs of **100** $20 \times$ ______ $2 \times$ ______

Factor Pairs of **1000** $200 \times$ ______ $20 \times$ ______ $2 \times$ ______

❷ What patterns do you see?

______

______

______

❸ Extend the pattern. Name four factor pairs for 10,000.

______

Mixed Review and Test Prep

❹ Use the rectangle if you need help. Which is **not** equal to one whole?

A. $\frac{1}{6} + \frac{1}{3} + \frac{1}{2}$

B. $\frac{1}{6} + \frac{1}{6} + \frac{2}{3}$

C. $\frac{1}{4} + \frac{1}{4} + \frac{1}{2}$

D. $\frac{1}{4} + \frac{1}{3} + \frac{1}{2}$

Name Date

Mathematical Thinking at Grade 5

The Right Tool

Circle the tools that can help you solve each multiplication problem. Add any others you need. Then solve.

Family Connection

Students have been exploring patterns and relationships among numbers. Now they are learning to use those relationships as tools when they multiply. Have your child tell you how he or she finds the answer for 26 × 5.

1. 26 × 5 = ☐

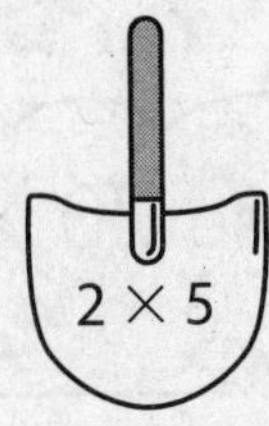

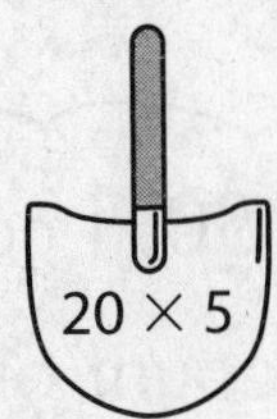

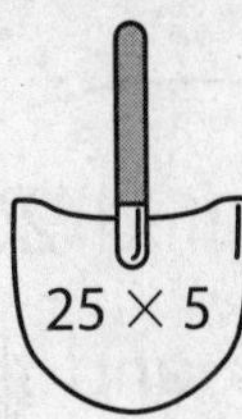

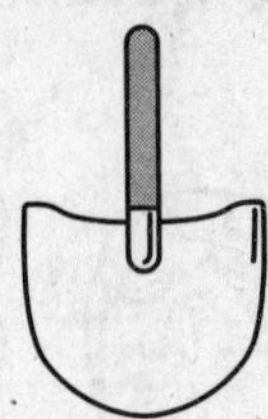

______

2. 36 × 40 = ☐

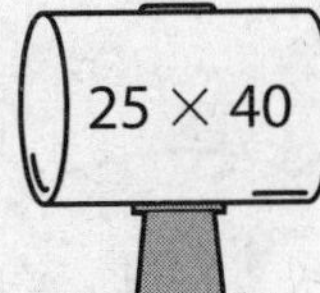

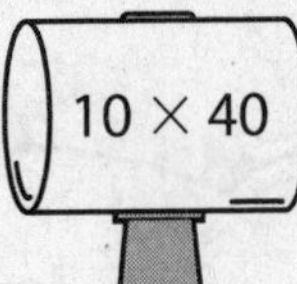

______

3. 279 × 4 = ☐

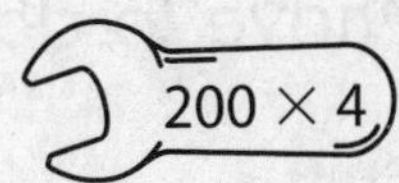

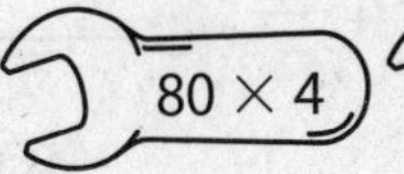

______

4. 356 × 5 = ☐

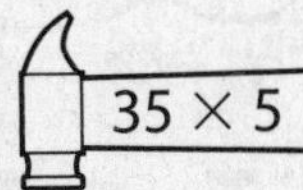

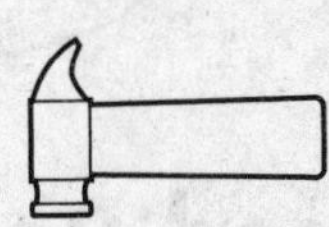

______

Mixed Review and Test Prep

5. How many teams of 8 can 32 students form?

A. 258 **B.** 40 **C.** 8 **D.** 4

6. If 18 people form 2 teams, how many people will be on each team?

A. 6 **B.** 9 **C.** 20 **D.** 36

Name Date

Mathematical Thinking at Grade 5

What Are You Thinking?

Finish each person's thoughts and solve the problem.

Family Connection

Students are finding strategies for multiplying "hard" numbers mentally. As aids, they are using multiplication facts, counting on, and some of the landmark numbers they have studied. **Questions you might ask your child:** "Is there a different way to find 23 × 50 than what is shown on this page?" "What is it?"

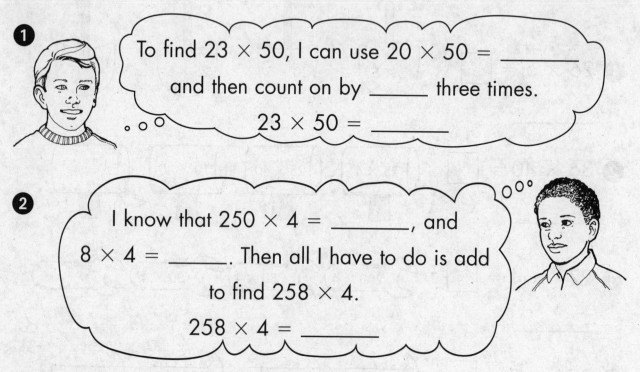

1

To find 23×50, I can use $20 \times 50 =$ ______ and then count on by _____ three times.

$23 \times 50 =$ ______

2

I know that $250 \times 4 =$ ______, and $8 \times 4 =$ _____. Then all I have to do is add to find 258×4.

$258 \times 4 =$ ______

Mixed Review and Test Prep

3 Joyce bought a box of crackers for $2.74. The clerk said, "seventy-five, three, four, five" as he gave back the change. Which shows the change Joyce got back?

A. 1 penny, 1 quarter, 2 dollars

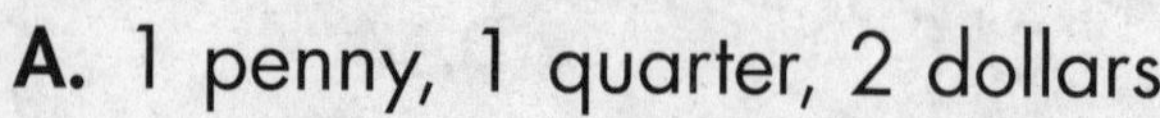

B. 1 penny, 1 quarter, 3 dollars

C. 3 quarters, 3 dollars

D. 3 quarters, 2 dollars

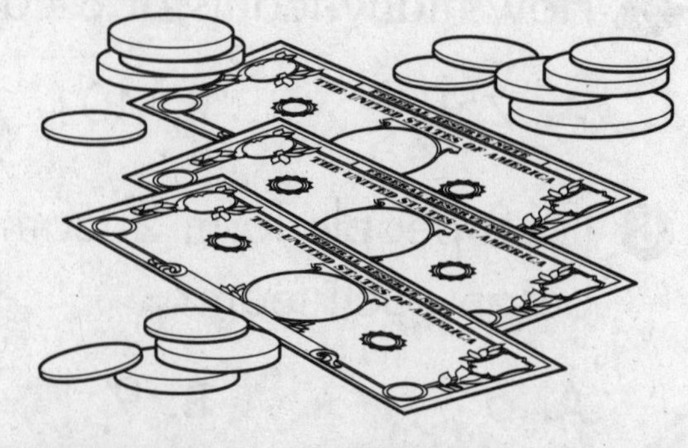

Name Date

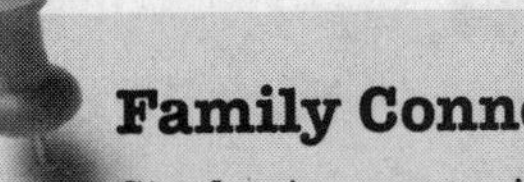

Petal Power

Use the problems on the petals to help you. Add any others you need. Solve the problem in the middle.

Family Connection

Students are using what they know about multiplication and division to solve harder division problems. Many students are less comfortable with division than they are with multiplication. It may be helpful for your child to think of related multiplication problems to help solve division problems. For example, instead of thinking "What is 240 divided by 6?", he or she might think "What number times 6 equals 240?"

1.
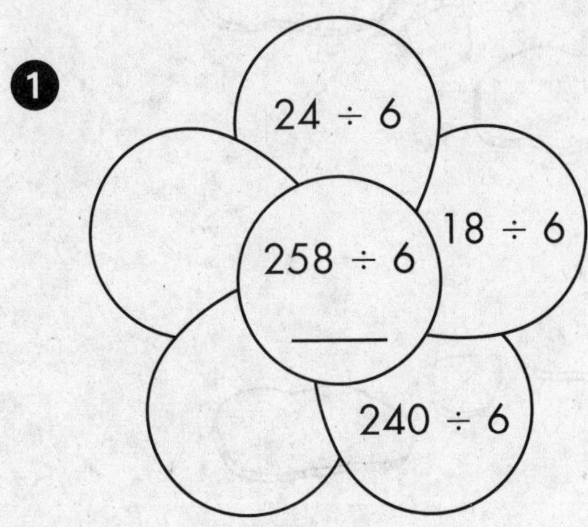

2.
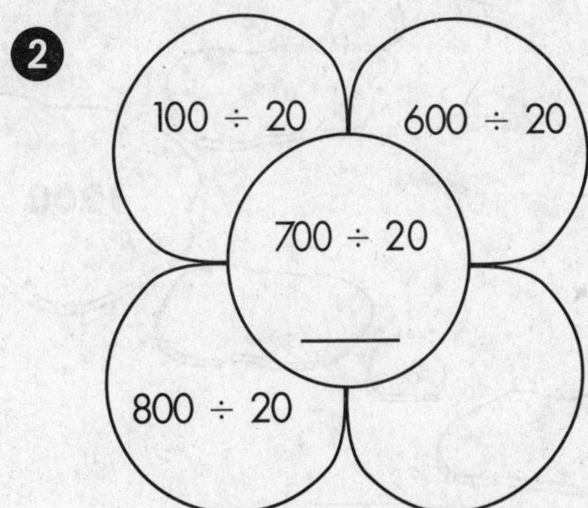

3.
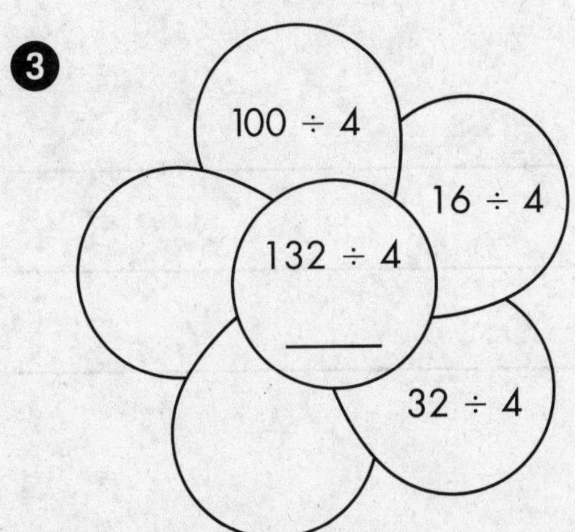

Interesting Tidbit

Hundreds of species of flowers have five petals. In fact, five is the most common number of petals on flowers.

Mixed Review and Test Prep

4. Pencils come in packages of 12. There are 26 students in Mark's class. How many packages of pencils do you have to open to give 3 pencils to everyone in Mark's class?

A. 3 **B.** 6 **C.** 7 **D.** 14

Name Date

Mathematical Thinking at Grade 5

Paths to 1200

Family Connection

In class, students found factor pairs for 1100. By explaining how they found the factor pairs, they demonstrated their understanding of important number relationships. Have your child describe his or her strategies for finding factor pairs to you.

1. Find factor pairs to complete each path to 1200.

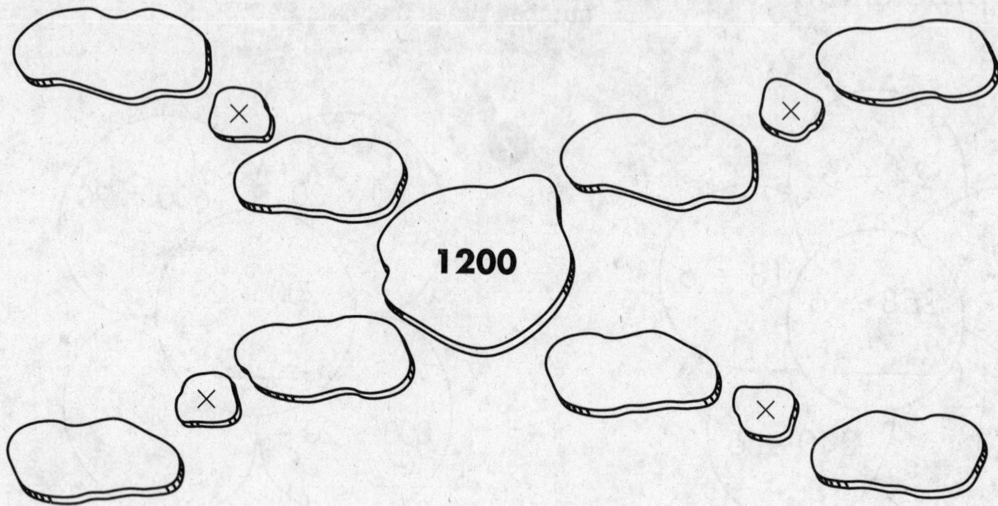

2. Tell how you found your factor pairs.

____

____

____

Mixed Review and Test Prep

3. Which shows how running faster and faster would look on a speed graph?

A. 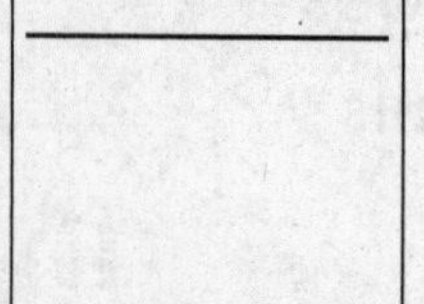 B. 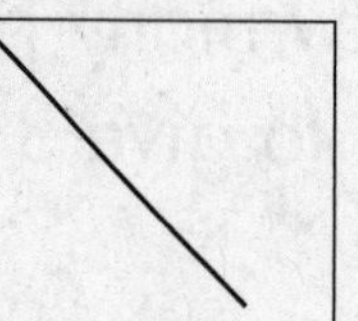 C. 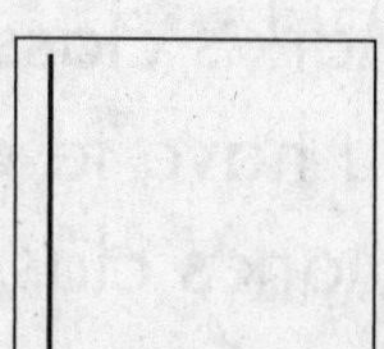 D. 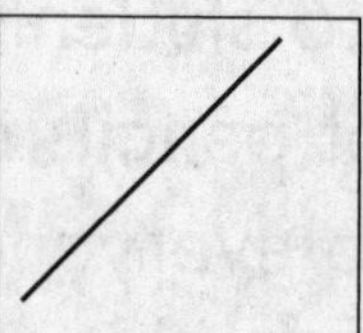

Name Date

Mathematical Thinking at Grade 5

Exactly 1000

Family Connection

Students have been playing a math game called "Close to 1000." The game involves arranging digits to make two three-digit numbers that have a sum as close as possible to 1000. You may enjoy working with your child to find as many sums of 1000 as you can using the numbers shown here.

Use the numbers in the circles to make 1000 in three different ways.

1. _____ + _____ = 1000
2. _____ + _____ = 1000
3. _____ + _____ = 1000
4. What strategies did you use to make sums of 1000?

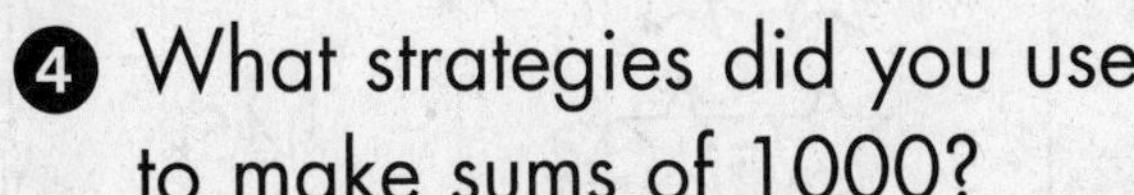

____

____

____

Mixed Review and Test Prep

5. In Margie's class, 11 out of 31 students wear glasses. What fraction do *not* wear glasses?

A. $\frac{31}{11}$

B. $\frac{31}{20}$

C. $\frac{20}{31}$

D. $\frac{11}{20}$

Name Date

The Dog Ate My Chart

Just as Mark finished writing 1451 on a 100-square-by-100-square chart, his dog grabbed it. Mark says he saved enough of the chart to finish his homework. Help him.

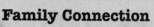

Family Connection

Students have been using number sense and patterns to locate numbers on a 10,000-square chart. In this activity your child will locate numbers on a portion of the chart. Ask your child how he or she knows what numbers are above and below 1451.

1. Label the numbers above and below 1451.
2. Label the number 6 rows below 1145.
3. Label the number that is 100 more than 1650.
4. How many squares are in the rectangle marked with stars? ________

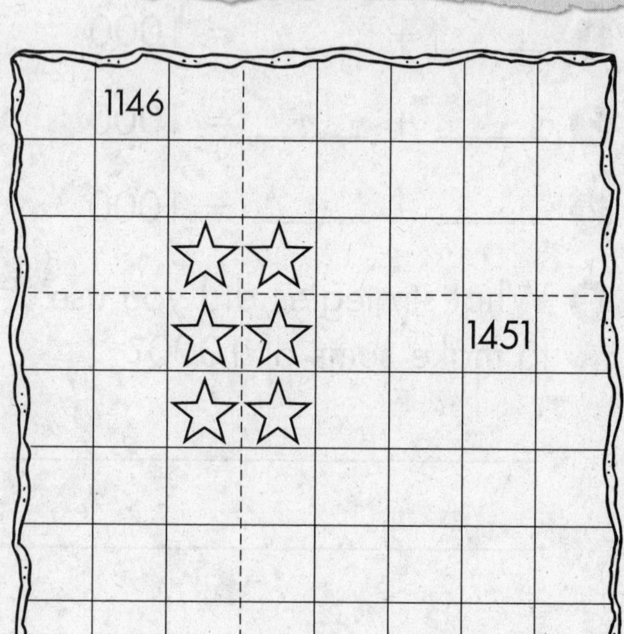

5. How many squares are in the whole 100 by 100 chart that are **not** in that rectangle? ________

Mixed Review and Test Prep

6. The dotted lines show where a shape is folded. In which shape is the dotted line a line of symmetry?

A. 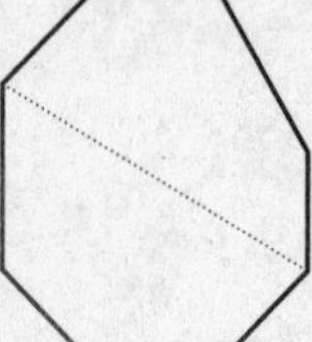
B. 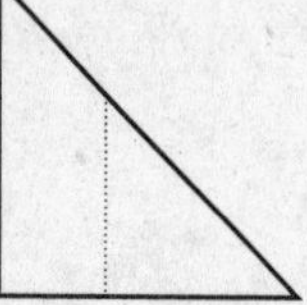
C. 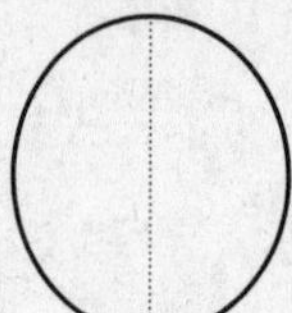
D. 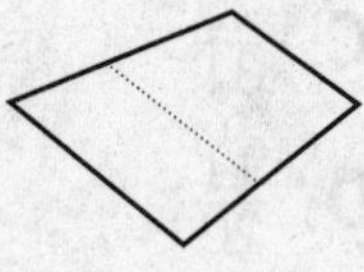

Name Date

Mathematical Thinking at Grade 5

My Number Is ...

Solve each puzzle.
Match each answer
to its description.

Family Connection

Students have been following clues to solve "What's My Number?" puzzles. They have discovered that for some puzzles the solution is one number. For some it is more than one number, and some puzzles are impossible. Ask your child to show you how he or she decides which category each of these puzzles falls into.

1 There is only one number that solves this puzzle. The number is ______.

2 There is more than one number that solves this puzzle. The numbers are:

______________________________.

3 This puzzle is impossible.
It is impossible because:

____

____

____

My number is
- a multiple of 100.
- greater than 300.
- a factor of 2000.
- an even number.

My number is
- a factor of 10,000.
- a prime number.
- a multiple of 25.
- a three-digit number.

My number is
- a factor of 100.
- a square number.
- a two-digit number.
- a multiple of 5.

Mixed Review and Test Prep

4 What is the median height for this group of fourth graders?

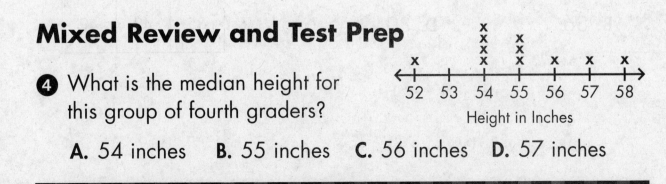

Height in Inches	52	53	54	55	56	57	58
Marks	x		xxxx	xxx	x	x	x

A. 54 inches **B.** 55 inches **C.** 56 inches **D.** 57 inches

Name Date

Mathematical Thinking at Grade 5

Get a Little Closer

Use the numbers in the circles to write subtraction problems.

Family Connection

Students have been playing a math game called **Close to 0**. This game is similar to **Close to 1000** except that students make two three-digit numbers that are subtracted to get a number as close as possible to zero. You may want to play this game with your child. Have your child tell you about his or her strategies for getting close to zero.

1           

8 1 2 5 6 9 0 2

902 – 865 = 37

_____ – _____ = _____

2           

5 3 2 5 8 2 7 9

532 – 529 = 3

_____ – _____ = _____

Mixed Review and Test Prep

3 The drawing shows a line of symmetry in part of the multiplication table. Use a pattern to find the missing number in the table.

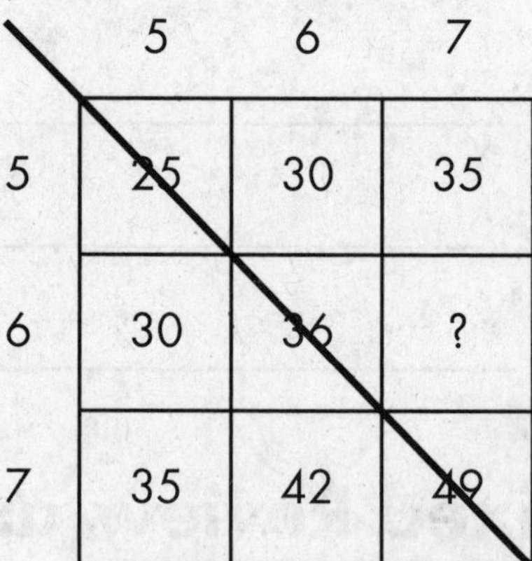

	5	6	7
5	25	30	35
6	30	36	?
7	35	42	49

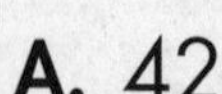

A. 42 **C.** 35

B. 36 **D.** 30

Name Date

Mathematical Thinking at Grade 5

The Final Clue

Each person found numbers that fit the first three clues in a puzzle. Complete the final clue so each puzzle has only one answer.

Family Connection

In class, students solved What's My Number? puzzles that have two or more answers. They then wrote another clue to create a puzzle with just one answer. For each puzzle on this page, have your child explain how his or her clue eliminates numbers so there is just one answer.

1 

The numbers that fit the first three clues are: 50, 100, and 200.

What is the final clue?

My number is ______________

______________________.

What is the answer? ________

2 

The numbers that fit the first three clues are: 40, 80, and 400.

What is the final clue?

My number is ______________

______________________.

What is the answer? ________

3 

The numbers that fit the first three clues are: 5, 25, 75, and 100.

What is the final clue?

My number is ______________

______________________.

What is the answer? ________

Mixed Review and Test Prep

4 Which is the best estimate of 48 + 502 + 156 + 98?

A. 500 **B.** 600 **C.** 700 **D.** 800

Name Date

Ask 10,000

Write **yes** or **no** to tell how 10,000 would answer each of these questions.

Family Connection

In class students were asked to write everything they knew about 10,000. The questions on this page show some of the terms students may have used. Ask your child what he or she wrote about 10,000.

1. Are you an even number? ________
2. Are you a multiple of 300? ________
3. Do you have 200 as a factor? ________
4. Are you a square number? ________
5. Are you ten times greater than 100? ________
6. Do you have 8 as a factor? ________
7. Can you make a rectangle 600 tiles wide? ________
8. Are you a multiple of 40? ________

Mixed Review and Test Prep

9. What does the top of this shape look like?

A. 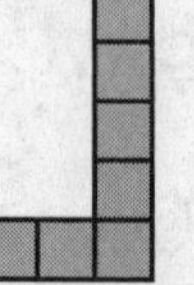

B. 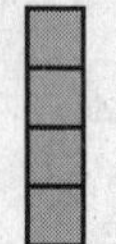

C. 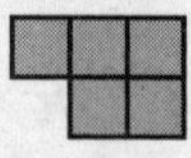

D. 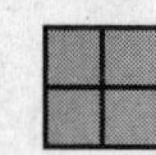

 Use after Investigation 4 (Reasoning About Landmarks up to 10,000), Sessions 5 and 6.

Name Date

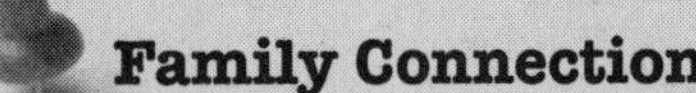

Find the Polygons

Is each shape a polygon? Write **yes** or **no** on the line to show your answer.

Family Connection

Students are learning how to decide if a flat shape is a polygon. Polygons are closed shapes with straight sides that do not cross. **Questions you might ask your child:** "What can you find in our kitchen that is shaped like a polygon?" "What is not shaped like a polygon?"

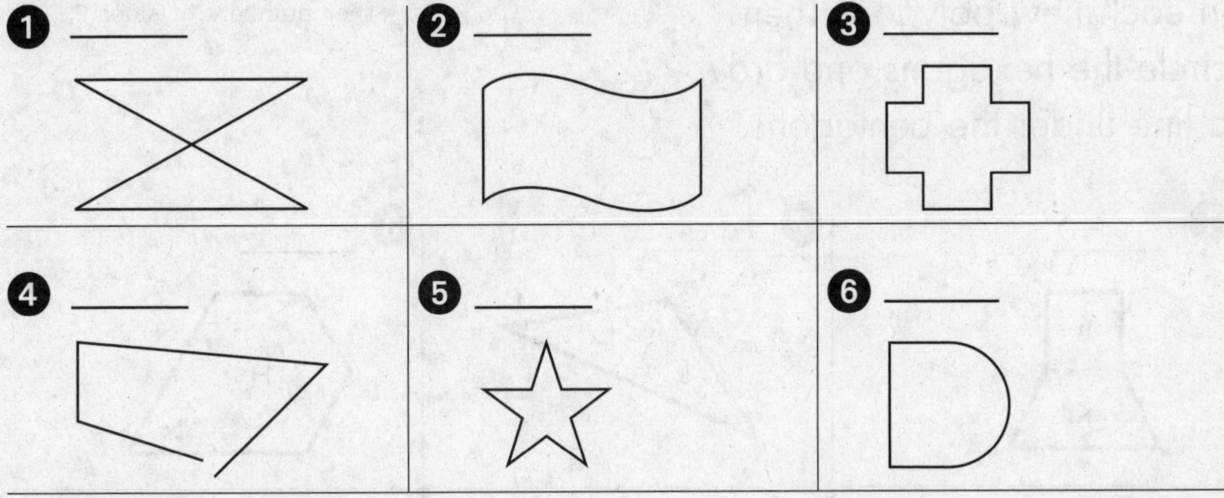

7 Draw two of each.

Polygons	Not Polygons

Mixed Review and Test Prep

8 Which two multiplication facts can you use to find the answer for 5×7?

A. 3×7 and 4×7

B. 3×7 and 2×7

C. 5×5 and 7×7

D. 5×5 and 5×12

Name Date

Picturing Polygons

Count the Sides

You can join shapes together to make a polygon.

Count the number of sides in each new polygon. Then circle the hexagons and draw a line under the pentagons.

Family Connection

Students have been using shape pieces called Power Polygons to make polygons with different numbers of sides. Students will see many examples of shapes with 4 sides in everyday life—doors, windows, books, and so on. Encourage your child to point out polygons with other numbers of sides.

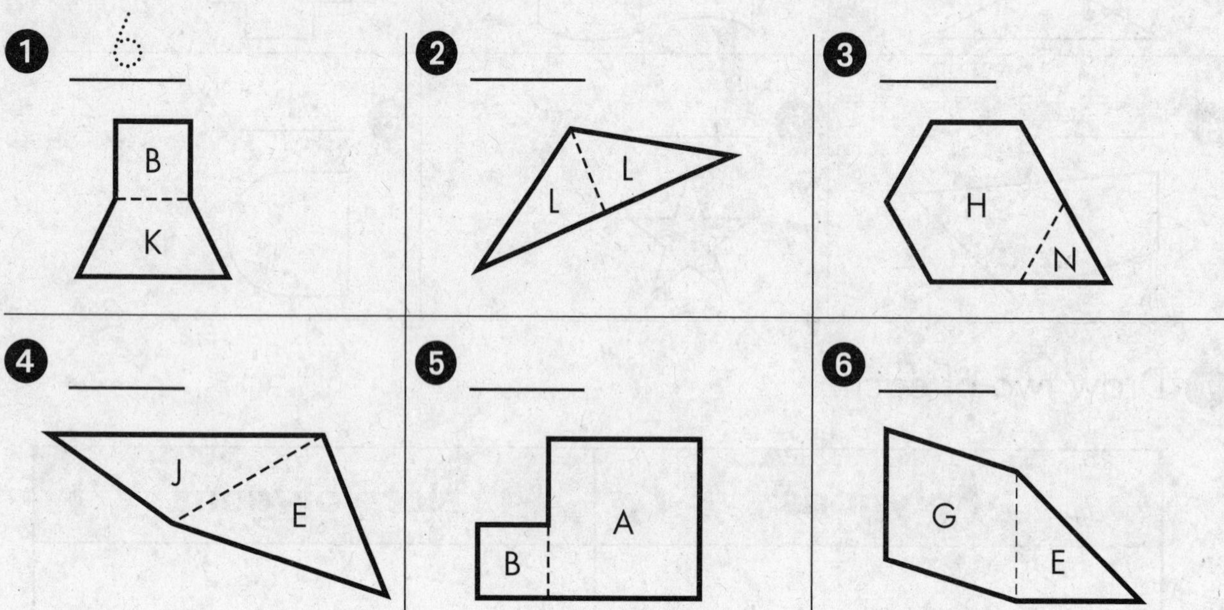

Mixed Review and Test Prep

7. Which number correctly completes the number sentence?

140 + _____ = 200

A. 60 **C.** 240

B. 160 **D.** 340

Name Date

Polygon Plots

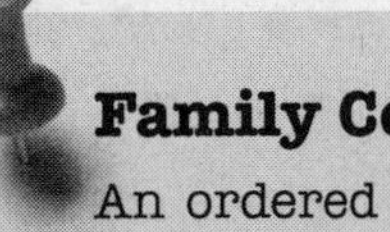

Family Connection

An ordered pair of numbers, such as (20, 40) shows a location on a grid. The 20 tells you to move 20 to the right on the grid and the 40 tells you to move 40 up. Students have been describing polygons by naming the ordered pairs at their corners (vertices).

Use ordered pairs for your answers. The first one is done for you.

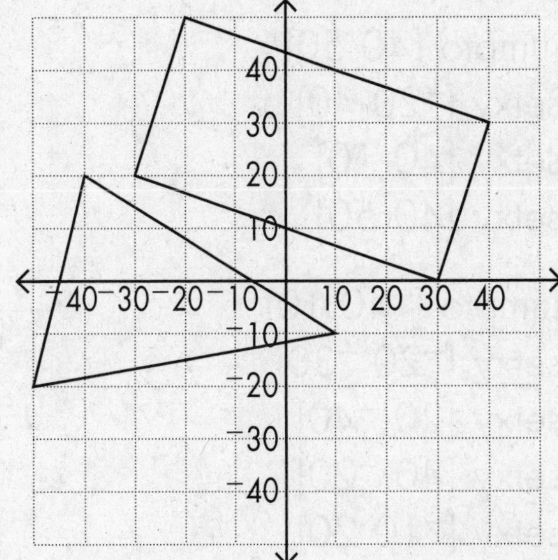

❶ Name the vertices of the rectangle.

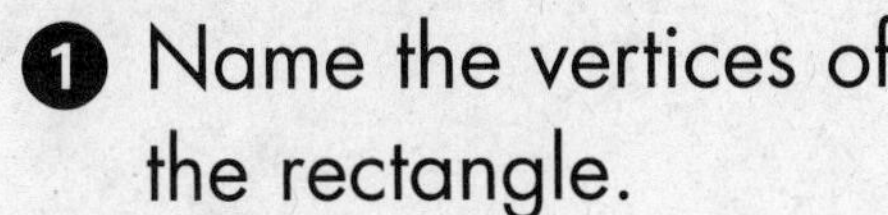

(−30, 20)

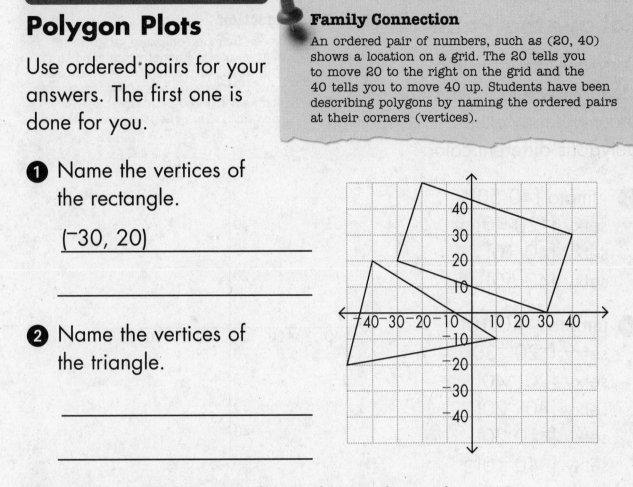

____

❷ Name the vertices of the triangle.

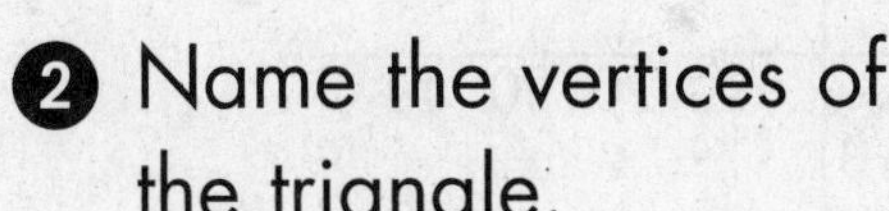

____

____

❸ Draw a polygon with four sides on the grid. Name its vertices.

____

Mixed Review and Test Prep

❹ Which number is a factor of 46?

A. 23 **B.** 10 **C.** 6 **D.** 4

❺ Which number is a multiple of 21?

A. 7 **B.** 36 **C.** 63 **D.** 70

Name Date

Follow the Paths

Draw the polygons that the turtle would make on a computer. Make the polygons different colors.

Family Connection

Students have been using a computer program to draw polygons. They use the jumpto command to give a starting location, such as [⁻30 10] to a turtle. Then they tell the turtle where to go next by typing a command such as setxy [20 ⁻40]. They keep typing commands until the turtle has gone all around the polygon.

1. jumpto [40 50]
   setxy [⁻20 40]
   setxy [40 10]
   setxy [40 50]

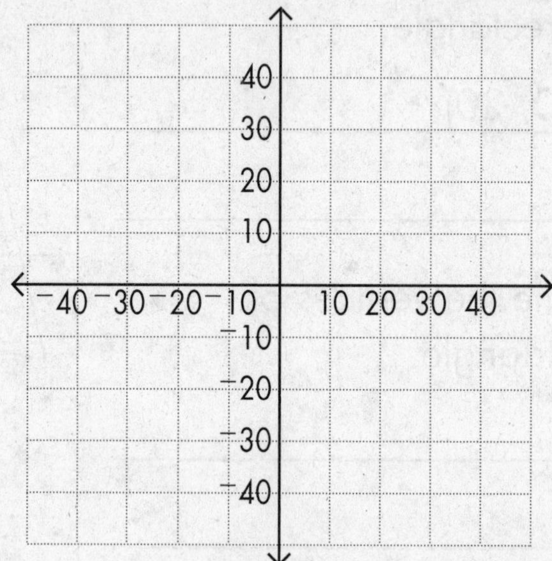

2. jumpto [⁻40 10]
   setxy [⁻20 ⁻30]
   setxy [20 ⁻40]
   setxy [40 ⁻20]
   setxy [⁻10 20]
   setxy [⁻40 10]

3. Circle the name of the polygon you drew in Exercise 2.

   hexagon quadrilateral

   octagon pentagon

Interesting Tidbit

A triangle of **any** shape can be used as floor tiles with no gaps or overlaps. See if you can "tile" a sheet of paper with triangles like the one in Exercise 1.

Mixed Review and Test Prep

4. Beverly has 2 coins. Which amount of money could she have?

   A. $0.25 **B.** $0.35 **C.** $0.40 **D.** $0.41

Name Date

Triangle Sort

Write the numbers of all the triangles that belong in each category. HINT: Use a square corner of a piece of paper as a "right-angle tester."

Family Connection

Students have been sorting shapes into categories. They have learned to sort triangles by the types of angles they contain. Ask your child to find examples at home of angles that are right (90°), obtuse (larger than 90°), or acute (smaller than 90°).

1. right triangles

___

2. triangles with 3 acute angles

___

3. triangles with 1 obtuse angle

___

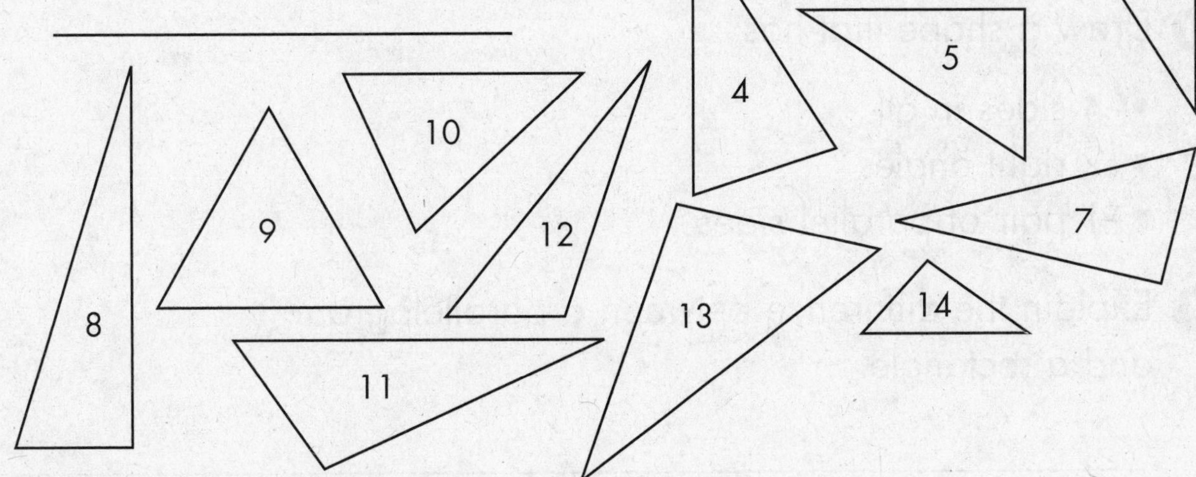

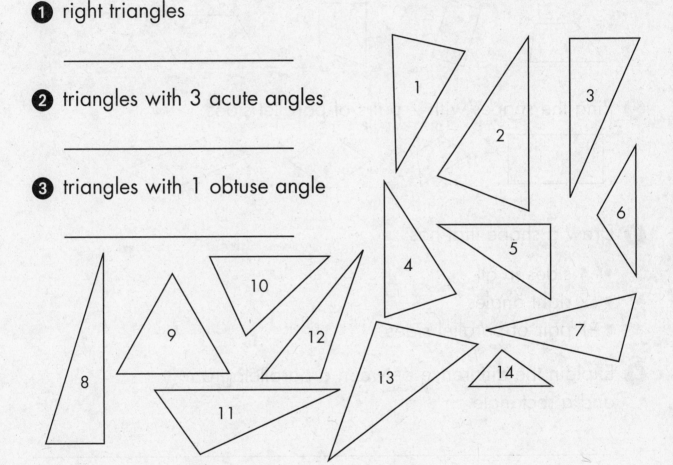

Mixed Review and Test Prep

4. Choose the best estimate for 43×68.

A. between 1000 and 1500

B. between 1500 and 2000

C. between 2000 and 2400

D. between 2400 and 3000

Name Date

Parallel or Not?

Parallel lines never meet. Parallel segments or sides are parts of parallel lines.

Family Connection

Students have been studying quadrilaterals—flat closed shapes with four sides. Parallelograms are important kinds of quadrilaterals. Examples of parallelograms include squares and rectangles.

1. Ring the shapes with exactly 1 pair of parallel sides.

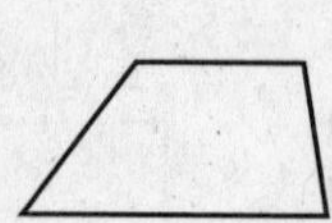   

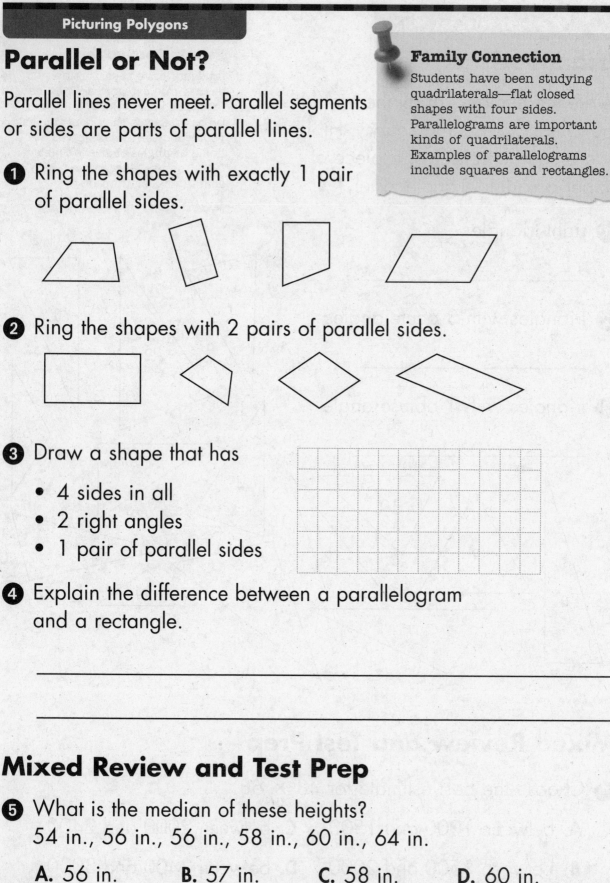

2. Ring the shapes with 2 pairs of parallel sides.

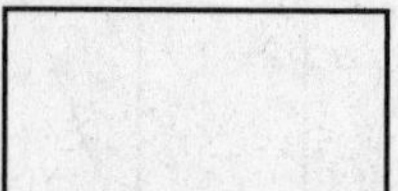 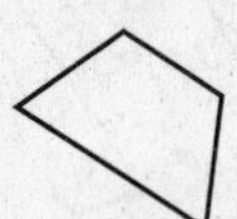  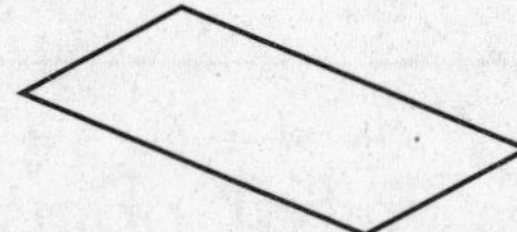

3. Draw a shape that has
   - 4 sides in all
   - 2 right angles
   - 1 pair of parallel sides

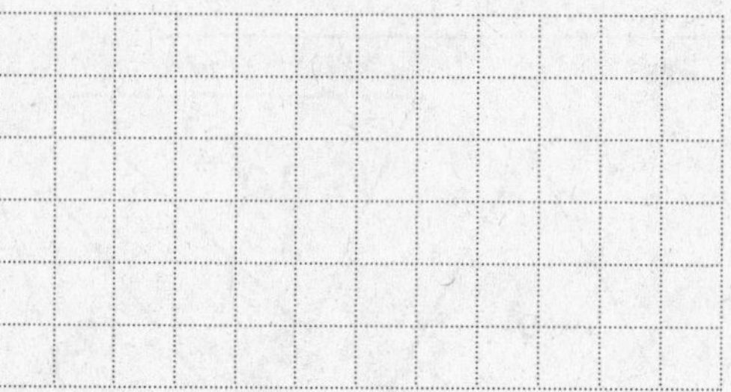

4. Explain the difference between a parallelogram and a rectangle.

____

____

Mixed Review and Test Prep

5. What is the median of these heights?
54 in., 56 in., 56 in., 58 in., 60 in., 64 in.

A. 56 in. **B.** 57 in. **C.** 58 in. **D.** 60 in.

 Use during Investigation 2 (Triangles and Quadrilaterals), Sessions 1, 2, and 3.

Name Date

Quad Sort

Write the numbers of all the quadrilaterals that belong in each category.

Family Connection

Students are learning to classify quadrilaterals. Some things they look for are right angles, parallel sides, and sides or angles of equal length. Talk with your child about which of these properties are shared by all squares or all rectangles.

1. 4 right angles

____

2. 2 pairs of parallel sides

____

3. 4 sides of equal length

____

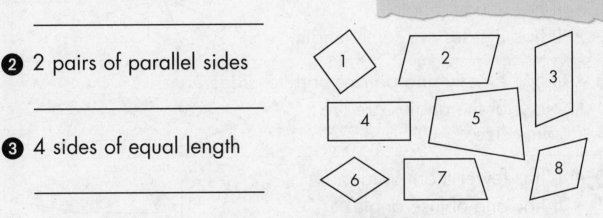

Draw a shape to prove each statement is **false.**

4. All rectangles are squares.

5. All quadrilaterals have at least 1 right angle.

Mixed Review and Test Prep

6. In Arnold's class, 13 out of 28 students are wearing sneakers. What fraction of the students are **not** wearing sneakers?

A. $\frac{13}{15}$ **B.** $\frac{15}{28}$ **C.** $\frac{13}{28}$ **D.** $\frac{13}{41}$

Name Date

Picturing Polygons

Follow the Rules

Ring the shape that follows each set of rules.

Family Connection

Students are studying the properties of triangles and quadrilaterals. They learn to look for angles and sides of equal measure, as well as pairs of parallel sides. Find different shapes around your home and ask your child to describe their properties.

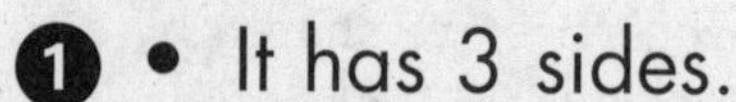

1
- It has 3 sides.
- It has 1 right angle.
- It has 2 sides the same length.

2
- It has exactly one pair of parallel sides.
- No 2 of the angles are the same size.

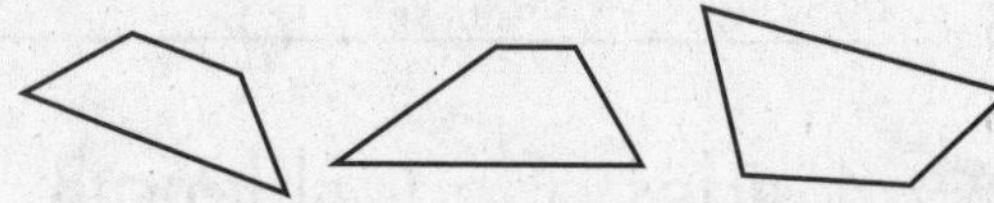

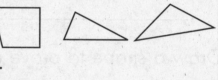

3
- It has fewer than 4 sides.
- It has one obtuse angle.
- It has 2 angles that are the same size.

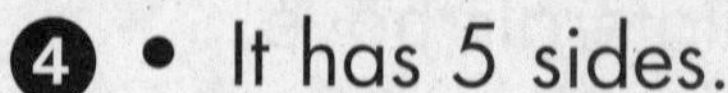

4
- It has 5 sides.
- It has 2 right angles.
- It has exactly one pair of parallel sides.

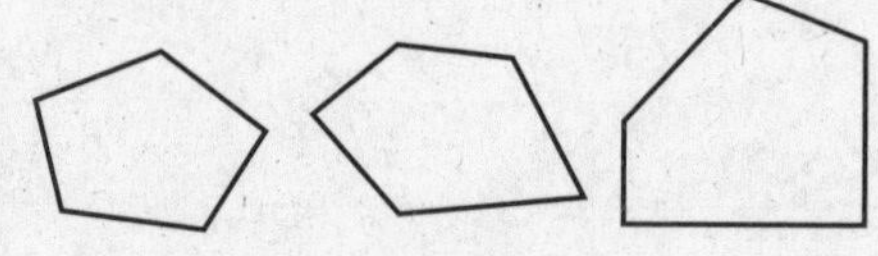

5
- It has exactly 2 pairs of parallel sides.
- It has 0 right angles.
- The sides are not the same length.

Mixed Review and Test Prep

6 Crystal ran 9.6 miles each week. How many miles did she run in the two weeks?

A. 4.8 mi **B.** 18.12 mi **C.** 18.2 mi **D.** 19.2 mi

Name Date

Picturing Polygons

Impossible Figures

Family Connection

Students are learning that some shapes are impossible to construct. For example, a triangle cannot have three right angles because the sum of all three angles must be 180°. Problems such as these help your child develop logical thinking skills.

Can you make each shape? Write **yes** or **no** in the right column.

	Number of sides	Sides	Angles	Possible?
1	3	your choice	1 angle larger than a right angle	
2	3	3 equal sides	1 right angle	
3	3	0 equal sides	2 equal angles	
4	3	2 equal sides	2 angles smaller than a right angle	
5	4	your choice	exactly 3 right angles	
6	4	2 equal sides	2 right angles	
7	4	3 equal sides	0 right angles	
8	4	1 pair parallel sides	exactly 1 right angle	
9	4	2 pairs parallel sides	0 right angles	

Mixed Review and Test Prep

10 The line plot shows the number of peas in 10 pods. Based on these data, which is the best guess of the number of peas that will be in the next pod?

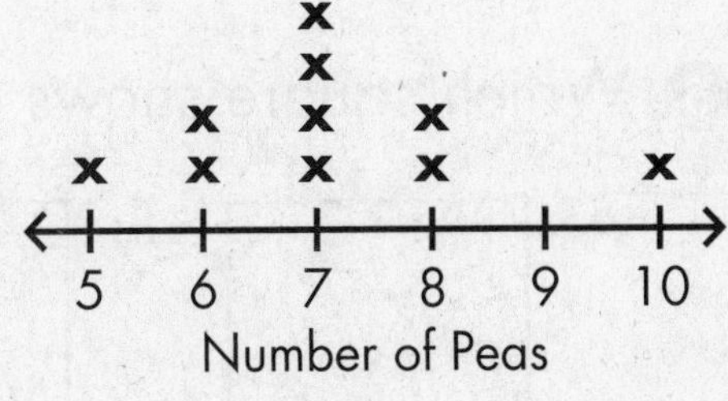

A. 5 **B.** 7 **C.** 9 **D.** 10

Name Date

Turning the Turtle

Find the angle the turtle would make. Write the correct problem number inside each angle to show your answers.

Family Connection

Students have been learning to use a computer program to make angles, rectangles, squares, and other shapes. To make an angle, they tell a turtle to turn a certain number of degrees. A 90-degree turn makes a right angle.

1 jumpto [$^{-}$10 10]
fd 30
rt 90
fd 30

2 jumpto [$^{-}$20 $^{-}$10]
lt 90
fd 30
lt 90
fd 20

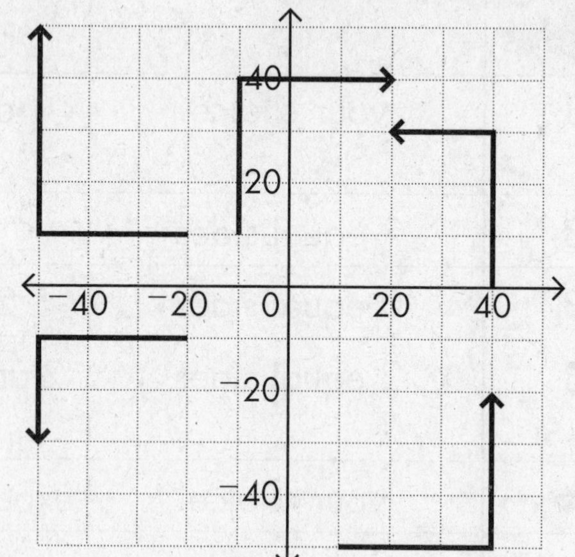

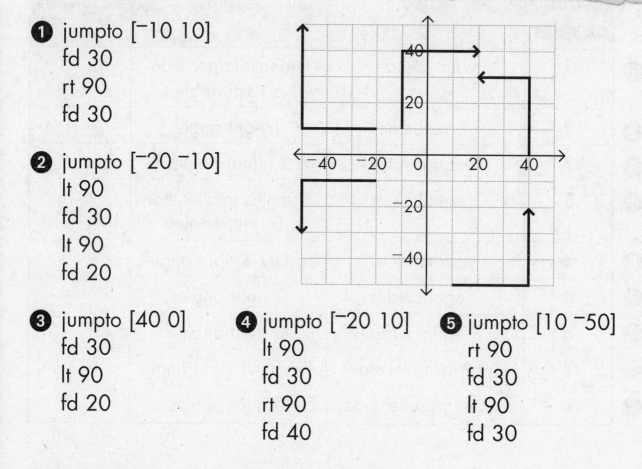

3 jumpto [40 0]
fd 30
lt 90
fd 20

4 jumpto [$^{-}$20 10]
lt 90
fd 30
rt 90
fd 40

5 jumpto [10 $^{-}$50]
rt 90
fd 30
lt 90
fd 30

Mixed Review and Test Prep

6 Which square shows fourths?

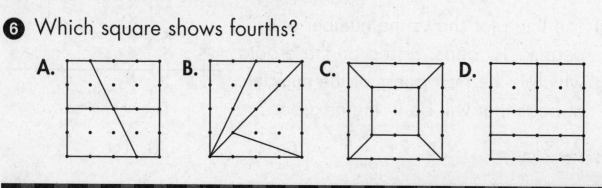

A.

B. 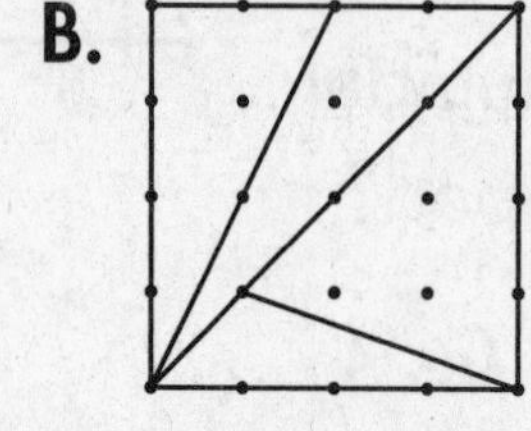

C. 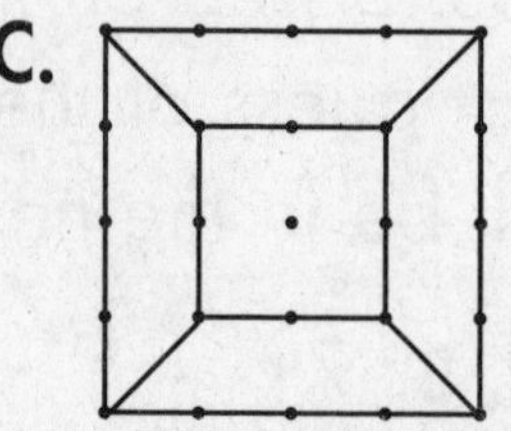

D. 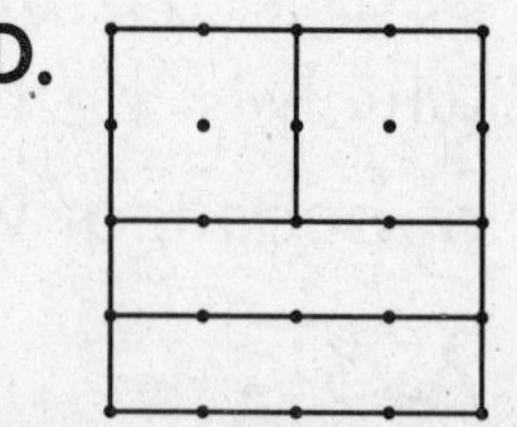

Name Date

Picturing Polygons

Category Search

Family Connection

Students are learning to classify triangles and quadrilaterals (shapes with 4 sides). To do this, they must learn the definitions of the various kinds of shapes; for example, a scalene triangle must have 3 sides that are all different lengths.

Some shapes fit many categories. For each shape, write the letters of **every** category to which it belongs.

Categories

A square	D trapezoid	G equilateral	J right
B rectangle	E parallelogram	H isosceles	K obtuse
C rhombus	F quadrilateral	I scalene	L acute

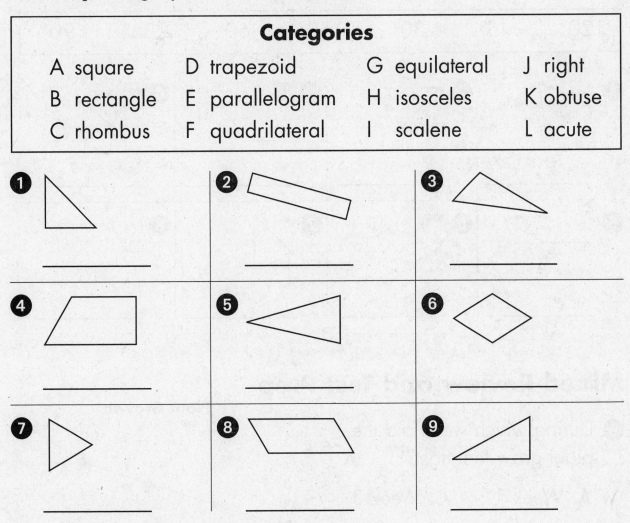

______

______

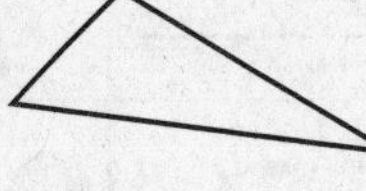

______

______

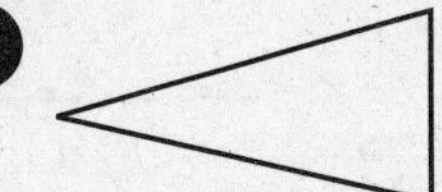

______

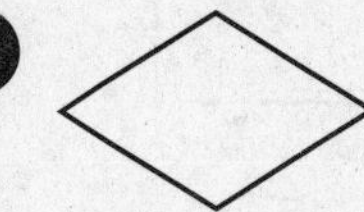

______

7 

______

8 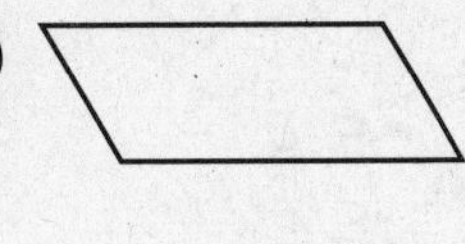

______

9 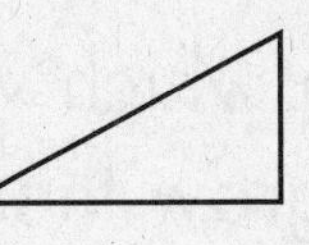

______

Mixed Review and Test Prep

10 Skip count by 2's. What is the next number?
64, 66, 68, 70, 72, ______

A. 73 **B.** 74 **C.** 78 **D.** 82

Name Date

Picturing Polygons

Measure Match

Match each angle to one of the measures in the box. One measure is used twice.

Family Connection

Students have been describing the sizes of angles in degrees. To make a 45-degree angle, help your child fold a piece of paper by lining up two adjacent edges of the paper. This can be used to solve the matching puzzle on this page.

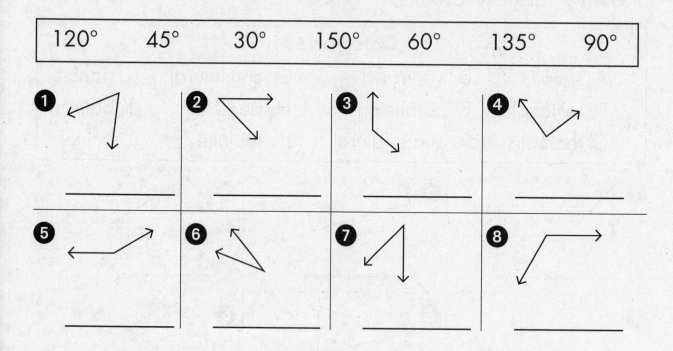

120°	45°	30°	150°	60°	135°	90°

1. ____________ 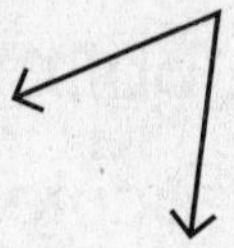
2. ____________ 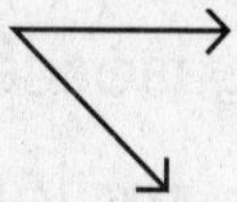
3. ____________ 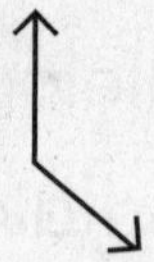
4. ____________ 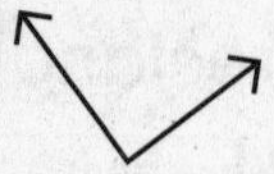
5. ____________ 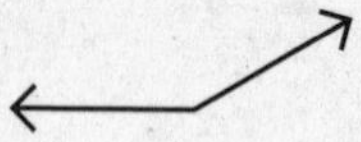
6. ____________ 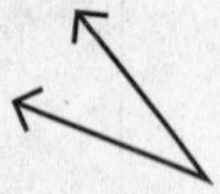
7. ____________ 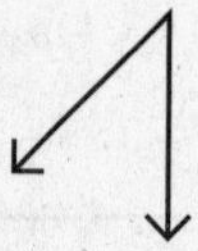
8. ____________

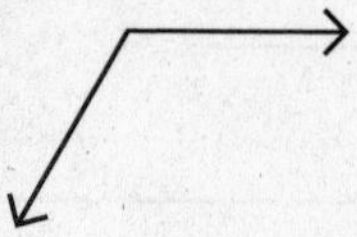

Mixed Review and Test Prep

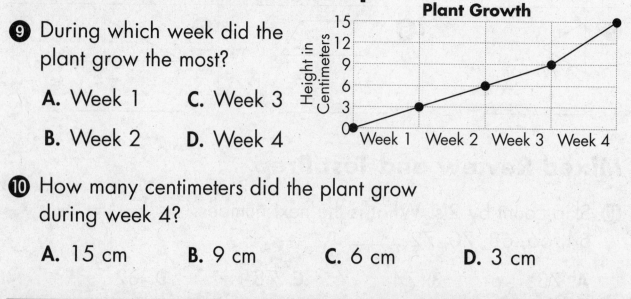

9. During which week did the plant grow the most?

A. Week 1 **C.** Week 3

B. Week 2 **D.** Week 4

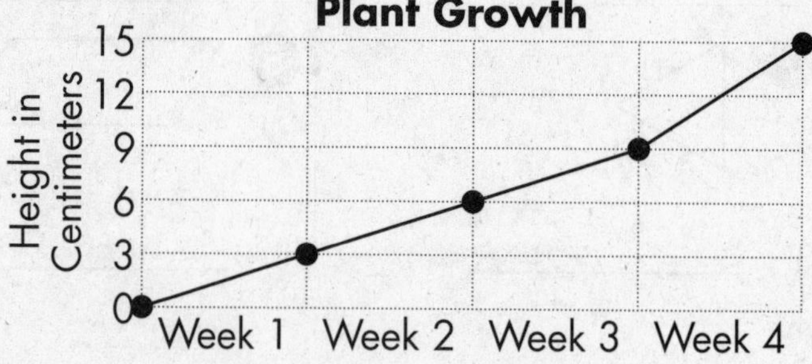

10. How many centimeters did the plant grow during week 4?

A. 15 cm **B.** 9 cm **C.** 6 cm **D.** 3 cm

Name Date

The Missing Measures

Write the measure of the missing angle in each drawing. The missing angle is marked with a question mark.

Family Connection

Students have been learning about supplementary angles. An angle and its supplement make a straight line, so their sum is 180 degrees.

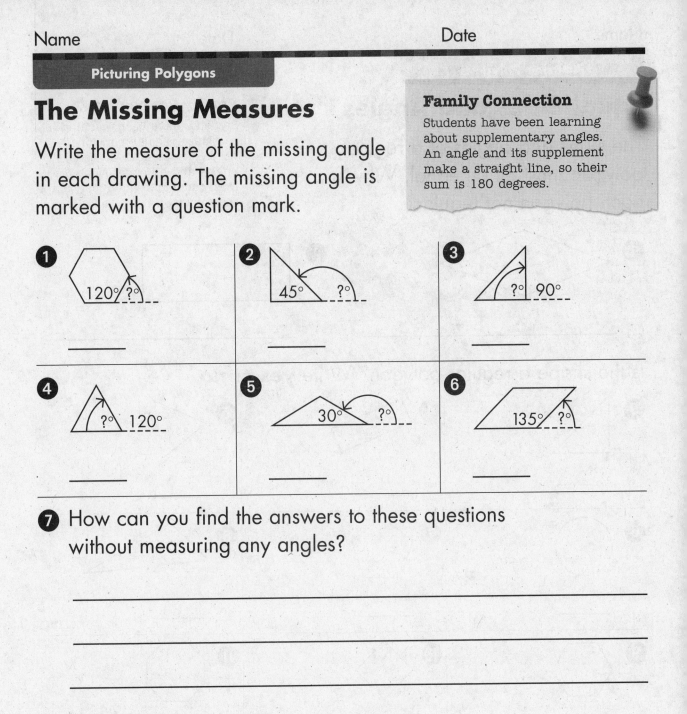

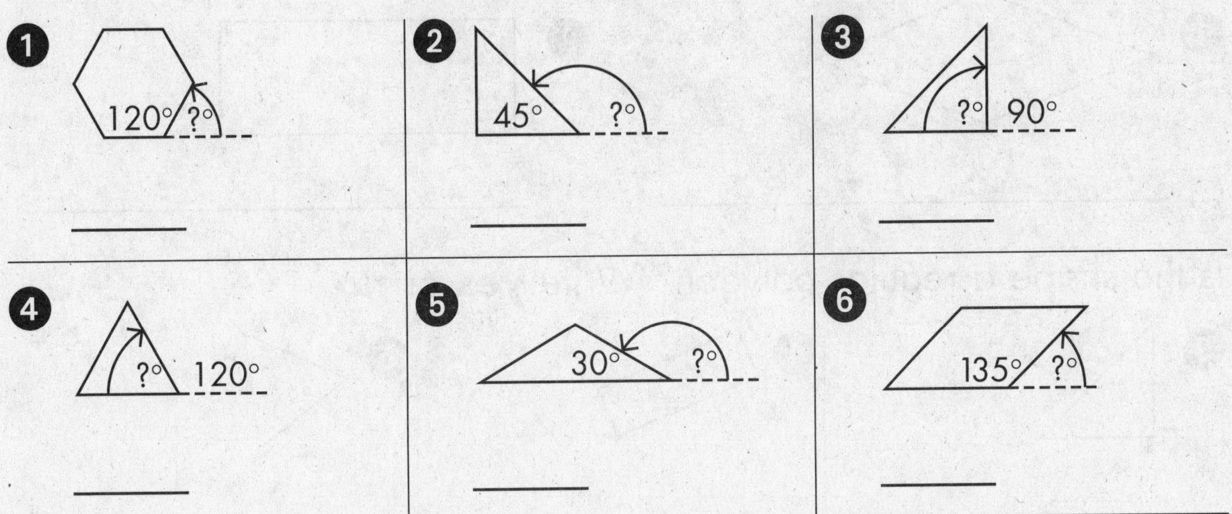

7 How can you find the answers to these questions without measuring any angles?

____

____

____

Mixed Review and Test Prep

8 In Alice's class, 3 out of 4 students read a book last week. There are 28 students in the class. How many students did **not** read a book last week?

A. 4 **B.** 7 **C.** 14 **D.** 21

Name Date

Equal Sides and Angles

The sides and angles of a regular polygon must all be equal. Why is each polygon not regular?

Family Connection

Students have been learning to recognize regular polygons. These shapes have all equal angles and all equal sides. The most familiar regular polygon is the square.

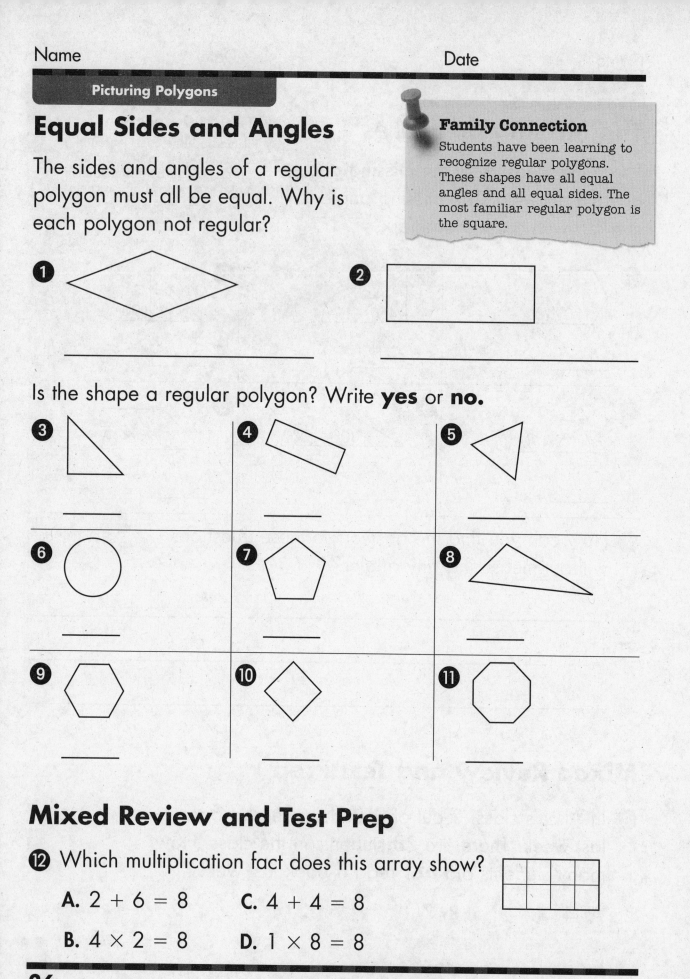

1 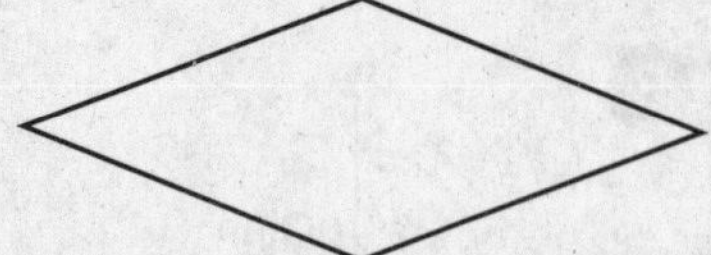

______

2  

______

Is the shape a regular polygon? Write **yes** or **no.**

3 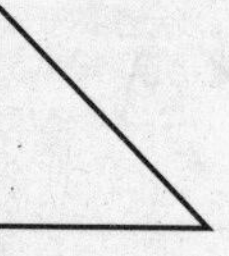 ______

4 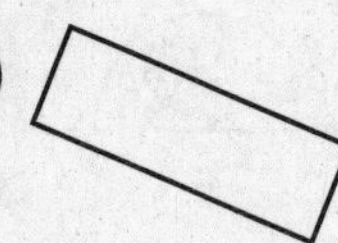 ______

5  ______

6 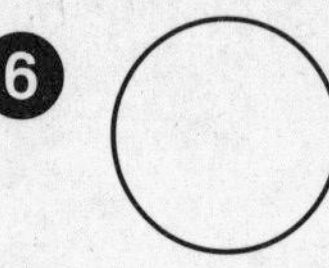 ______

7 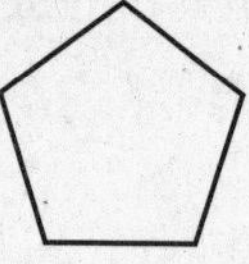 ______

8 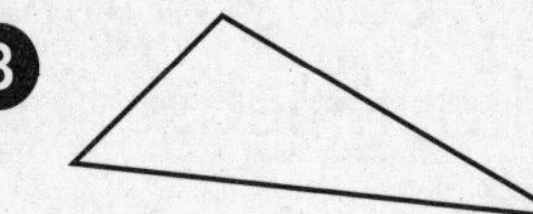 ______

9 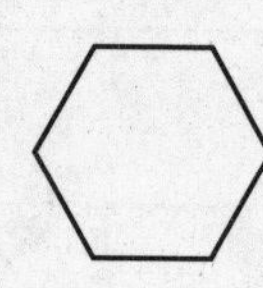 ______

10 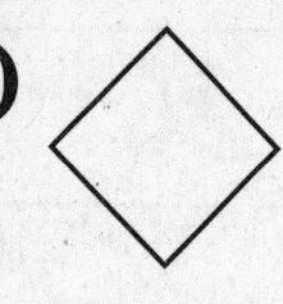 ______

11 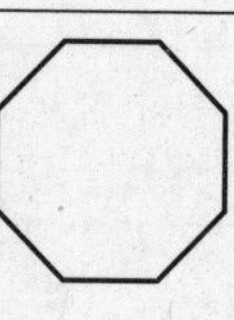 ______

Mixed Review and Test Prep

12 Which multiplication fact does this array show?

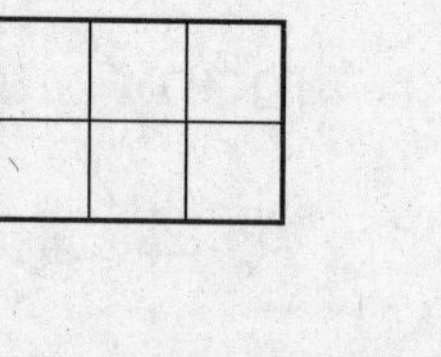

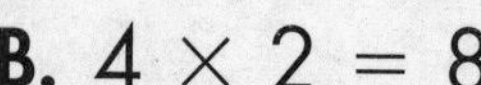

A. $2 + 6 = 8$ **C.** $4 + 4 = 8$

B. $4 \times 2 = 8$ **D.** $1 \times 8 = 8$

 Use during Investigation 3 (Regular Polygons and Similarity), Sessions 1 and 2.

Name Date

Picturing Polygons

Angle Patterns

Family Connection

Students have been using a computer program to look for angle patterns in regular polygons. After your child completes the page, ask him or her to describe some of the patterns in the chart.

Use what you have learned about regular polygons to complete the chart. Use patterns to help.

	Name of regular polygon	Number of sides	Size of each angle	Sum of angles
1	equilateral triangle	3		180°
2		4	90°	
3		5		540°
4	hexagon			720°
5		8		1080°
6	nonagon		140°	
7	decagon			1440°

Mixed Review and Test Prep

8 James surveyed his fifth grade class to decide what the best movie was last year. Whose opinion was **not** considered in the survey?

A. boys **C.** 18-year-olds

B. James **D.** fifth-graders

Name Date

Making Regular Polygons

Family Connection

Students have used the Power Polygons (shown below) to make both regular and nonregular polygons. Be on the lookout for regular hexagons. They can be spotted in floor tiles and chicken wire!

Find three different ways to use Power Polygons to make each regular polygon.

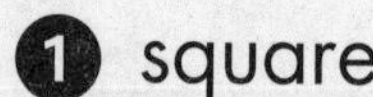

1. square

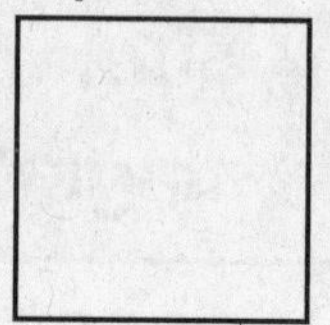  

2. equilateral triangle

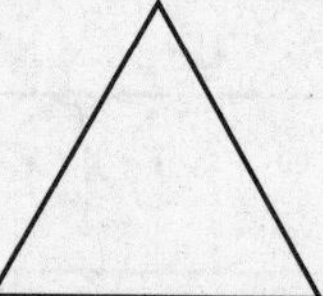  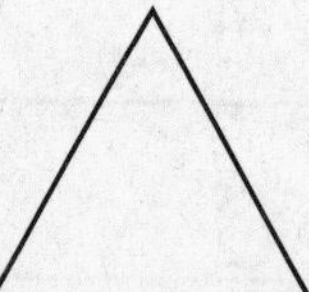

3. regular hexagon

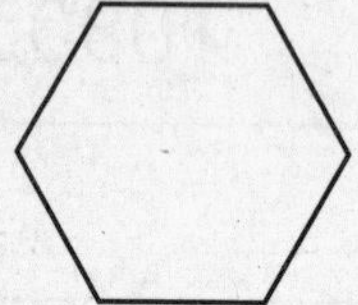 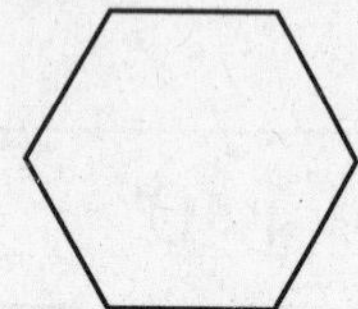 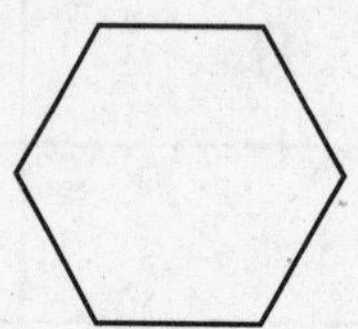

4. Why is neither polygon regular?

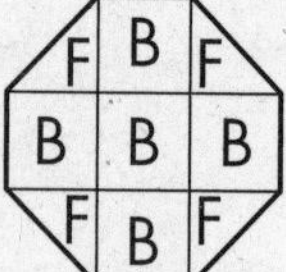

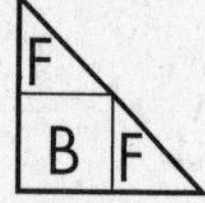

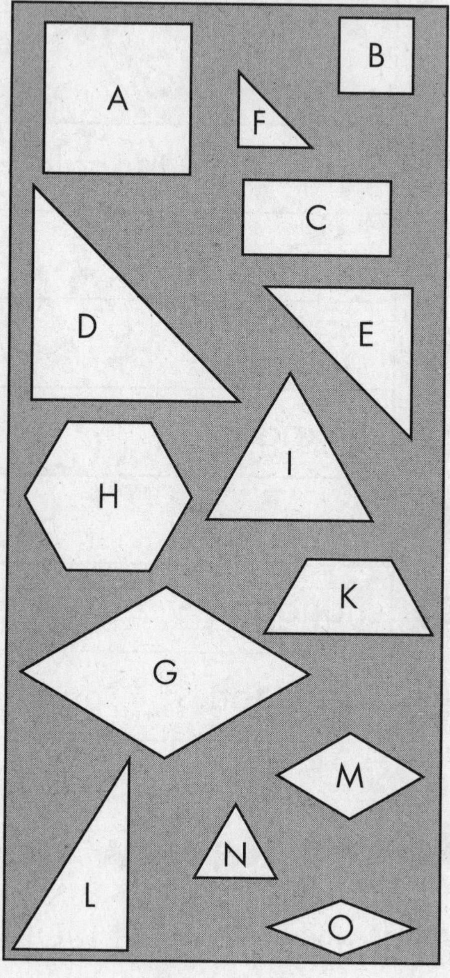

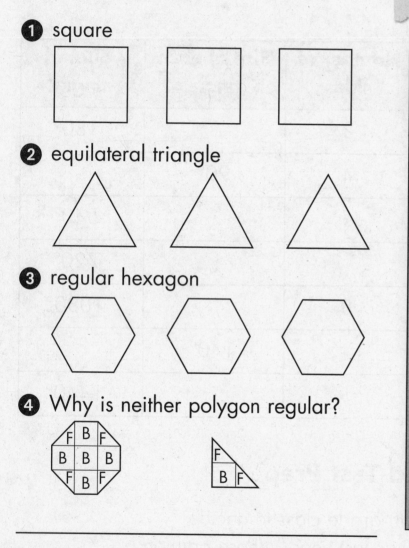

Mixed Review and Test Prep

5. Ben ordered items costing $2.35, $1.49, and $1.10 from a restaurant menu. What was the total cost?

A. $4.84 **B.** $4.94 **C.** $5.12 **D.** $5.94

Name Date

Similar Shapes

Are the shapes similar?
Write **yes** or **no.**

Family Connection

Students are learning to identify pairs of shapes that are mathematically similar. These shapes have corresponding angles that are equal, and corresponding sides that are proportional.

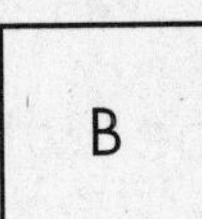

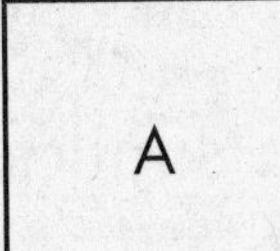

______

______

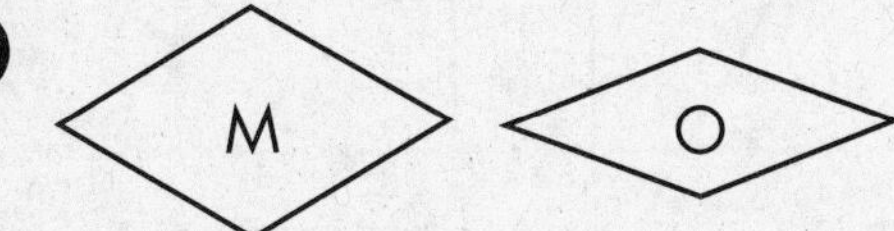

______

4
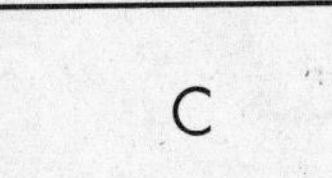

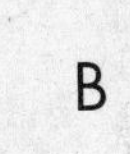

______

5
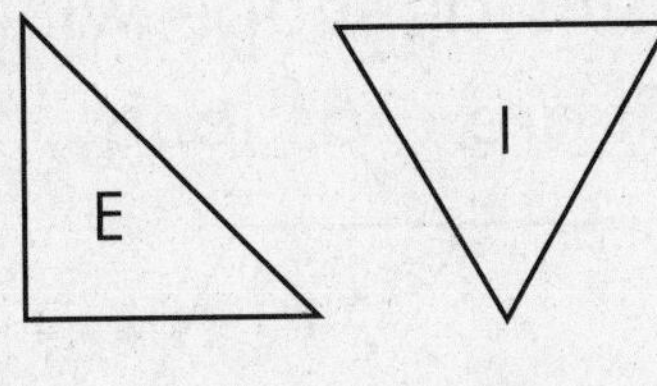

______

6
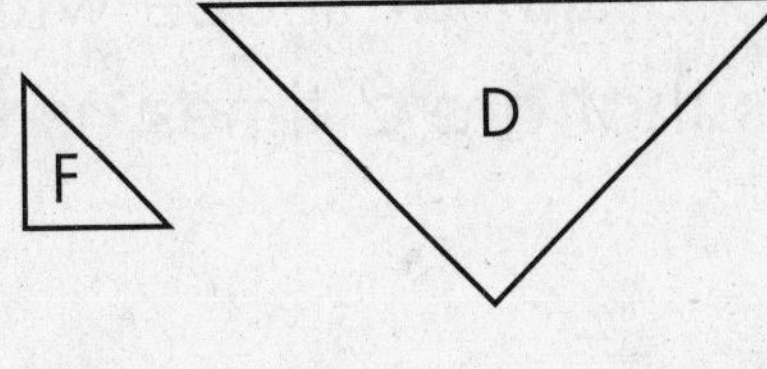

______

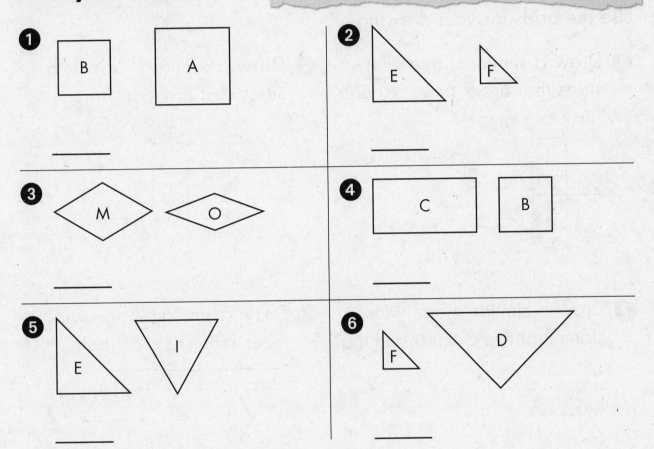

Mixed Review and Test Prep

7 The graph shows a car's speed over time. What does a line going up mean?

A. The car is accelerating.

B. The driver is buying gas.

C. The car is going up hill.

D. The car is heading north.

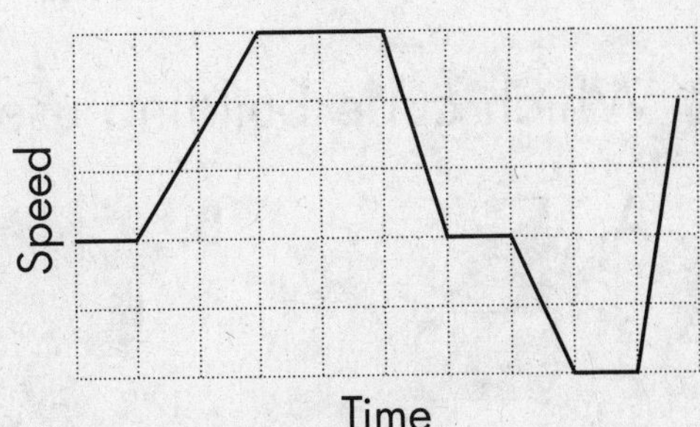

Name Date

Drawing Similar Shapes

Family Connection
Students have been building pairs of similar shapes with plastic pieces and on the computer. This page gives them a chance to draw similar shapes on grids.

Use the grids for your drawings.

1. Draw a similar shape with sides that are 2 times as long.
2. Draw a similar shape with sides that are $\frac{1}{2}$ as long.

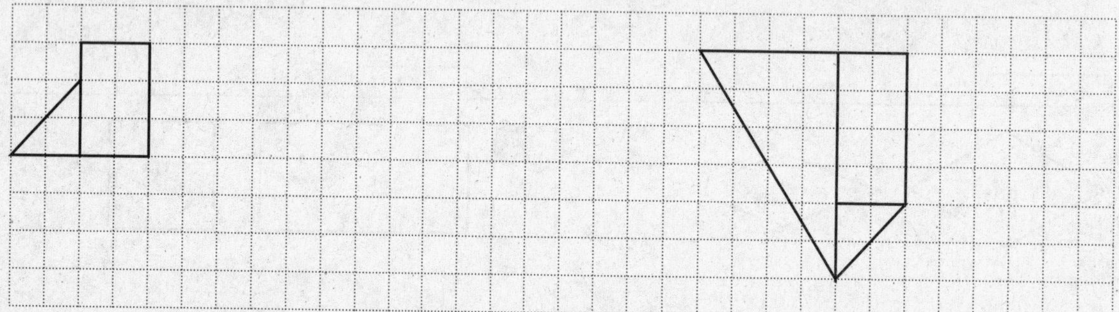

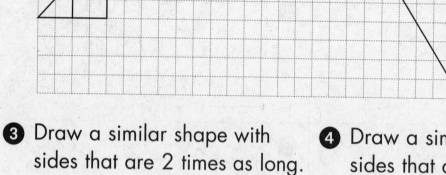

3. Draw a similar shape with sides that are 2 times as long.
4. Draw a similar shape with sides that are $\frac{1}{2}$ as long.

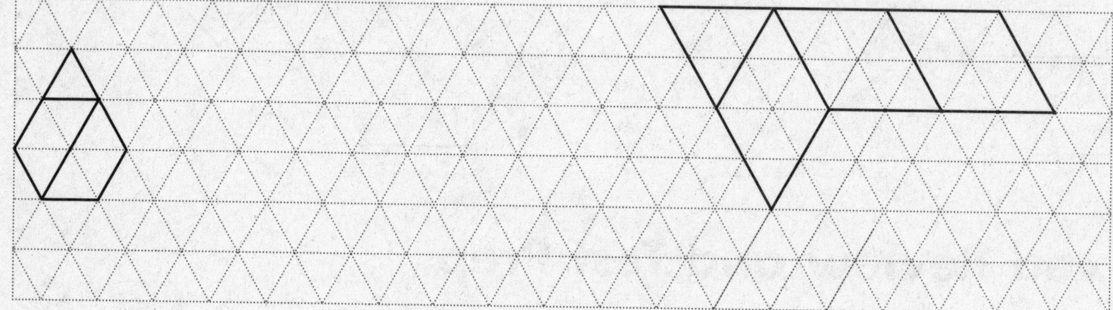

Mixed Review and Test Prep

5. Which cube building uses the fewest cubes?

A. 

B. 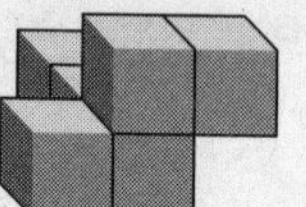

C. 

D. 

Name Date

Area Patterns

Count small squares or small triangles to find the areas.

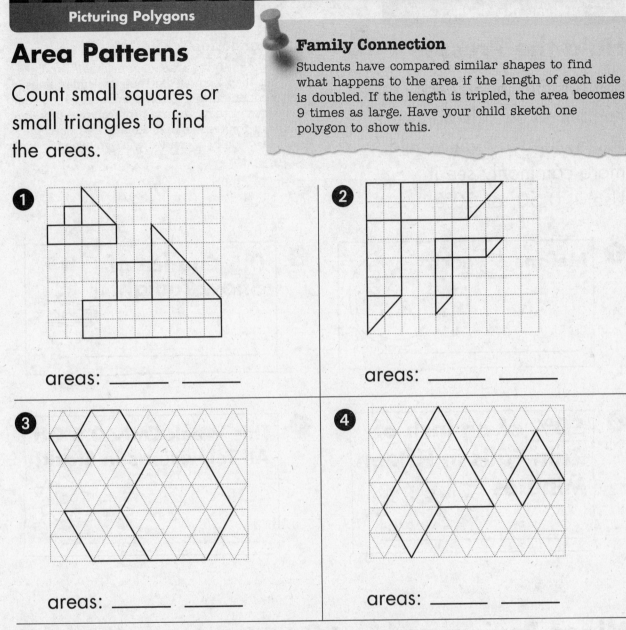

Family Connection

Students have compared similar shapes to find what happens to the area if the length of each side is doubled. If the length is tripled, the area becomes 9 times as large. Have your child sketch one polygon to show this.

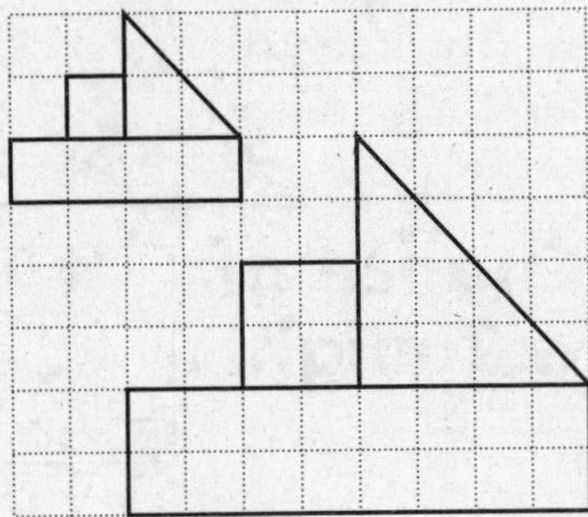

areas: ______ ______

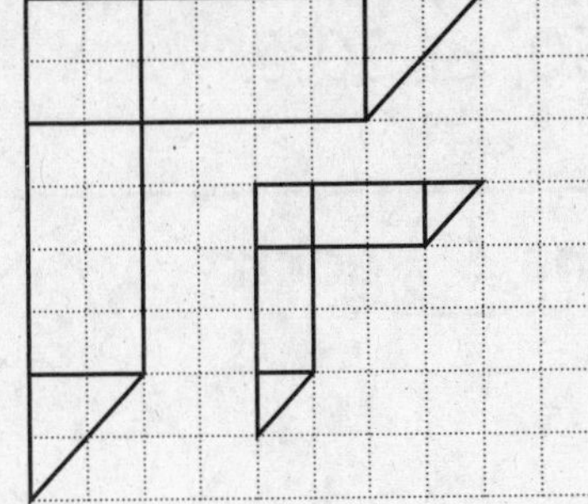

areas: ______ ______

areas: ______ ______

areas: ______ ______

5 In a pair of similar polygons, the polygon with sides that are 2 times as long as the other has an area that is ______ times as large.

Mixed Review and Test Prep

6 Complete this equation: $\frac{1}{2} + \frac{1}{6} =$ ______

A. 1 **B.** $\frac{2}{3}$ **C.** $\frac{1}{3}$ **D.** $\frac{3}{12}$

Name Date

Name That Portion

Hold the Presses

Rewrite the underlined number in each headline so it is the way you would more commonly see it. Use $\frac{1}{2}$, 0.50, or 50%.

Family Connection

Students are identifying fractions, decimals, and percents that they know from their everyday lives. They are becoming aware of situations in which each is used and when they are used interchangeably. Be on the lookout for fractions, decimals, and percents in the course of daily activities with your child.

1. 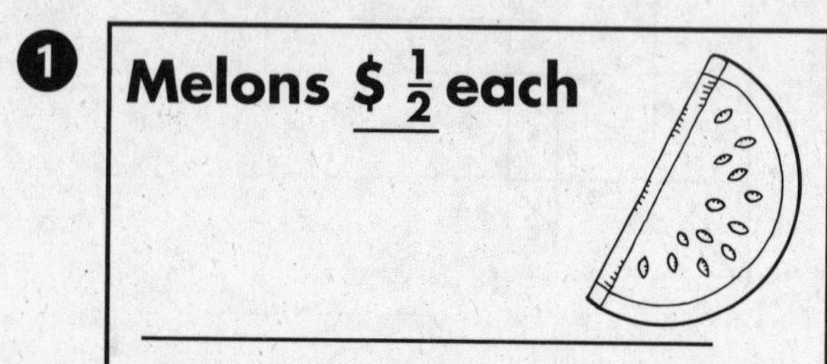

____

2. **$\underline{0.5}$ Chance of Snow Tonight**

____

3. 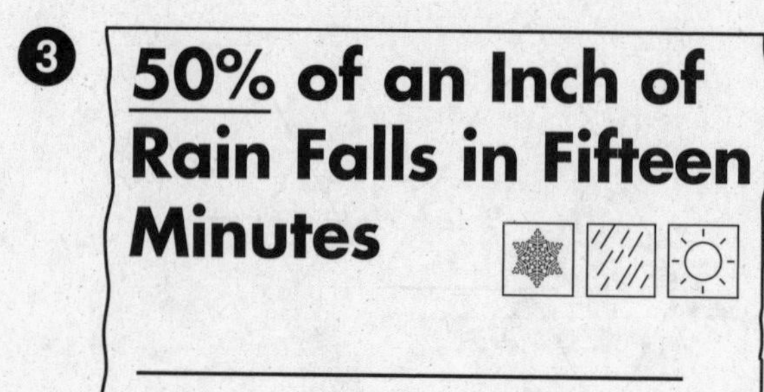

$\underline{50\%}$ of an Inch of Rain Falls in Fifteen Minutes

____

4. **This Week Only $\underline{0.5}$ Off All Televisions in Stock!**

Sale!

____

Mixed Review and Test Prep

5. Which list of numbers was used to make this line plot?

A. 15, 16, 16, 17, 17, 18, 18, 18

B. 15, 16, 16, 17, 18, 18, 18

C. 15, 16, 16, 17, 17, 18, 18

D. 15, 16, 16, 17, 18, 18, 18, 19

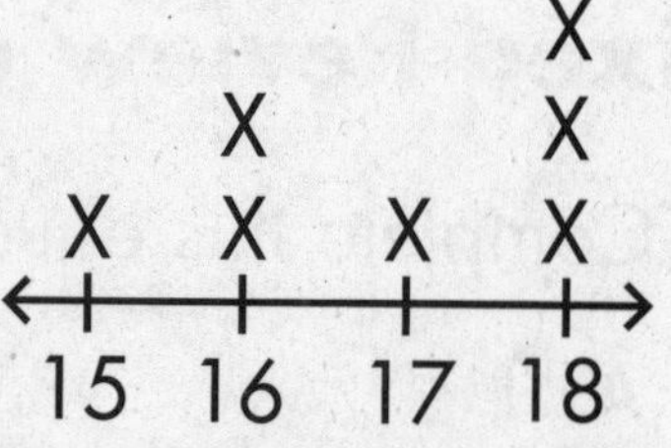

Name Date

Name That Portion

The 40% Pattern

1 Color 40% of the squares. Make a pattern.

2 Write a fraction for the part of the grid that is colored.

____

3 What percent of the grid is **not colored?**

____

4 How many more squares would you need to color to have 50% colored?

____

Family Connection

Students learned that just as \$20 **per hour** means "\$20 for each hour," 20 **percent** means "20 for each hundred." Percents can be written as fractions with 100 as the denominator. For example, 20% = $\frac{20}{100}$. In this activity, your child will make a pattern by coloring 40% of a 10-by-10 grid.

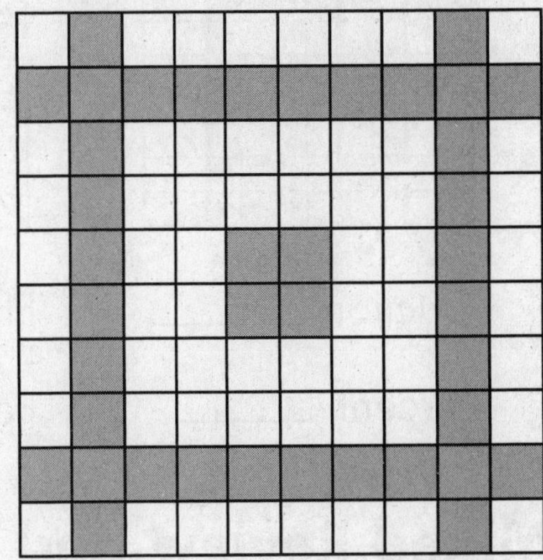

Mixed Review and Test Prep

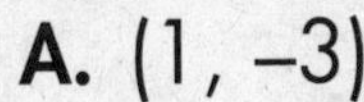

5 Each square on the grid represents 1 square block. Which location is fewer than 5 blocks from the circle?

A. (1, –3) **C.** (0, 3)

B. (2, –2) **D.** (1, 0)

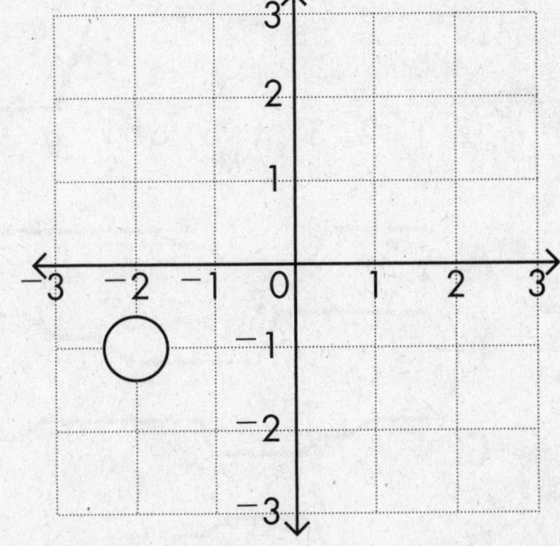

Name Date

Fractions of 100

Write the fraction for the shaded part of each grid. Then write the percent.

Family Connection

In class, students used 100-square grids to find percents for fractions. For example, they colored $\frac{1}{3}$ of the grid and found that it is $33\frac{1}{3}$ squares. Have your child tell you the percent for $33\frac{1}{3}$ out of 100.

1. 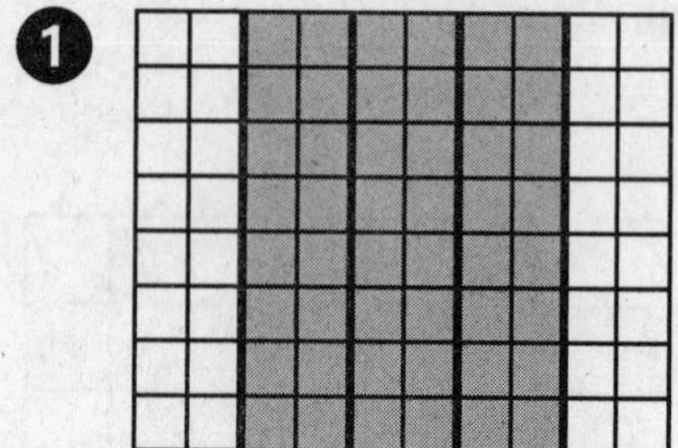

   Fraction ______

   Percent ______

2. 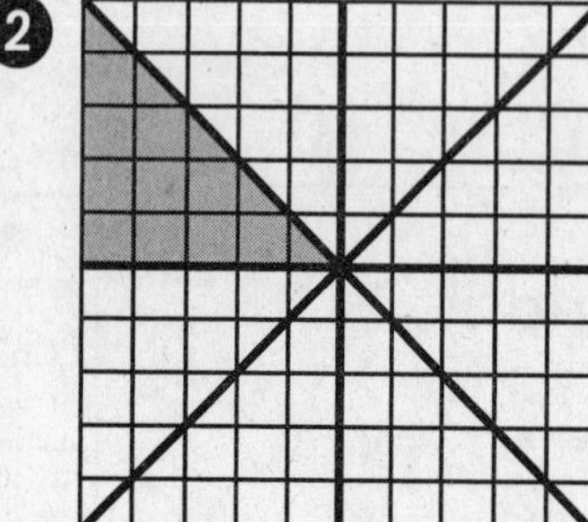

   Fraction ______

   Percent ______

3. 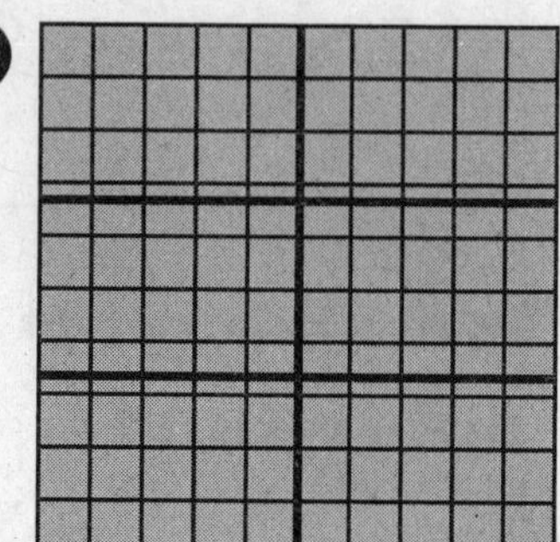

   Fraction ______

   Percent ______

Mixed Review and Test Prep

4. Which shows the pattern this graph might show over 3 days?

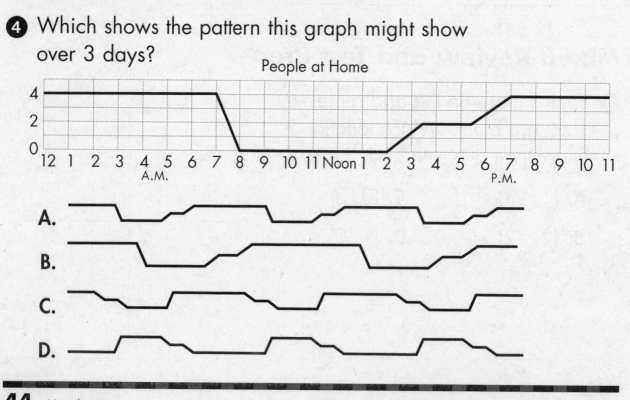

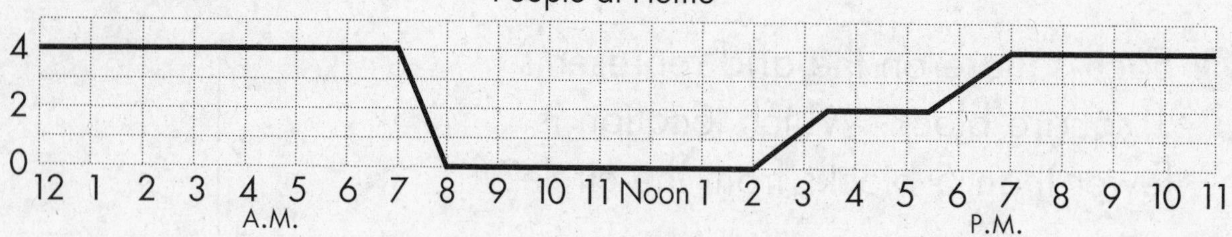

A.

B.

C.

D.

 Use during Investigation 1 (Exploring Percents and Fractions), Sessions 3 and 4.

Name Date

Name That Portion

It's All the Same

1 Match each grid to the fractions and percent that describe the shaded part of the grid.

Family Connection

Students are learning to identify fractions and percents that have the same value. For example $\frac{1}{2}$ is equal to $\frac{2}{4}$ or $\frac{3}{6}$ or $\frac{50}{100}$ or 50%. Ask your child if he or she knows other fractions equal to $\frac{1}{2}$.

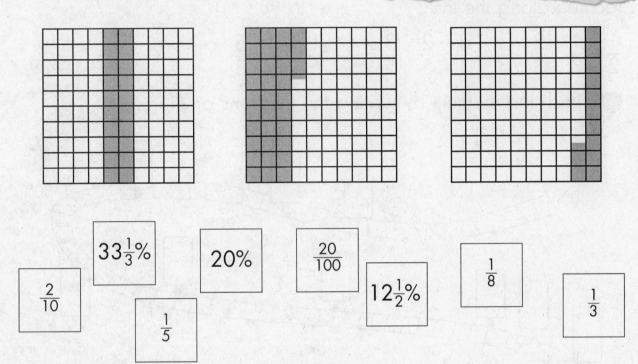

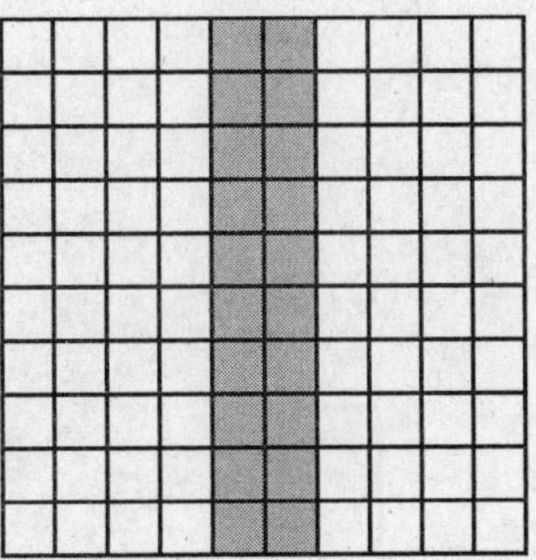

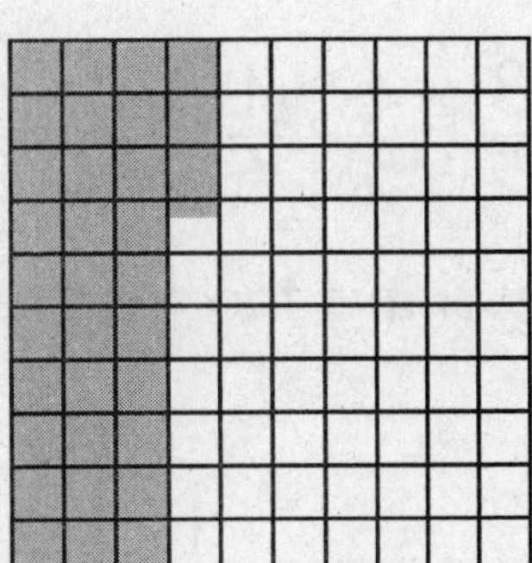

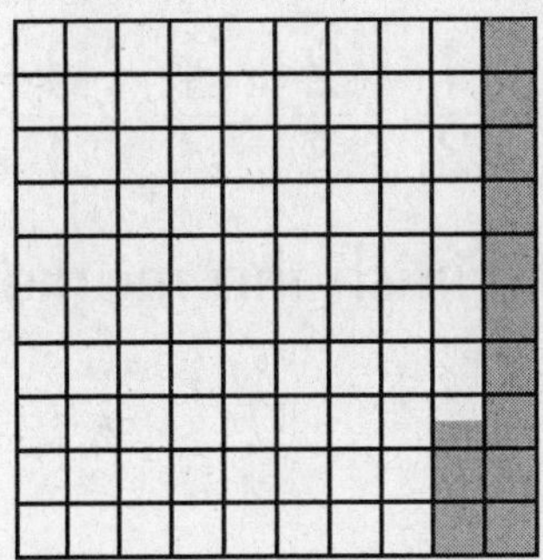

$\frac{2}{10}$ | $33\frac{1}{3}\%$ | $\frac{1}{5}$ | 20% | $\frac{20}{100}$ | $12\frac{1}{2}\%$ | $\frac{1}{8}$ | $\frac{1}{3}$

Mixed Review and Test Prep

2 Which two numbers total 100?

A. 28 + 62 **C.** 43 + 57

B. 71 + 39 **D.** 16 + 94

3 What is the sum of these two numbers? 38 + 26

A. 12 **C.** 62

B. 54 **D.** 64

Name Date

Name That Portion

Strolling the Percent Trail

Family Connection

In class, students made Percent Equivalent Strips. The strips and the trail shown here provide visual images of equivalent fractions and percents. Have your child tell you the percent for each fraction as he or she labels the signs along this trail.

Markers show where these fractions are located along the trail.

$\frac{1}{2}$ $\frac{1}{3}$ $\frac{2}{3}$ $\frac{1}{4}$ $\frac{3}{4}$ $\frac{2}{5}$ $\frac{3}{5}$ $\frac{4}{5}$ $\frac{1}{6}$ $\frac{1}{8}$ $\frac{5}{8}$

1 Finish the markers by writing the fractions on them.

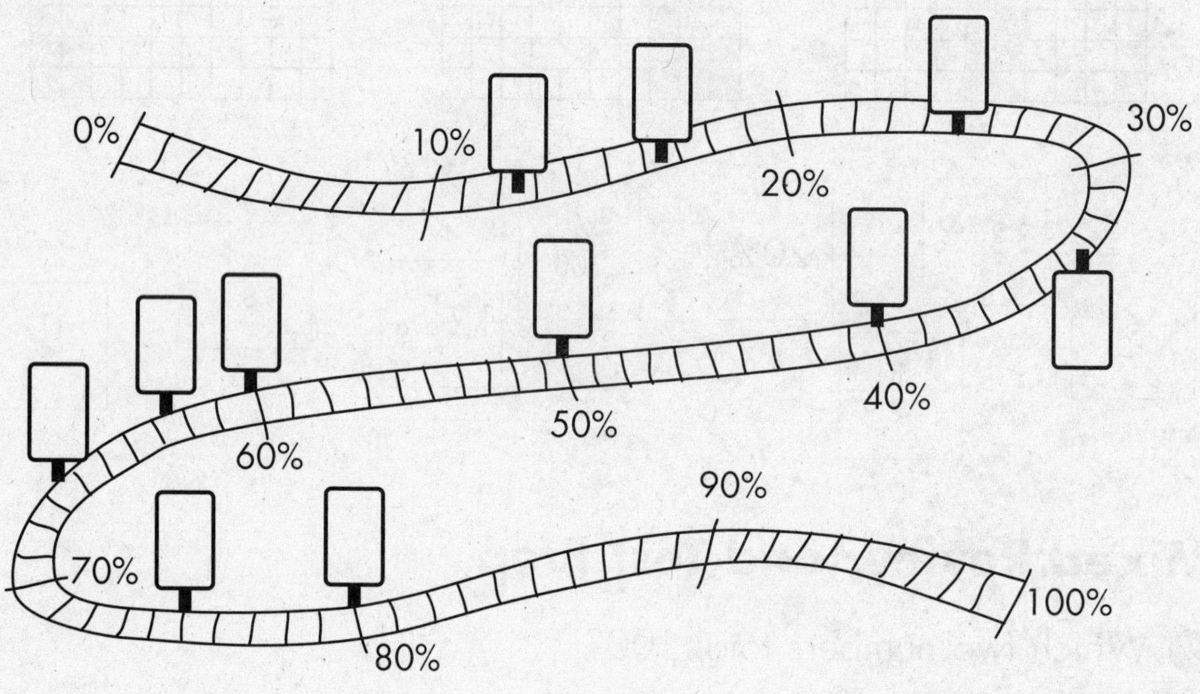

Mixed Review and Test Prep

2 Which of these is a factor of 225?

A. 9 **B.** 20 **C.** 22 **D.** 55

Name Date

Name That Portion

Ordering Fractions

Family Connection

Students have been playing the **In-Between Game.** This game provides practice comparing fractions and finding equivalent fractions and percents.

1. Write the above fractions in order. Some are done for you.

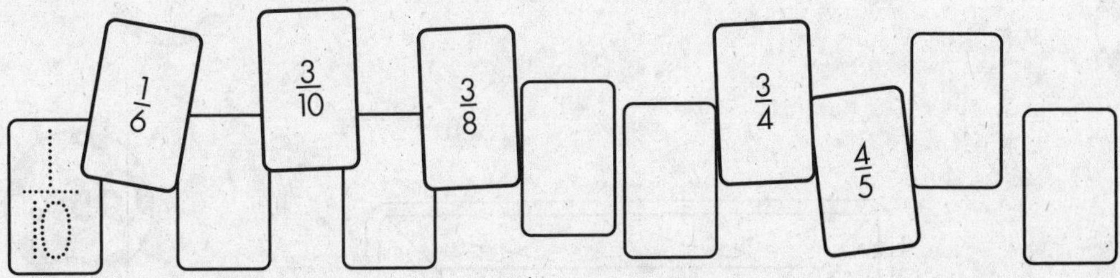

Mixed Review and Test Prep

2. Compare one half of the two shapes. Which statement is correct?

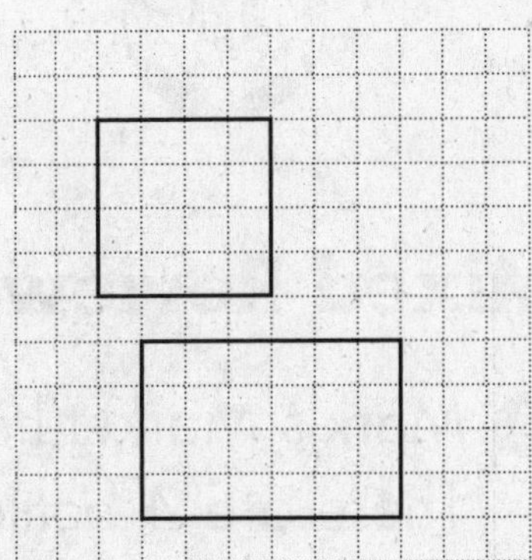

A. $\frac{1}{2}$ is 8 squares for both

B. $\frac{1}{2}$ is 12 squares for both

C. $\frac{1}{2}$ is the same size for both

D. $\frac{1}{2}$ of the bottom rectangle is bigger

Name Date

Name That Portion

Goal!

1 Draw lines to put each ball in the correct goal.

> **Family Connection**
>
> Students are learning to use $\frac{1}{2}$ and 1 as reference points for putting fractions and percents in order. Ask your child how he or she knows whether a percent or fraction is more than or less than $\frac{1}{2}$.

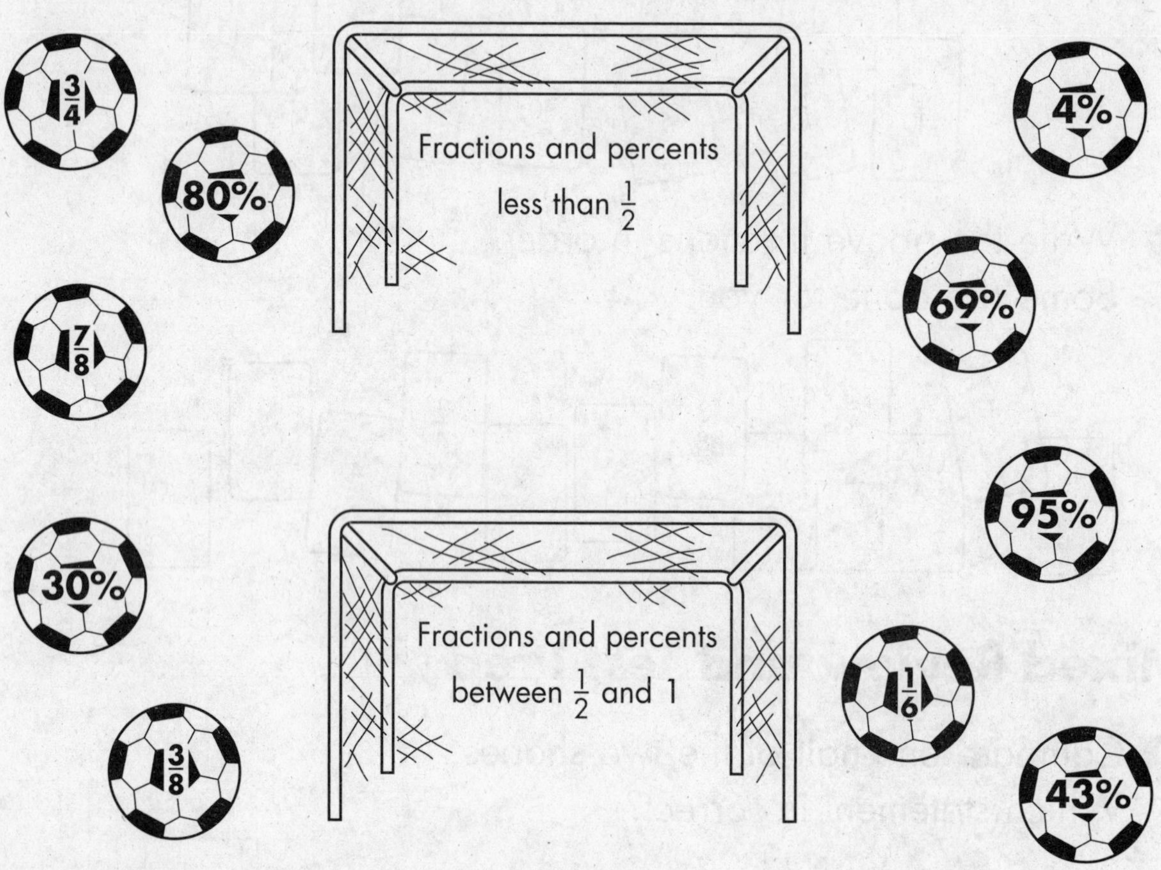

Mixed Review and Test Prep

2 Mark's Market has 27 cartons of iced tea in stock. There are 4 bottles in a carton. How many bottles of iced tea does Mark's Market have?

A. 31 **B.** 88 **C.** 108 **D.** 828

Name Date

Name That Portion

Round and Round

Laurie is the last person to get on the Ferris wheel. Everyone else has ridden part of the way around. Use the Ferris wheel to answer the questions.

Family Connection

In class, students used a clock to show fractions as rotation around a circle. This Ferris wheel shows fractions in the same way. Choose a name on the Ferris wheel and have your child tell you what fraction of the way around that person has ridden.

1. Who has ridden $\frac{2}{3}$ of the way around?

____

2. What fraction of the way around has Ike ridden?

____

3. Write at least two fractions to tell what part of the trip around Finn has made.

____

4. Who rode farthest? What fraction of the way around did he or she ride?

____

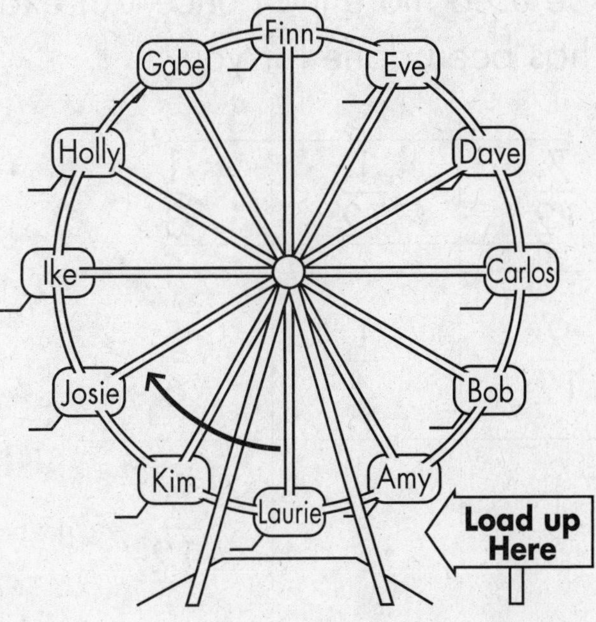

Interesting Tidbit

The original Ferris wheel was built in 1893 at a cost of $380,000.

Mixed Review and Test Prep

5. Which fraction is greater than $\frac{3}{4}$?

A. $\frac{11}{20}$ **B.** $\frac{15}{22}$ **C.** $\frac{25}{32}$ **D.** $\frac{3}{5}$

Name Date

Get One

Family Connection

Students have been playing a game called **Roll Around the Clock.** The object of the game is to add fractions to get a sum as close to 1 as possible. Have your child show you how he or she uses the clock face provided here to add fractions.

1 Use the clock face to add fractions. Draw a ring around sets of fractions that add up to 1. Use only fractions that are next to each other in a column or row. Some fractions will be used more than once. An example has been done for you.

$\frac{7}{12}$	$\frac{1}{12}$	$\frac{1}{3}$
$\frac{9}{12}$	$\frac{1}{4}$	$\frac{5}{6}$
$\frac{1}{6}$	$\frac{2}{3}$	$\frac{2}{12}$

Mixed Review and Test Prep

2 Which interval shows a hole in the data?

A. 250–274 lb **C.** 300–324 lb

B. 275–299 lb **D.** 325–349 lb

3 Seven people weigh less than Sam. Which could be Sam's weight?

A. 327 lb **C.** 265 lb

B. 304 lb **D.** 230 lb

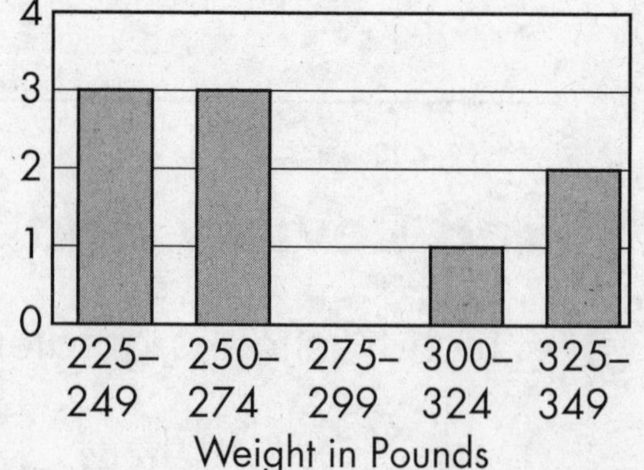

Name Date

Name That Portion

Down and Across

Add or subtract to fill in the boxes in the diagram. Use the fraction strips to help you.

Family Connection

Students made their own sets of fraction strips like those shown below. They have been using the fraction strips to help them add and subtract fractions. Have your child show you how he or she uses the fraction strips to find $\frac{5}{6} - \frac{2}{3}$.

1. $\frac{1}{6}$ $+\frac{2}{3}$ = ☐

2. $\frac{1}{2}$ $-\frac{1}{3}$ = ☐

$\frac{1}{6}$	$\frac{1}{6}$	$\frac{1}{6}$	$\frac{1}{6}$	$\frac{1}{6}$	$\frac{1}{6}$
$\frac{1}{3}$		$\frac{1}{3}$		$\frac{1}{3}$	
$\frac{1}{2}$			$\frac{1}{2}$		

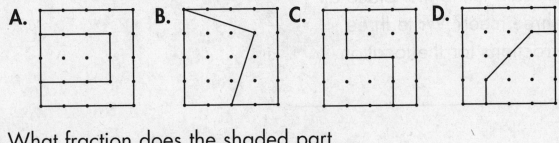

Mixed Review and Test Prep

3. Which square is divided in half?

A. **B.** 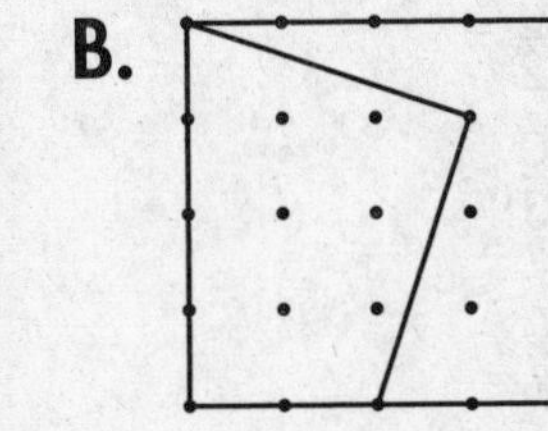 **C.** 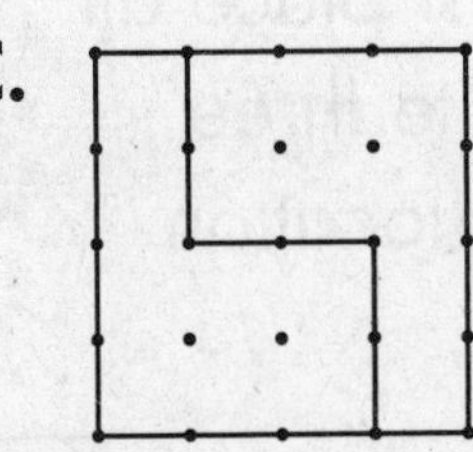 **D.** 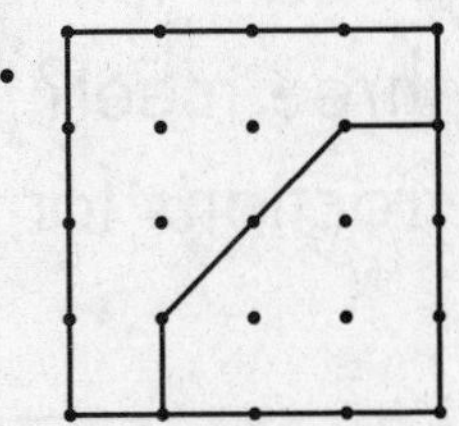

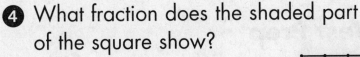

4. What fraction does the shaded part of the square show?

A. $\frac{1}{4}$ **C.** $\frac{3}{4}$

B. $\frac{1}{2}$ **D.** 8

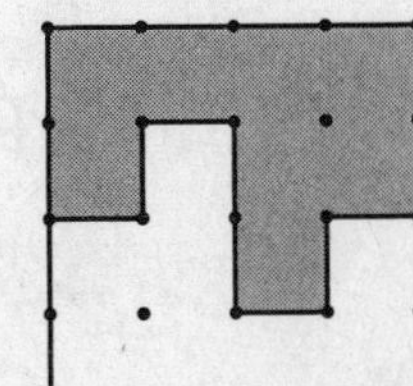

Name Date

Name That Portion

Where Shall We Meet?

Three fleas are trying to decide where to meet. Dottie Daryl leaps by $\frac{1}{2}$. Solid Sara leaps by $\frac{1}{3}$. Dashing Dora leaps by $\frac{1}{6}$.

Family Connection

Students have been counting by fractions, looking for equal fractions, and finding patterns among fractions. Have your child point out how the jumps of the fleas in this activity show counting by halves, thirds, and sixths.

1. Use fractions to label where Sara and Dora land. Daryl's landings have been done for you.
2. Where is the first place Daryl and Dora meet? Write two fractions for the location.

 ____

3. Where is the first place Sara and Dora meet? Write two fractions for the location.

 ____

4. Where is the first place all three meet? Write three fractions for the location.

 ____

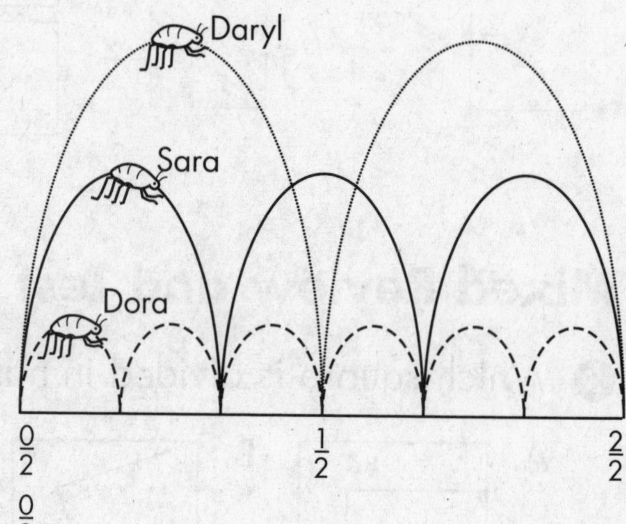

Mixed Review and Test Prep

5. What is the next number in this pattern?

 15, 25, 35, 45, ...

 A. 46 **B.** 50 **C.** 54 **D.** 55

Name Date

Name That Portion

Order Up

❶ Connect the dots in order from least to greatest. Then connect the last dot to the first.

Family Connection

Students have been learning how to put fractions in order. In the process they are using what they have learned about equal fractions and fraction patterns. If your child has trouble ordering the fractions to connect the dots in this puzzle, suggest that he or she use the Fraction Tracks worksheet from class to help.

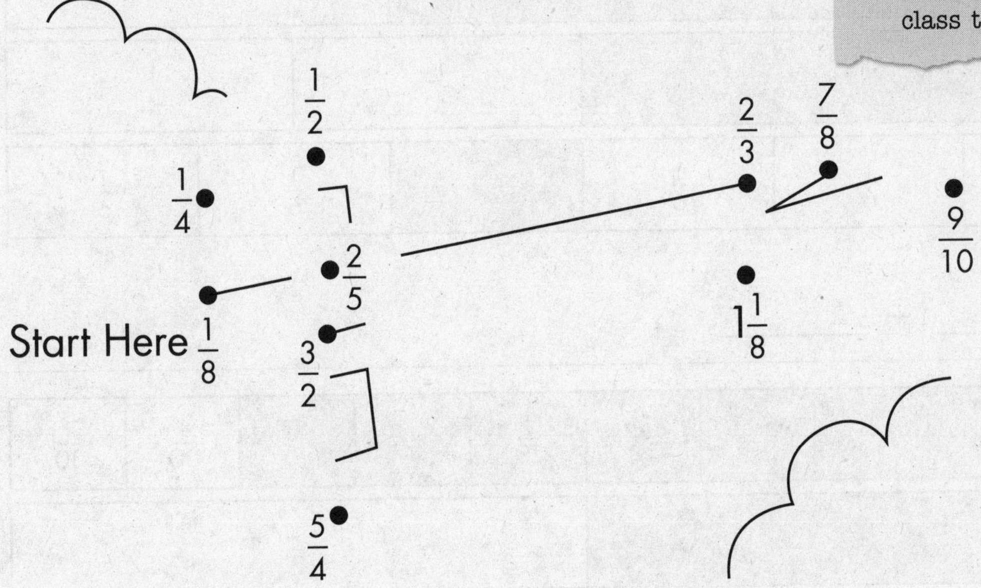

Mixed Review and Test Prep

❷ Which is the silhouette of the top of this shape?

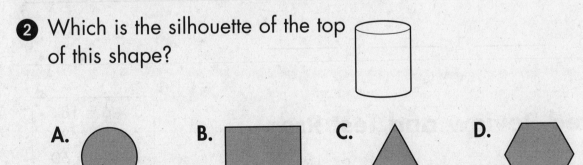

A. 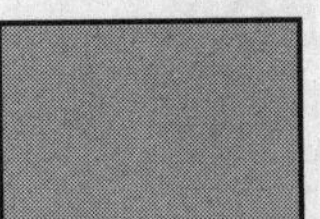 **B.**  **C.** **D.** 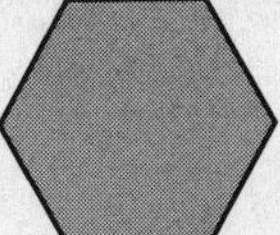

Name Date

Name That Portion

Breaking Apart Fractions

In Exercise 1, the fraction $\frac{2}{3}$ has been broken into two parts. In Exercise 2, the fraction $\frac{8}{10}$ has been broken into 3 parts. Finish the two equations.

Family Connection

Students have been playing the **Fraction Track Game.** This game requires them to break fractions into parts, find equal fractions, and add fractions. This page gives your child a different model of equivalent fractions and fraction addition.

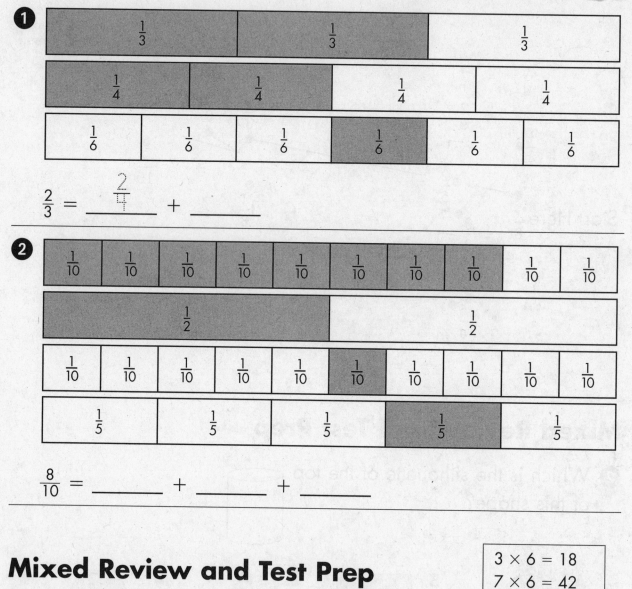

1

$\frac{1}{3}$	$\frac{1}{3}$	$\frac{1}{3}$

$\frac{1}{4}$	$\frac{1}{4}$	$\frac{1}{4}$	$\frac{1}{4}$

$\frac{1}{6}$	$\frac{1}{6}$	$\frac{1}{6}$	$\frac{1}{6}$	$\frac{1}{6}$	$\frac{1}{6}$

$\frac{2}{3}$ = $\frac{2}{4}$ + ______

2

$\frac{1}{10}$	$\frac{1}{10}$	$\frac{1}{10}$	$\frac{1}{10}$	$\frac{1}{10}$	$\frac{1}{10}$	$\frac{1}{10}$	$\frac{1}{10}$	$\frac{1}{10}$	$\frac{1}{10}$

$\frac{1}{2}$	$\frac{1}{2}$

$\frac{1}{10}$	$\frac{1}{10}$	$\frac{1}{10}$	$\frac{1}{10}$	$\frac{1}{10}$	$\frac{1}{10}$	$\frac{1}{10}$	$\frac{1}{10}$	$\frac{1}{10}$	$\frac{1}{10}$

$\frac{1}{5}$	$\frac{1}{5}$	$\frac{1}{5}$	$\frac{1}{5}$	$\frac{1}{5}$

$\frac{8}{10}$ = ______ + ______ + ______

Mixed Review and Test Prep

3 Use the cluster problems to find 37×6.

$3 \times 6 = 18$
$7 \times 6 = 42$
$10 \times 6 = 60$
$30 \times 6 = 180$
$37 \times 6 = ?$

A. 178 **B.** 222 **C.** 240 **D.** 242

Name Date

Name That Portion

Comparing Fractions

Family Connection
Students have been playing a game called **Capture Fractions.** In this game, the person who has the fraction with the higher value gets both fraction cards. This page gives your child additional practice comparing fractions.

Circle the greater fraction.

1. $\frac{1}{3}$ $\frac{3}{5}$	2. $\frac{5}{6}$ $\frac{2}{3}$	3. $\frac{1}{2}$ $\frac{1}{8}$
4. $\frac{3}{10}$ $\frac{3}{5}$	5. $\frac{4}{5}$ $\frac{1}{2}$	6. $\frac{7}{10}$ $\frac{1}{4}$
7. $\frac{3}{8}$ $\frac{5}{8}$	8. $\frac{2}{3}$ $\frac{3}{4}$	9. $\frac{1}{4}$ $\frac{3}{8}$
10. $\frac{4}{8}$ $\frac{3}{5}$	11. $\frac{9}{10}$ $\frac{4}{5}$	12. $\frac{2}{8}$ $\frac{1}{3}$

Mixed Review and Test Prep

13. Which shows the fractions in order from least to greatest?

A. $\frac{1}{2}, \frac{3}{8}, \frac{1}{6}$ **C.** $\frac{3}{8}, \frac{1}{2}, \frac{1}{6}$

B. $\frac{1}{6}, \frac{3}{8}, \frac{1}{2}$ **D.** $\frac{1}{6}, \frac{1}{2}, \frac{3}{8}$

Name Date

Name That Portion

Which Is Closer to 1?

Find the two totals.
Then circle the one that is closer to 1.

Family Connection

Students are continuing to play fraction games to improve their skills adding fractions, comparing fractions, and finding equal fractions.

1. $\frac{1}{2} + \frac{7}{12} =$ ______ $\frac{1}{6} + \frac{2}{3} =$ ______

2. $\frac{1}{4} + \frac{1}{3} =$ ______ $\frac{1}{6} + \frac{1}{2} =$ ______

3. $\frac{5}{10} + \frac{2}{5} =$ ______ $\frac{4}{12} + \frac{2}{4} =$ ______

4. $\frac{3}{4} + \frac{1}{4} =$ ______ $\frac{2}{8} + \frac{2}{4} =$ ______

5. $\frac{1}{8} + \frac{3}{4} =$ ______ $\frac{4}{6} + \frac{1}{3} =$ ______

Mixed Review and Test Prep

6. One mile is 5280 feet.
How many feet is $\frac{1}{10}$ of a mile?

A. 52,800 **B.** 580 **C.** 528 **D.** 52.8

7. One mile is 1760 yards.
How many yards is $\frac{2}{10}$ of a mile?

A. 3.52 **B.** 35.2 **C.** 352 **D.** 3520

Name Date

Name That Portion

What Do You Say About That?

Read the first statement and then use what that person said to complete the other statements.

Family Connection

Students are using what they have learned about fractions and percents to solve problems and describe events. Include fractions and percents in conversations with your child and encourage him or her to use fractions or percents to describe situations like these.

1

There were 12 muffins. Ben ate $\frac{1}{4}$ of them.
Ben ate ________ muffins.
There are ________ muffins left.
We still have ________% of the muffins.
Ben ate ________% of the muffins.

2

Shanna won 8 out of 10 tennis games.
Shanna won ________ of the games.
Shanna won ________% of the games.
Shanna lost ________% of the games.
Shanna lost ________ of the games.

Mixed Review and Test Prep

3 Match 7×6 with the expression that will give the same product.

A. $3 \times 6 + 4 \times 6$ **C.** $3 \times 4 + 3 \times 2$

B. $7 \times 4 + 7 \times 6$ **D.** $4 \times 4 + 3 \times 3$

Name Date

Name That Portion

Coming Through

1 0.5, 0.25, and 0.1 each want to get to the opposite side of the maze. They can move horizontally, vertically, or diagonally, but must always be on fractions equal to themselves. Find a path through the maze for each of them.

Family Connection

Students have discovered that fractions and decimals are two ways of naming the same number. They found that they can think of fractions as division. For example, $\frac{1}{5}$ is the same as $1 \div 5$. To find the decimal that is equal to $\frac{1}{5}$, students divided 1 by 5, $\frac{1}{5} = 1 \div 5 = 0.2$. In this activity, your child will identify fractions that are equal to the common decimals 0.5, 0.25, and 0.1.

0.25

$\frac{6}{20}$	$\frac{5}{10}$	$\frac{4}{40}$	$\frac{9}{10}$	$\frac{1}{4}$
$\frac{4}{8}$	$\frac{10}{100}$	$\frac{10}{20}$	$\frac{50}{100}$	$\frac{3}{12}$
$\frac{1}{2}$	$\frac{10}{40}$	$\frac{3}{30}$	$\frac{25}{100}$	$\frac{9}{18}$
$\frac{4}{16}$	$\frac{8}{10}$	$\frac{5}{20}$	$\frac{1}{10}$	$\frac{2}{3}$

Mixed Review and Test Prep

2 Which sum is closest to 100?

A. 24 + 52 + 4 **C.** 163 + 12 + 9

B. 7 + 86 + 55 **D.** 33 + 34 + 35

Name Date

Name That Portion

Tenths and Hundredths

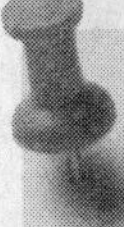

Family Connection
Students have been playing a fraction game called **Fill Two.** In this game decimal addition is modeled on hundred-square grids.

1. Color 0.40 and 0.25.

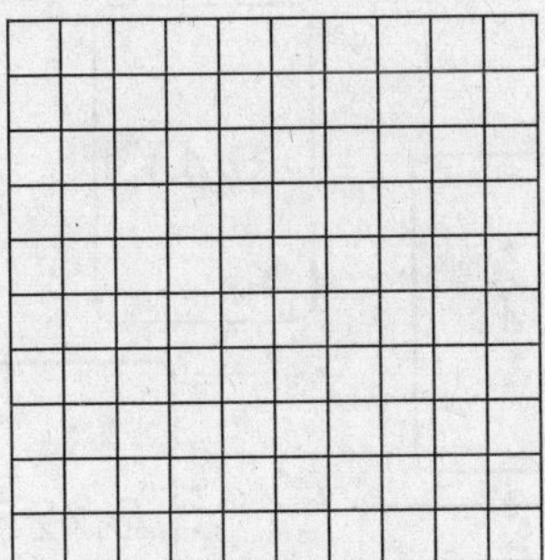

2. Color 0.45 and 0.15.

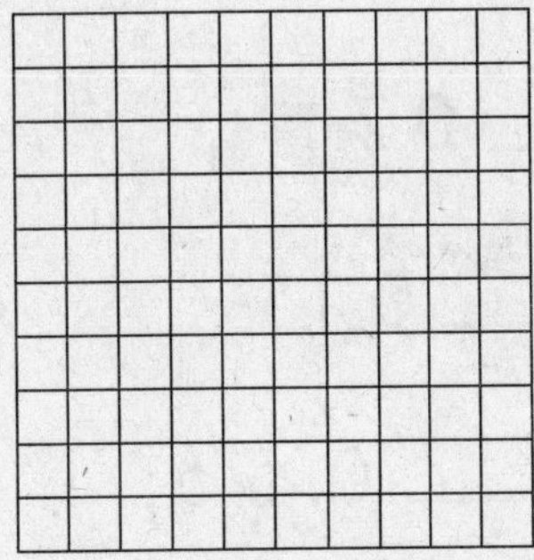

0.40 + 0.25 + 0.45 + 0.15 = ________

3. Color 0.18 and 0.70.

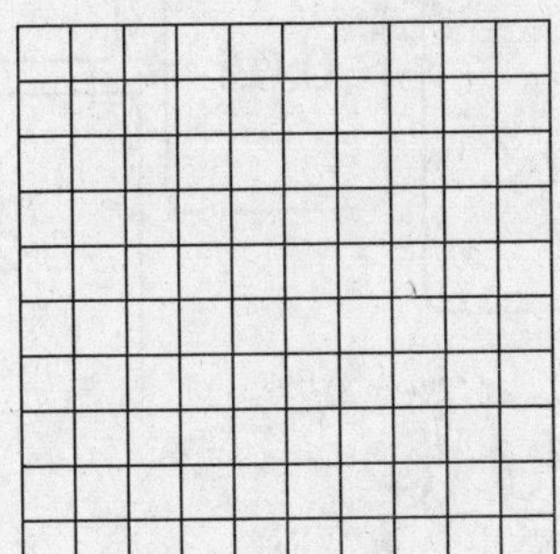

4. Color 0.55 and 0.30.

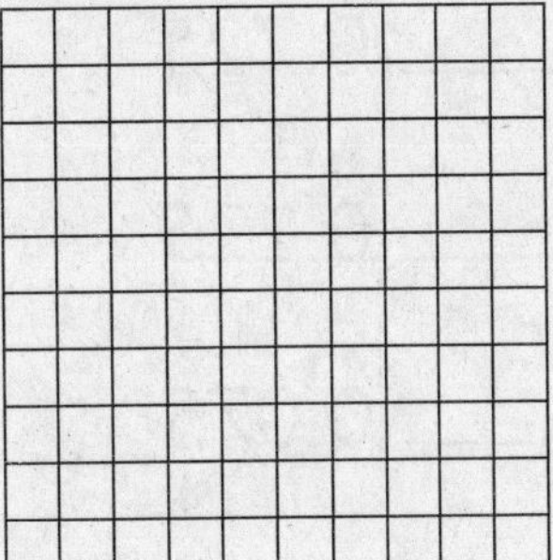

0.18 + 0.70 + 0.55 + 0.30 = ________

Mixed Review and Test Prep

5. Which is the next multiple of 60?
60, 120, 180, 240, 300, _____

A. 320 **B.** 340 **C.** 360 **D.** 400

Name Date

Name That Portion

Squeeze Between

Fit one of the decimals shown on the cards between the pair of decimals in each exercise. Two decimals will be left over.

Family Connection

In class, students are playing games in which they compare decimals and put them in order. Watch for everyday examples of decimals such as rainfall. **Questions you might ask your child:** "Did we get more rain on Tuesday or Wednesday?" "How can you tell?"

1. 0.6 ______ 0.7
2. 0.25 ______ 0.15
3. 0.425 ______ 0.475
4. 0.075 ______ 0.125
5. 0.55 ______ 0.5
6. 0.675 ______ 0.725
7. 0.275 ______ 0.225
8. 0.025 ______ 0.075
9. 0.715 ______ 0.8
10. 0.4 ______ 0.3

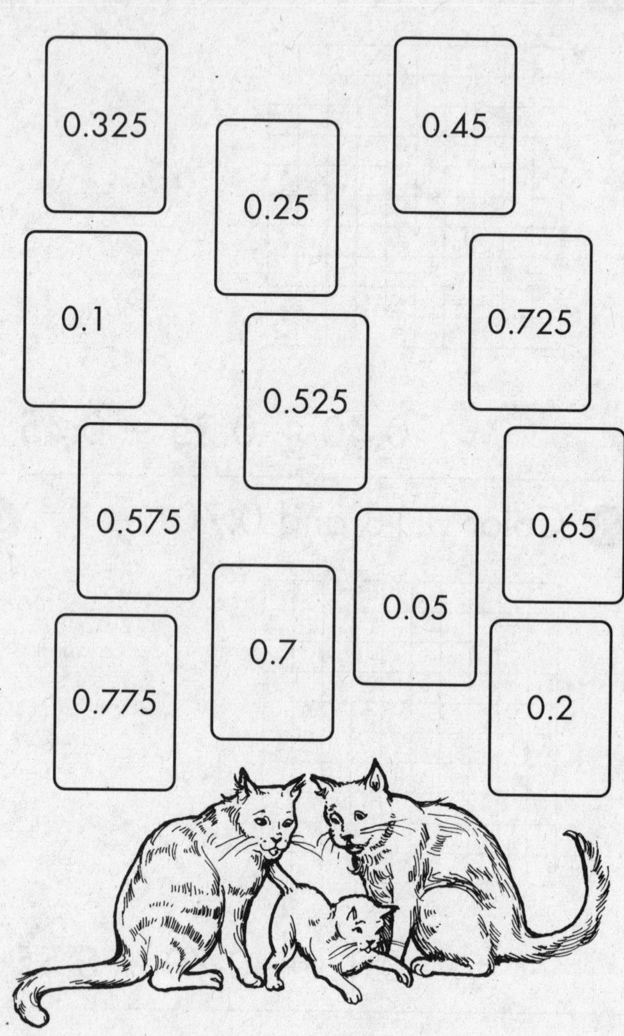

Mixed Review and Test Prep

11. Which fraction is between 0 and $\frac{1}{2}$?

A. $\frac{3}{2}$ **B.** $\frac{6}{8}$ **C.** $\frac{4}{6}$ **D.** $\frac{3}{8}$

Name Date

Name That Portion

Going Up

Family Connection
In class, students are playing a game called **Smaller to Larger** in which they order fractions in a grid like the one shown here. Ask your child to share his or her strategies for putting the decimals in order.

❶ Arrange the decimals in the grid so that each row from left to right and each column from top to bottom is in increasing order.

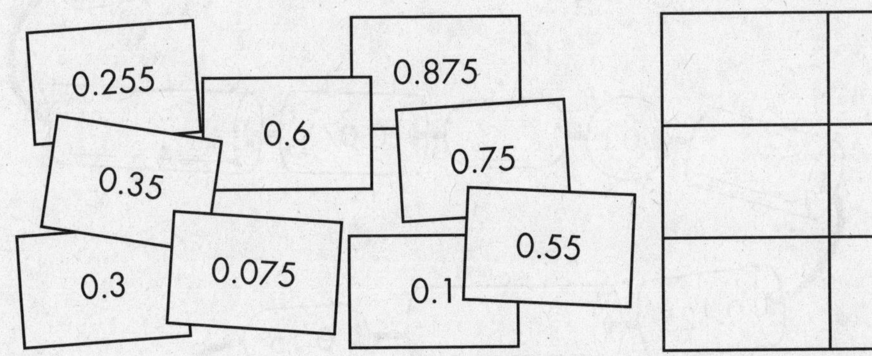

Mixed Review and Test Prep

❷ Which shows the fewest coins for this amount of money?

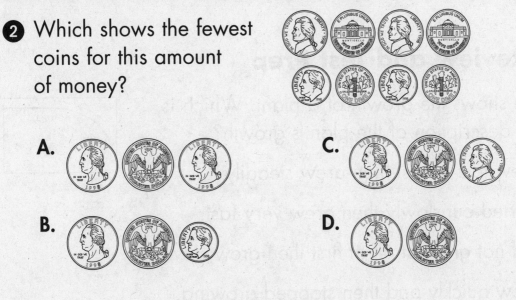

A. 

C. 

B. 

D. 

Name Date

Name That Portion

Stringing Along

Each number fits between two of the numbers in the string. Write the numbers where they belong.

Family Connection

Students are finding decimals with values between two given decimals. For example, 0.93 and 0.942 are decimals between 0.925 and 0.95. Ask your child how he or she knew where to put 0.13 on the string of numbers shown here.

1. 0.13
2. 0.015
3. 0.09
4. 0.062
5. 0.158
6. Write a decimal for any unnumbered bead.

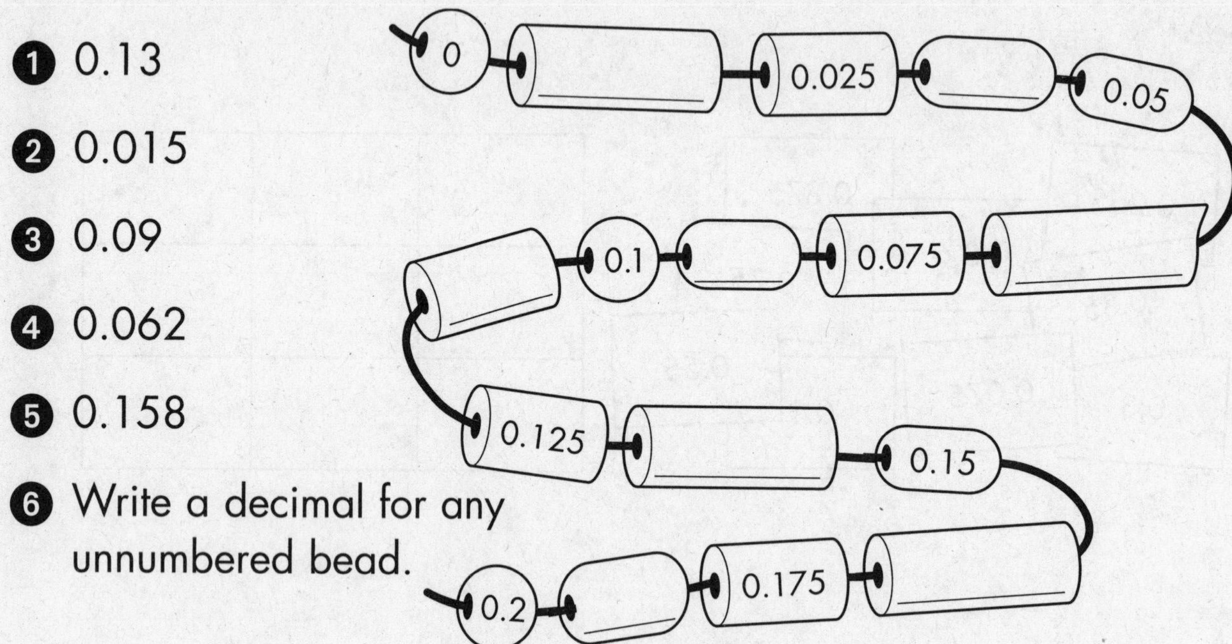

Mixed Review and Test Prep

7. This line shows the growth of a plant. Which is the best description of the plant's growth?

   A. It grew fast at first then grew steadily.

   B. It started out slowly then grew very fast.

   C. It did not grow at all at first then grew slowly.

   D. It grew quickly and then stopped growing.

Name Date

Name That Portion

More or Less

Tell if the decimal is a little more or a little less than its closest fraction on the number line. The first one is done for you.

Family Connection

Students continue to study the relationship between fractions and decimals. They are learning to relate decimals to landmark fractions such as those shown on this number line. Ask your child what the decimal is for each of these landmark fractions.

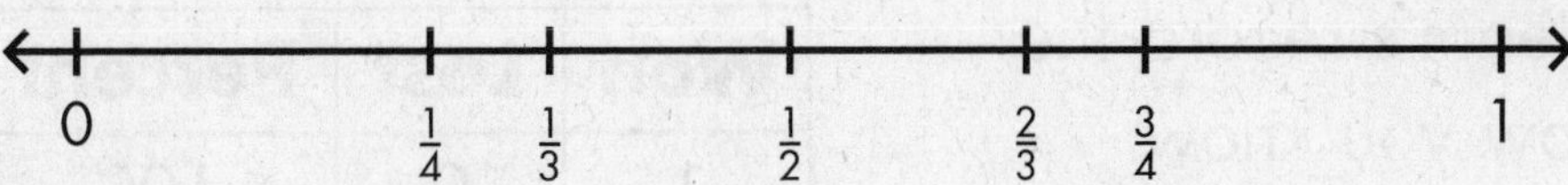

1. 0.22 is a little less than $\frac{1}{4}$.
2. 0.342 is a little ________ than $\frac{1}{3}$.
3. 0.772 is a little ________ than $\frac{3}{4}$.
4. 0.98 is a little ________ than 1.
5. 0.626 is a little ________ than $\frac{2}{3}$.
6. 0.553 is a little ________ than $\frac{1}{2}$.

Mixed Review and Test Prep

7. Which number sentence can be used to solve this problem:

   How many capes can Mandy make from 42 yards of fabric if she needs 6 yards of fabric for each cape?

   A. $42 \div 6 =$ ____ **C.** $42 + 6 =$ ____

   B. $42 - 6 =$ ____ **D.** $42 \times 6 =$ ____

Name Date

Name That Portion

Go Team!

After each game, Ben recorded how many games his team had won, how many they lost, and what percent of the games they won.

Family Connection

Students are using what they have learned about fractions, decimals, and percents to answer questions about sports records. For the record shown here, have your child explain how the percent of games won was calculated.

1. When was the team's record the best? Explain how you know.

Won	Lost	Percent
1	0	100
2	0	100
2	1	$66\frac{2}{3}$
3	1	75
3	2	60
3	3	50

2. How did the record change as the team played more games?

Mixed Review and Test Prep

3. Which shape could NOT make this silhouette? 

A. 

B. 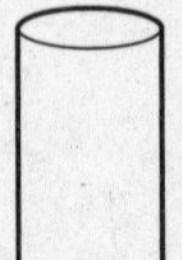

C. 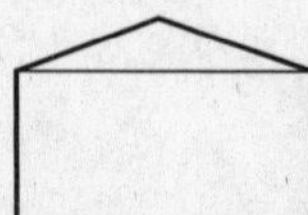

D. 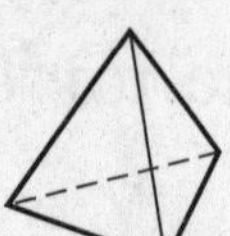

Name Date

Name That Portion

Compare Fractions

Family Connection
Students have been working on posters showing that one fraction is greater than another. The posters show some of the ways you can think about fractions to help you decide which is greater. Here your child will write an explanation for someone else's work.

1. Kelly drew the pictures for her poster on comparing fractions. Title the poster to tell what fractions Kelly is comparing. Then compare the fractions by explaining each drawing.

____

____

____

____

____

____

____

0.6666666

0.75

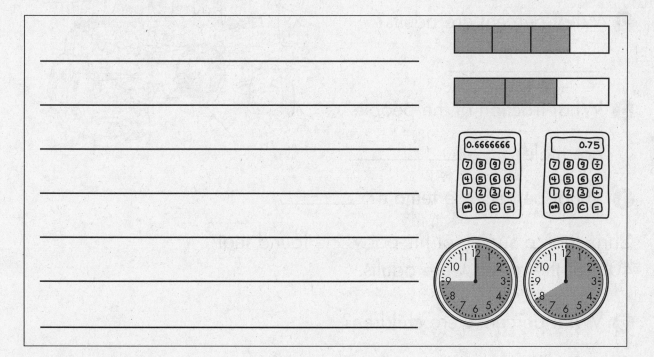

Mixed Review and Test Prep

2. Choose the best estimate for 27 × 34.

A. between 600 and 800

B. between 900 and 1,000

C. between 1,000 and 1,200

D. between 1,200 and 1,600

Name Date

Name That Portion

Party Survey

Use this picture to answer questions 1–4.

Family Connection

In class, students planned surveys they will be taking over the next few days. Their surveys will compare the interests and activities of adults and children, and males and females. Ask your child what his or her survey is about.

1. What fraction of the people are children? ______________

2. What percent are adults? ______________

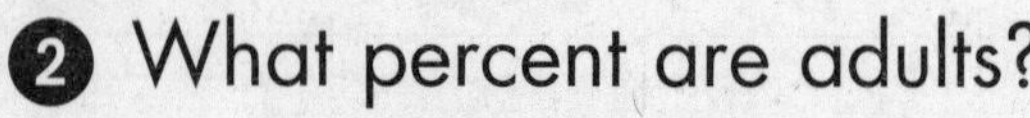

3. What fraction of the people are male? ______________

4. What percent are female? ________

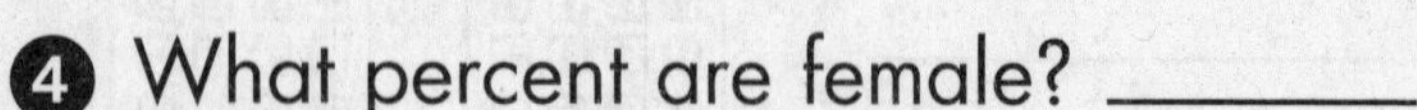

Chris took a survey at his party. He found that 40% of the guests were adults.

5. What percent were children? ________

6. What fraction of the guests were children? ______________

Mixed Review and Test Prep

7. A number ends in the digit 4. Which is always a factor of this number?

A. 3 **B.** 2 **C.** 8 **D.** 12

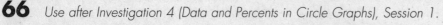

Name Date

Name That Portion

Graphing Around

Draw and color a graph for each set of data.

Family Connection

Students are learning how to draw circle graphs for two groups of data. Watch for examples of simple circle graphs in newspapers or magazines. Talk with your child about what the circle graphs show. Encourage your child to interpret the graphs using fractions and percents.

1. Children on the swings:

   6 girls

   4 boys

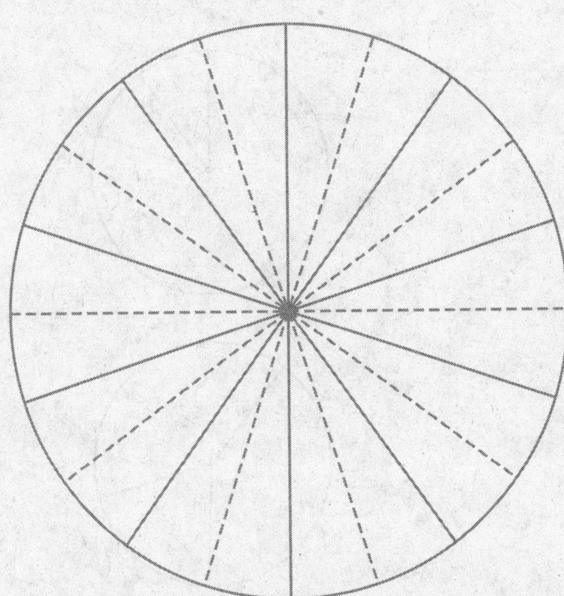

2. People on the bus:

   35% adult

   65% children

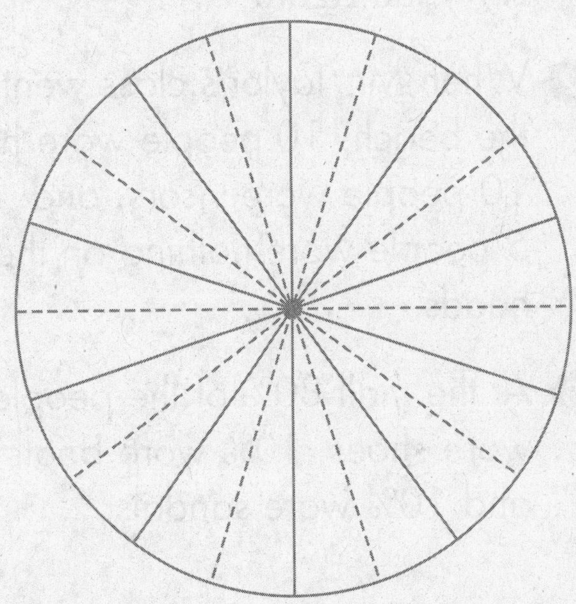

Mixed Review and Test Prep

3. What is the 7th number in this pattern?

   4, 24, 44, 64, ___, ___, ___

   A. 124 **B.** 94 **C.** 84 **D.** 74

Name Date

Name That Portion

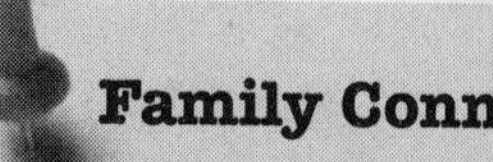

Slicing the Pie

Draw lines to match each graph with its description.

Family Connection

Students are learning to recognize the relationship between the way the data is divided and the way the circle graph is divided. Ask your child to tell you how he or she decided which of the graphs shown here match each set of data.

1 A survey about favorite class animal showed $\frac{1}{6}$ of the class liked Bill the Banana Slug, $\frac{1}{2}$ liked Mark the Mouse, and $\frac{1}{3}$ liked Larry the Lizard.

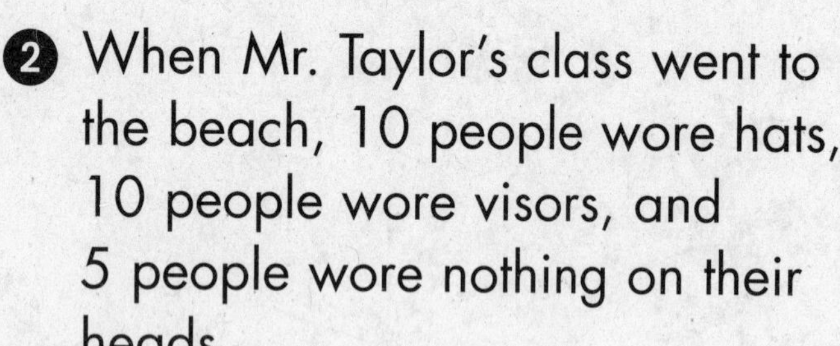

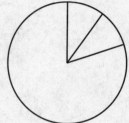

2 When Mr. Taylor's class went to the beach, 10 people wore hats, 10 people wore visors, and 5 people wore nothing on their heads.

3 At the mall 80% of the people wore shoes, 10% wore boots, and 10% wore sandals.

Mixed Review and Test Prep

4 Which shape is at (0, −2)?

A. (cross shape) C. (triangle)

B. (circle) D. (pentagon)

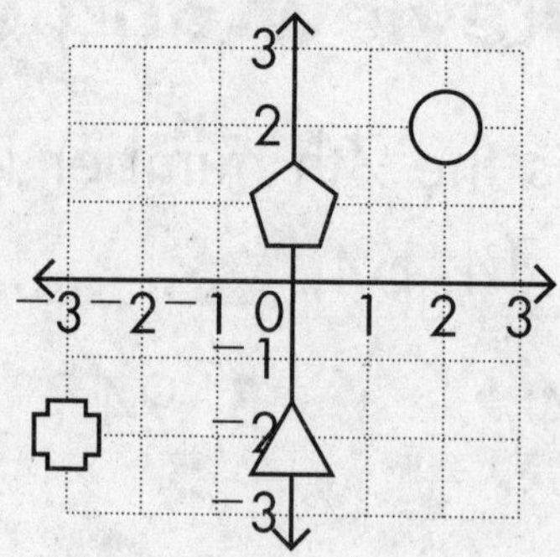

Name Date

Can It Be?

Decide if each statement is possible or impossible. Tell why.

Family Connection

Students have been deciding if descriptions of everyday situations involving percent make sense mathematically. Ask your child to explain how he or she decided if each of these statements is possible or impossible.

1. At the water park, 60% of the people are female. 50% of the females wear goggles.

____

____

2. 65% of the people at the park are under age ten. 55% are ten or older.

____

____

3. One day 100% of the people at the water park rode the super slide and 100% of the people swam in the pool.

____

____

Mixed Review and Test Prep

4. Which fraction is the greatest?

A. $\frac{2}{3}$ **B.** $\frac{4}{2}$ **C.** $\frac{5}{6}$ **D.** $\frac{1}{2}$

Name Date

Name That Portion

Story-Time Survey

Jason and Julia counted people who attended story time at the city library. Answer these questions about the results of their survey.

Family Connection

Students are working on reports showing the results of the surveys they took. Students begin with the raw data (the results of the survey), and write fractions and percents showing how the data is divided. Ask your child to share the results of his or her surveys with you.

Survey results:

Adults: 15 Children: 45 Total: 60 people

1. Report these results as fractions.

2. Report the results as familiar fractions and as percents.

3. If the people who come to the next story time are surveyed, do you think the results will be the same? Why or why not?

Mixed Review and Test Prep

4. Which is the best estimate of the total cost of a $3.49 box of cereal and a $2.89 carton of yogurt?

A. $5.00 **B.** $6.50 **C.** $8.00 **D.** $8.50

Name Date

Name That Portion

Right or Wrong?

Answer the questions about the survey shown.

Family Connection

Students are continuing to work on their survey reports. In the reports, they compare the results of their survey to their original hypothesis. Ask your child to tell you how his or her results compared to the group's original hypotheses.

Hypothesis: More men than women go to the auto parts store.
Predictions: Men 90% Women 10%

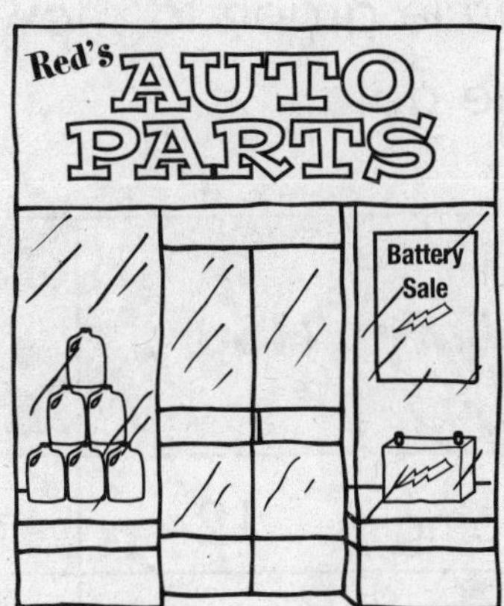

Survey results:
Wednesday between 3 P.M. and 5 P.M.
People entering Red's Auto Parts:
Men: 32 Women 8

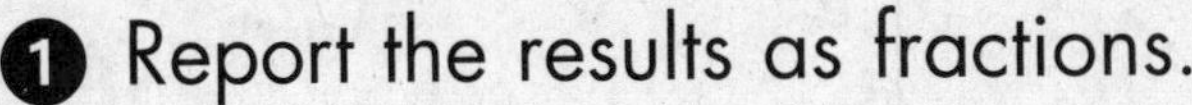

1. Report the results as fractions.

____

2. Report the results as percents.

____

3. Did the results match the hypothesis? Explain.

____

____

____

Mixed Review and Test Prep

4. How much money do you need to buy two items priced $2.88 and $1.29?

A. $3.07 **B.** $3.17 **C.** $4.07 **D.** $4.17

Name Date

Name That Portion

Make a Circle Graph

1 This chart shows a day in Kitty's life. Complete the chart. Then draw a circle graph to show the data.

Family Connection

Students have been making tables and drawing circle graphs to show how they spend their days now and how they imagine they will spend their days at age 30. Ask your child to explain how he or she made this circle graph for a day in Kitty's life.

Category	Hours	Fraction of Day	Percent of Day
Sleeping	12	$\frac{12}{24}$ or $\frac{1}{2}$	50%
Playing	6		
Bird Watching	3		
Grooming and Eating	3		

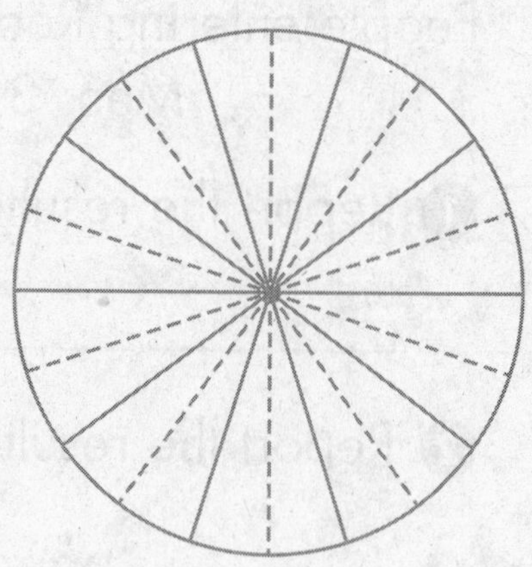

Mixed Review and Test Prep

2 Suppose you have 230 cubes in a box. How many groups of 5 cubes can you take out of the box?

A. 406 **B.** 64 **C.** 46 **D.** 23

3 How many groups of 10 can you take out of the box?

A. 230 **B.** 64 **C.** 23 **D.** 13

Name Date

Between Never and Always

Chancy Events

1. Draw a line to show how likely you think each event is.

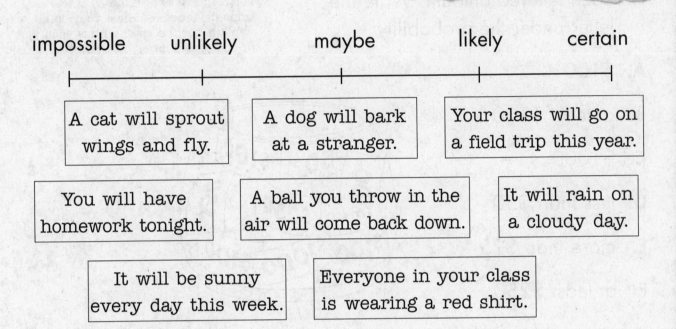

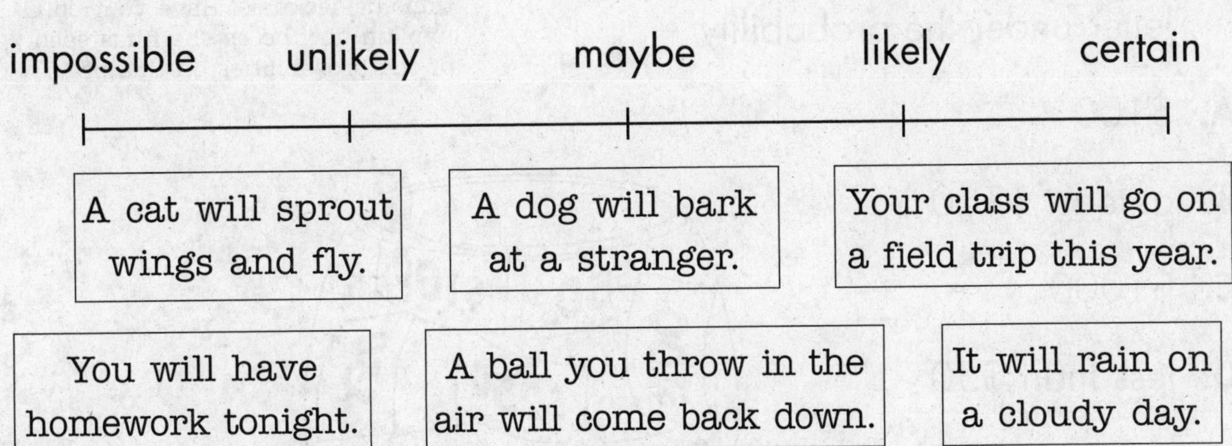

impossible
unlikely
maybe
likely
certain
A cat will sprout wings and fly.
A dog will bark at a stranger.
Your class will go on a field trip this year.
You will have homework tonight.
A ball you throw in the air will come back down.
It will rain on a cloudy day.
It will be sunny every day this week.
Everyone in your class is wearing a red shirt.

Mixed Review and Test Prep

2. A class of 32 students rides a tram. Each of the tram's cars holds 5 people. How many tram cars does the class need?

A. 160 **B.** 37 **C.** 7 **D.** 6

3. Fancy Farms packs 6 apples in a box. How many boxes will 39 apples fill?

A. 6 **B.** 7 **C.** 45 **D.** 234

Name Date

Dollar Draw

1 Hannah won a chance to draw a gift certificate from the bowl. Find the probability that Hannah will get each lettered amount. Write the letter under the probability.

A. $100

B. at least $100

C. $1000

D. less than $50

E. more than $25

F. at least $250

Family Connection

Students are learning how to express the likelihood of an event as a number. An event that is impossible has a probability of zero. An event that is certain to happen has a probability of one. Events with probabilities in between are expressed as fractions or decimals. Have your child explain how he or she finds each of the probabilities on this page.

impossible unlikely maybe likely certain

0 $\frac{1}{8}$ $\frac{1}{4}$ $\frac{1}{2}$ $\frac{3}{4}$ 1

0.25 0.5 0.75

Mixed Review and Test Prep

2 Count by 25's. What number comes next?

525, 550, 575, 600, 625, ____

A. 626 **B.** 630 **C.** 650 **D.** 675

Name Date

Between Never and Always

Spin to Win

Family Connection

Students have been comparing the actual results of spinning a spinner to expected results. They are discovering that the actual results are often not the same as the expected results.

The fifth-grade booth at the school fair features this wheel.

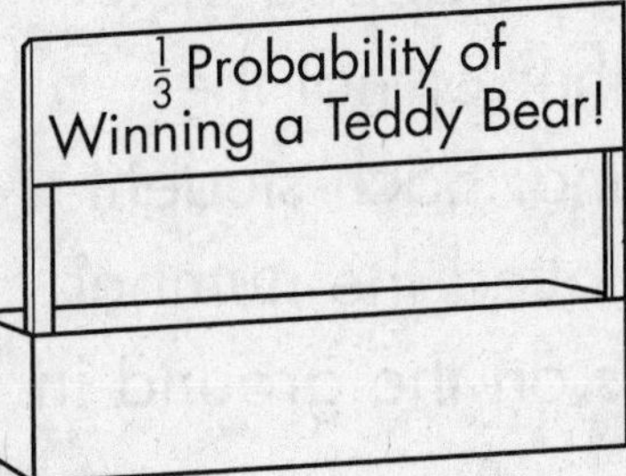

1. How many times would you expect to get a teddy bear out of 60 spins? ____

Teddy Bear	22
Sorry	38
Total	60

2. The table shows the last 60 spins of the wheel. Compare the actual results to the expected results.

____

____

3. How would you expect the results of the next 60 spins to compare to these results?

____

____

Mixed Review and Test Prep

4. Which solid is a cube?

A. 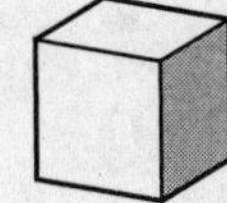 **B.** 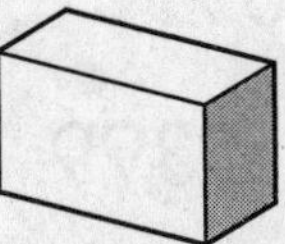 **C.**  **D.** 

Name Date

Between Never and Always

What's Down?

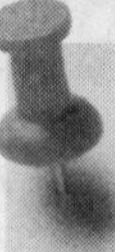

Family Connection

Students are learning that using a large number of trials gives you results that cluster around the expected results that you compute mathematically.

Thirteen students colored $\frac{1}{4}$ of the front wheels of their bicycles. Each time they stopped their bicycles, they recorded whether or not the colored part was on the ground. Each student did this for 50 stops. They plotted the number of times the colored part was on the ground in this line plot:

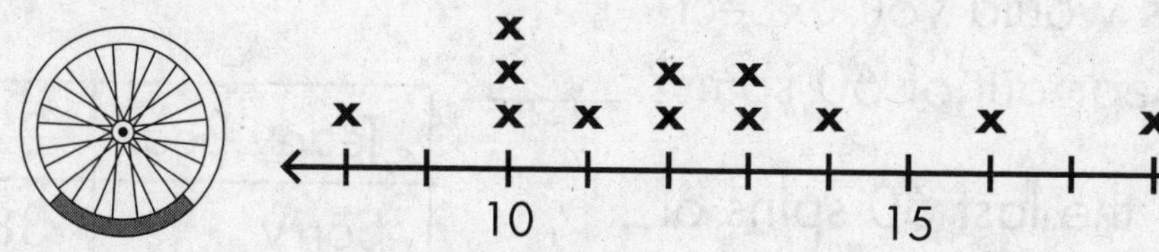

1. How many times out of 50 stops would you expect the colored part of the tire to be on the ground? Why? ______________________

2. What is the middle number in the line plot? ______

3. Between what two numbers are most of the results? ____________

4. Compare the group's results to expected results.

____

Mixed Review and Test Prep

5. Which number is greater than 5839?

A. 5850 **B.** 5804 **C.** 5399 **D.** 5340

Name Date

Between Never and Always

Guess Test

Family Connection

Students have been testing their guessing skills and comparing their results to predictions they made based on probability. You may enjoy comparing your guessing skills with your child's using this test.

1. Choose an answer for each question.

   What is a dumka?

   A. a song **B.** an animal **C.** a fruit **D.** a vehicle

   How much does a baseball weigh?

   A. 3 oz **B.** 5 oz **C.** 7 oz **D.** 9 oz

   Which of these is **not** a unit of measure?

   A. weber **B.** tesla **C.** henry **D.** meyer

   Which river is **not** in India?

   A. Luni **B.** Murat **C.** Son **D.** Yamuna

2. What is the probability of answering a question correctly if you guess? ______

3. How many questions would you expect to get right by guessing? ______

4. The answers to the test are A, B, D, B. Tell if you were guessing. Then compare your results to just guessing.

____

Mixed Review and Test Prep

5. Which fraction is equivalent to $\frac{3}{6}$?

   A. $\frac{2}{4}$ **B.** $\frac{4}{7}$ **C.** $\frac{4}{5}$ **D.** $\frac{6}{3}$

Name Date

Between Never and Always

Mystery Plot

Mandy found this line plot on the bus. What can you tell about this unidentified line plot?

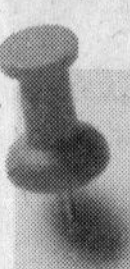

Family Connection

Students are learning to interpret and describe data based on how it is distributed on a line plot. **Questions you might ask your child:** "How did you find the median on the line plot?" "How did you find the mode?"

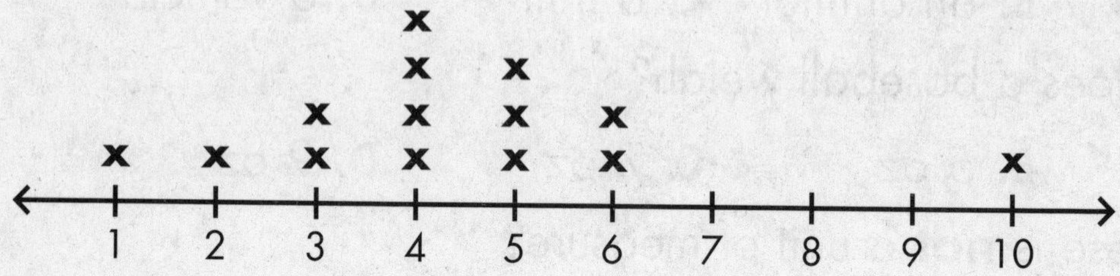

❶ What is the range? ________________

❷ What is the median? ________________

❸ What is the mode? ________________

❹ Are there outliers? ________________

❺ Describe the shape of this data.

____

____

____

Mixed Review and Test Prep

❻ Use the cluster problems to find 47×60.

A. 2240 **C.** 2820

B. 2640 **D.** 3060

$7 \times 60 = 420$
$4 \times 60 = 240$
$40 \times 60 = 2400$
$47 \times 60 = ?$

Name Date

Between Never and Always

Winning Option

Family Connection

Students have been reviewing number properties and using probability to play games. On this page, they are looking for a winning game strategy. You may wish to use this page to play a game with your child.

Gloria first chooses one of the options below and then draws a ball from the jar.

Find the probability for each option.

1. a multiple of 5 ________
2. a factor of 6 ________
3. a factor of 5 ________
4. a one-digit number ________
5. a number less than 25 ________

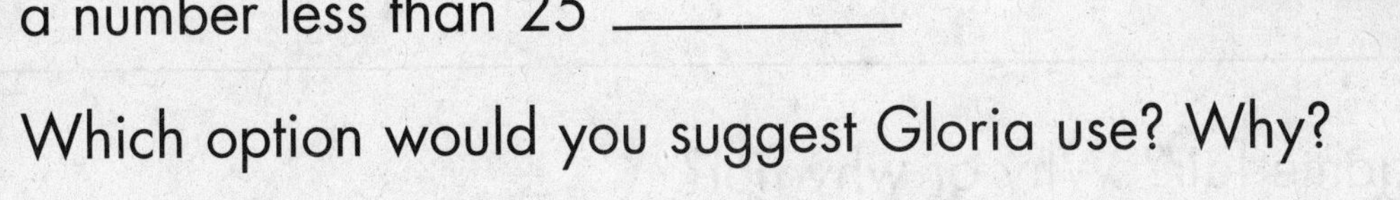

6. Which option would you suggest Gloria use? Why?

____

____

Mixed Review and Test Prep

7. Which situation fits this graph?

A. A music concert

B. A school day

C. Lunch count

D. Sleeping habits

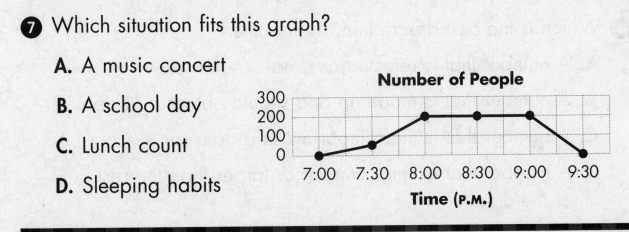

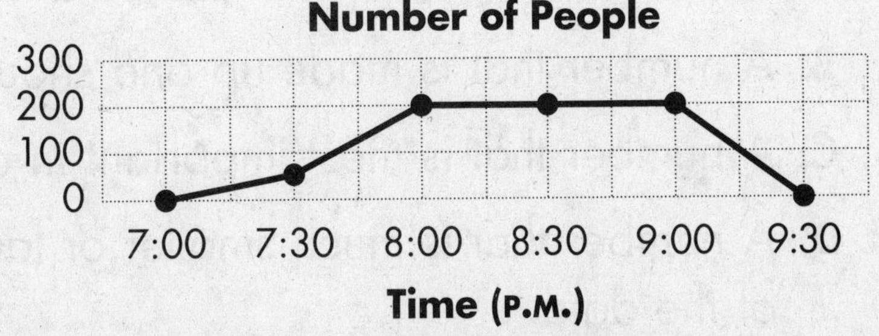

Name Date

Between Never and Always

Fair Toss?

The Game:

Toss a penny and a nickel.

Scoring:

Two heads: Player 1 gets a point.
Two tails: Player 2 gets a point.
One head, one tail: Player 3 gets a point.

Family Connection
Students are learning how to analyze games to decide if they are fair. One way is to make an organized list to compare the ways each player can win. You may want to help your child make a list for this game.

1 Complete the table to make an organized list of all the ways the coins can come up.

Penny	Nickel
Heads	Heads
Heads	

2 How many ways can each person get a point?

____

____

3 Is the game fair? Why or why not?

____

____

Mixed Review and Test Prep

4 Which is the best description of an outlier?

A. A number that is rejected as data
B. A number that is made up and should not be in a data set
C. A number that is most important in a data set
D. A number that is much smaller or larger than the rest of the data

Name Date

Between Never and Always

No Fair!

Family Connection

Students have been working in groups to modify the rules of an unfair game to make it fair. You may want to work with your child to make up other games and figure out ways to make them fair.

The Game:

Toss a penny, a nickel, and a dime.

Scoring:

All heads or all tails: Player 1 wins.

Two heads or two tails: Player 2 wins.

1. April made this table to show all the ways the coins can come up. How can you tell the game is not fair?

Penny	Nickel	Dime
Head	Head	Head
Head	Head	Tail
Head	Tail	Head
Head	Tail	Tail
Tail	Head	Head
Tail	Head	Tail
Tail	Tail	Head
Tail	Tail	Tail

2. How can you change the rules of the game so that it is fair?

3. How do you know your game is fair?

Mixed Review and Test Prep

4. Which number on the fraction strip is less than $\frac{1}{2}$?

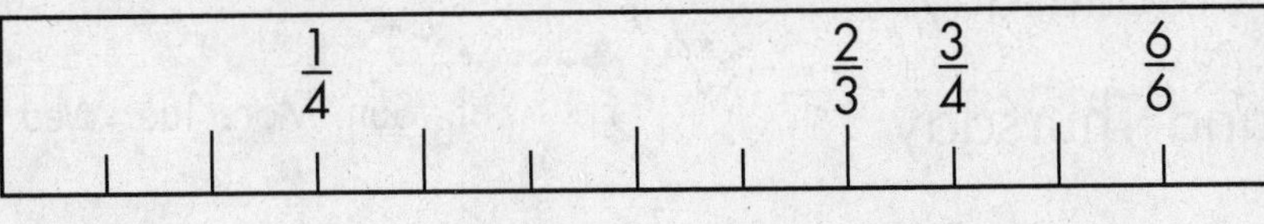

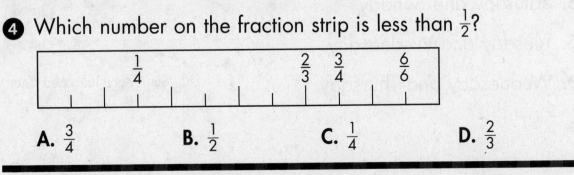

A. $\frac{3}{4}$ B. $\frac{1}{2}$ C. $\frac{1}{4}$ D. $\frac{2}{3}$

Name Date

Between Never and Always

Fair and True

Write **True** or **False** for each statement.

Family Connection
Students are continuing their study of what it means for a game to be fair. These true or false questions highlight some of the things they have learned.

1. Each player in a fair game will win the same number of times. __________

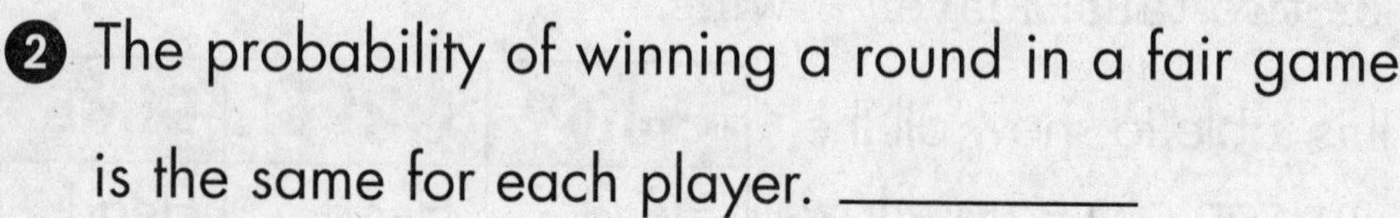

2. The probability of winning a round in a fair game is the same for each player. __________

3. Players in a fair game will take turns winning. __________

4. In a fair game, the same player can win four times in a row. __________

5. The player who goes first always wins a fair game. __________

Interesting Tidbit

The oldest board game ever discovered is The Royal Game of Ur. It was invented in a region of southwest Asia about 5000 years ago!

Mixed Review and Test Prep

6. Between what two days did the plant shown by the solid line grow more than the other plant?

   A. Friday and Saturday

   B. Saturday and Sunday

   C. Tuesday and Wednesday

   D. Wednesday and Thursday

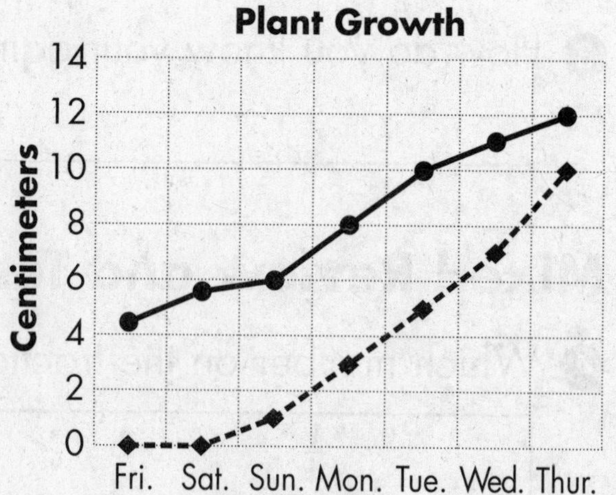

Name Date

Between Never and Always

Unfair, but Fair

The spinner is $\frac{3}{4}$ shaded. Suppose players take turns spinning it. Decide if each game is fair and tell why.

Family Connection

In class, students designed fair games for unfair spinners. They wrote rules for scoring the game that made the game fair. Have your child tell you how his or her group made their game

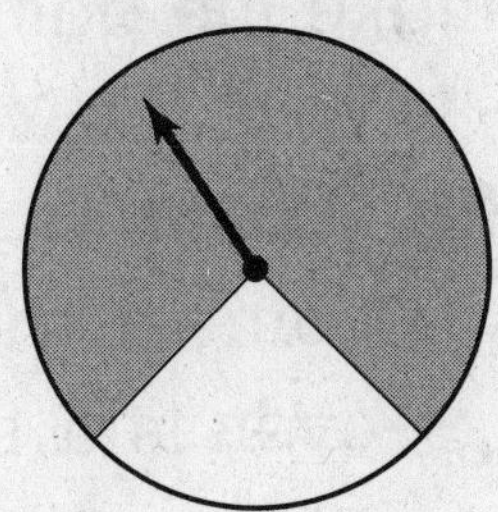

1. Game: On his or her turn, a player scores a point for spinning white, no points for shaded. The first person to get ten points is the winner.

____

____

2. Game: For each turn, Player 1 gets 3 points for white, Player 2 gets 1 point for shaded. The first person to get 12 points is the winner.

____

____

____

Mixed Review and Test Prep

3. Which shape could **not** have a triangle for a silhouette?

A. 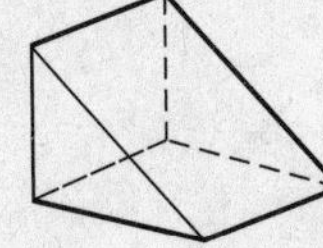

B. 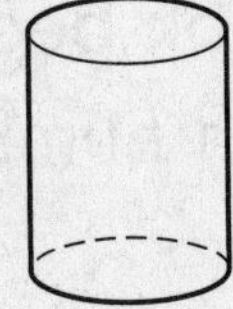

C. 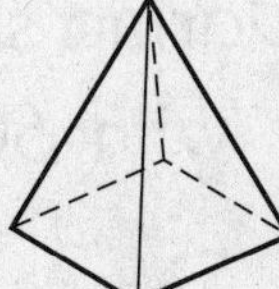

D. 

Name

Date

Face Down

For each game below, the cards are placed face down in a pile and two players take turns turning over a card. Match each game with the set of cards that can be used to make the game fair.

Family Connection

Students have learned methods for judging the fairness of games. **Questions you might ask your child:** "What is your favorite game?" "Is the game fair?" "How do you know?"

1. **Game 1:** Player 1 gets a point if the card turned over is a square number. Player 2 gets a point if it is a one digit number.

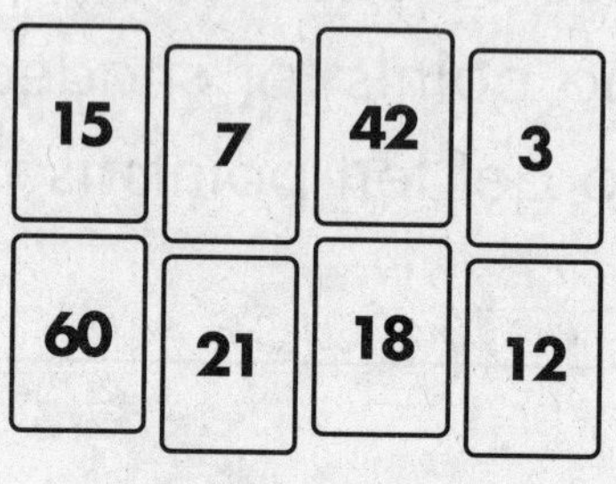

2. **Game 2:** Player 1 gets a point if his or her card is odd. Player 2 gets a point if his or her card is a multiple of 6.

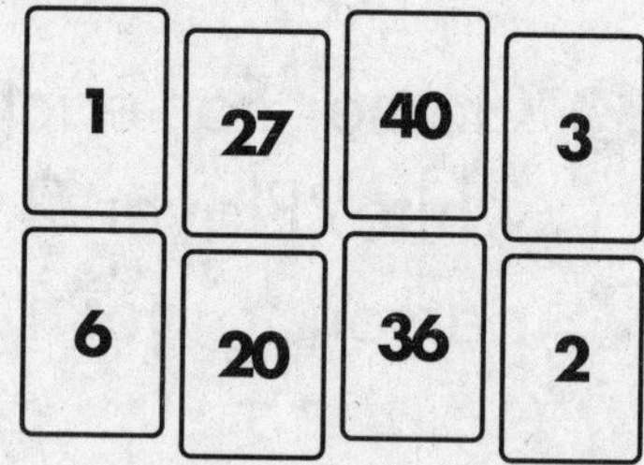

3. **Game 3:** Player 1 gets a point if the card turned over is a factor of 3. Player 2 gets a point if it is a multiple of 10.

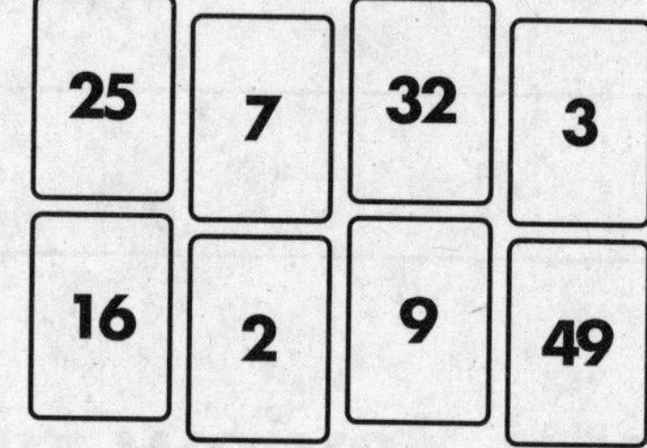

Mixed Review and Test Prep

4. The sixth page of Darma's 1000 book begins with 501 and ends with 600. Which number is on this page?

A. 105 **B.** 115 **C.** 155 **D.** 511

Name Date

Building on Numbers You Know

Missing Multiples and Factors

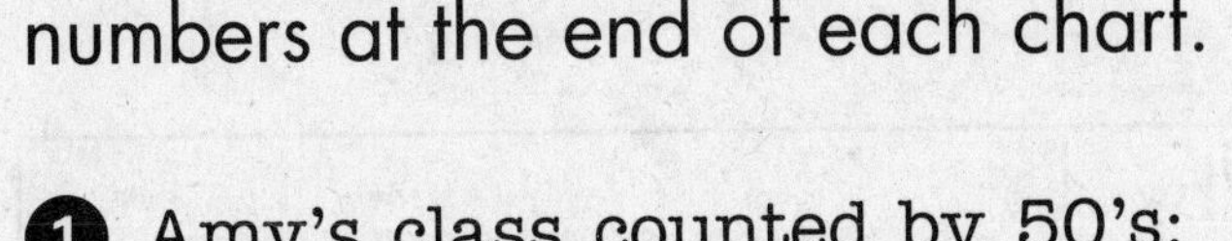

The middle section of each counting chart is omitted. Fill in the missing numbers at the end of each chart.

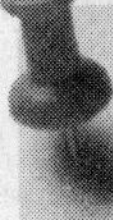

Family Connection

Students are looking at counting patterns and using multiplication to relate the final number to the number of students who counted. For example, if 27 students count by 50's, the final number equals 27 × 50. Have your child explain this relationship in his or her own words.

1. Amy's class counted by 50's: 50, 100, 150, and so on.

Student Number	1	2	3	4	25	26	27
Number Said	50	100	150	200	1250		

2. Bill's class counted by 300's: 300, 600, 900, and so on.

Student Number	1	2	3	4	29		31
Number Said	300	600	900	1200	8700	9000	

3. Kim's class counted by 20's: 20, 40, 60, and so on.

Student Number	1	2	3	4	32		34
Number Said	20	40	60	80		660	

4. Armando's class counted by 75's: 75, 150, 225, and so on.

Student Number	1	2	3	4	22	23	
Number Said	75	150	225	300	1650		1800

Mixed Review and Test Prep

5. Which fraction is greater than $\frac{1}{3}$?

A. $\frac{1}{30}$ B. $\frac{4}{15}$ C. $\frac{10}{27}$ D. $\frac{19}{60}$

Name Date

Building on Numbers You Know

Counting Puzzles

One number in each puzzle is missing. Try to find it without actually counting.

Family Connection

Students continue working with multiples of familiar numbers. For these puzzles, students can check their answers by listing the counting numbers from the starting number to the stopping number.

	Start at	Stop at	Count by	
1	225	525	25's	Say ______ numbers.
2	600	1050	15's	Say ______ numbers.
3	4300	5500	200's	Say ______ numbers.
4	960	1200	______	Say 20 numbers.
5	1600	1920	______	Say 8 numbers.

6. Choose one puzzle. On another sheet of paper, explain how you solved it.

Mixed Review and Test Prep

7. Dave started at 54 on a 100 chart and jumped by 1's to 100. How many jumps did he make?

A. 46 **B.** 54 **C.** 56 **D.** 154

Name Date

Building on Numbers You Know

Find the Counting Numbers

For each problem, circle all the numbers you could count by to get from the **Start** number to the **End** number.

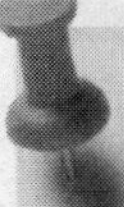

Family Connection

Students use their skills in skip counting to identify factors of numbers. A **factor** divides evenly into a number with no remainder. Every number has at least two factors, itself and 1.

	Start	Count by	End
1	0	8 15 24 36 90	180
2	0	15 30 25 80 200	400

	Start	Count by	End
3	250	40 50 75 120 125	0
4	840	16 25 70 120 400	0

	Start	Count by	End
5	300	15 23 25 115 225	875
6	520	9 25 30 90 160	1000

	Start	Count by	End
7	250	32 75 100 128 160	890
8	2500	70 130 140 150 350	6000

Mixed Review and Test Prep

9. Which number added to 16 makes 100?

A. 116 B. 94 C. 86 D. 84

10. Which number expression does **not** have a sum of 100?

A. 24 + 76 B. 92 + 8 C. 43 + 77 D. 68 + 32

Name Date

Building on Numbers You Know

1116
1085
1054
1023
992
961
930<
899
868
837
806
775
744
713
682
651
620<
589
558
527
496
465
434
403
372
341
310<
279
248
217
186
155
124
93
62
31

The 31 Tower

The tower shows multiples of 31. Use the tower for these questions.

Family Connection
Students have been working in class with multiples of 21. This page has questions using multiples of 31. Ask your child to tell you another multiplication or division problem that can be solved with the 31 tower.

Find these multiples in the tower.

1. $20 \times 31 =$ ______
2. $30 \times 31 =$ ______
3. $15 \times 31 =$ ______
4. $26 \times 31 =$ ______

How many 31's are there in each number?

5. 589 ______
6. 248 ______
7. 124 ______
8. 1054 ______
9. 837 ______
10. 434 ______

Use the tower to help you divide.

11. $341 \div 31 =$ ______
12. $775 \div 31 =$ ______
13. $682 \div 31 =$ ______
14. $155 \div 31 =$ ______

Mixed Review and Test Prep

15. Three corners of a square are at (−2, 1), (1, 2) and (2, −1). Where is the fourth corner?

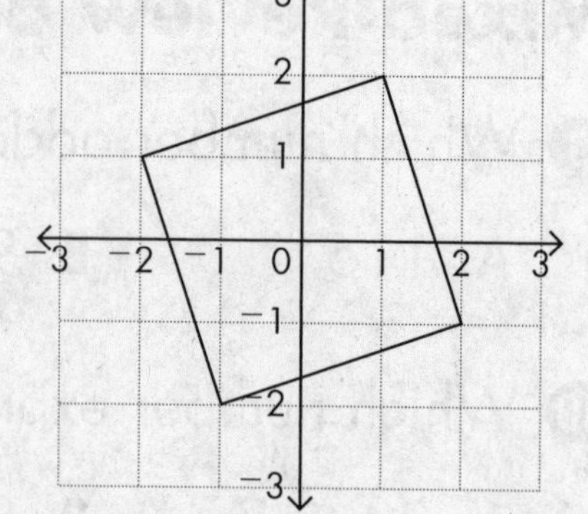

A. (−1, −2) **C.** (−1, −1)

B. (−2, −1) **D.** (−2, −2)

Name Date

Building on Numbers You Know

Tower Building

Write the missing numbers in each tower.

Family Connection

Students have been building "towers" of numbers by writing multiples of the bottom number. This activity relates skip counting to multiplication and division. Have your child describe some patterns in the ones digits in these towers.

1

520 <
____
468
442
416
390
364
338
312
286
260 <
234
____
182
156
130
104
____
52
26

2

1440 <
1368
1296
1224
1152
____
1008
936
864
____
720 <
648
576
504
____
360
288
216
144
72

3

2460 <
2337
2214
2091
____
1845
1722
1599
____
1353
1230 <
1107
984
861
738
____
492
369
246
123

4

4020 <
____
3618
3417
3216
3015
2814
2613
____
2211
2010 <
1809
1608
1407
1206
1005
804
603
____
201

Use the towers to help you multiply or divide.

5 $26 \times 13 =$ ______

6 $1152 \div 72 =$ ______

Mixed Review and Test Prep

7 A number ends in 7. What cannot be a factor of the number?

A. 1 **B.** 5 **C.** 7 **D.** 9

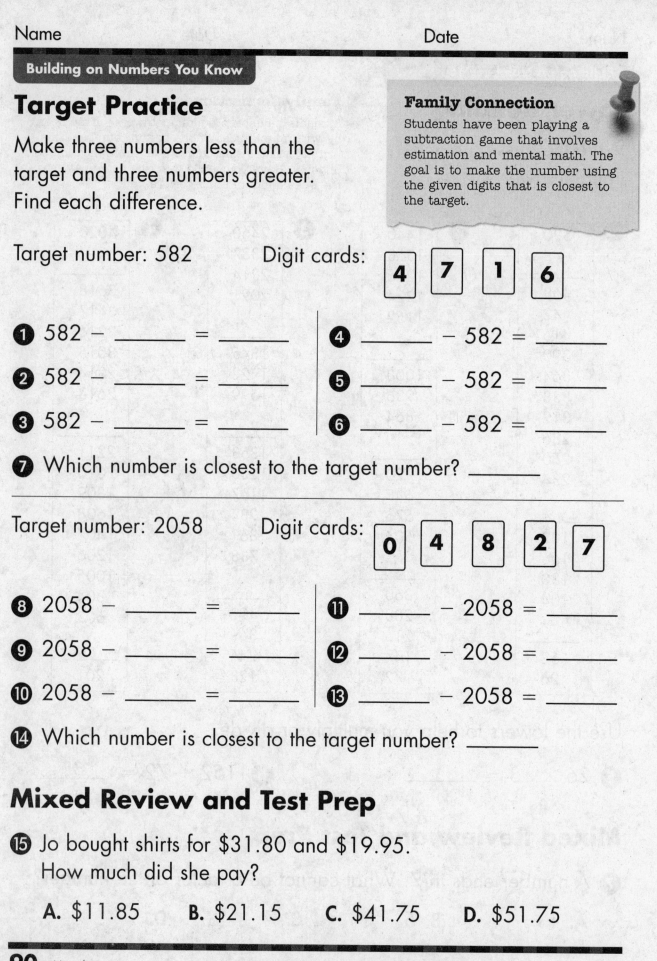

Name Date

Building on Numbers You Know

Target Practice

Make three numbers less than the target and three numbers greater. Find each difference.

Family Connection
Students have been playing a subtraction game that involves estimation and mental math. The goal is to make the number using the given digits that is closest to the target.

Target number: 582 Digit cards:

6

1. 582 − ______ = ______
2. 582 − ______ = ______
3. 582 − ______ = ______
4. ______ − 582 = ______
5. ______ − 582 = ______
6. ______ − 582 = ______
7. Which number is closest to the target number? ______

Target number: 2058 Digit cards:

2

8. 2058 − ______ = ______
9. 2058 − ______ = ______
10. 2058 − ______ = ______
11. ______ − 2058 = ______
12. ______ − 2058 = ______
13. ______ − 2058 = ______
14. Which number is closest to the target number? ______

Mixed Review and Test Prep

15. Jo bought shirts for $31.80 and $19.95. How much did she pay?

A. $11.85 **B.** $21.15 **C.** $41.75 **D.** $51.75

Name Date

Building on Numbers You Know

Closest to the Target

Try different arrangements of the digits given until you find the numbers closest to the target number.

Family Connection

Students continue playing **The Digits Game.** Your child may need to try several possible arrangements of the digits before finding the ones closest to the target number. Write the digits on slips of paper so your child can move them around.

Target number: 382 Digits: 1 5 3 6

1. Make the closest number less than the target. ______
2. Make the closest number greater than the target. ______
3. Which number is closer? ______
4. How close is it? ______

Target number: 2651 Digits:    

5. Make the closest number less than the target. ______
6. Make the closest number greater than the target. ______
7. Which number is closer? ______
8. How close is it? ______

Mixed Review and Test Prep

9. Which shape could **not** have a circle for a silhouette?

A. 

B. 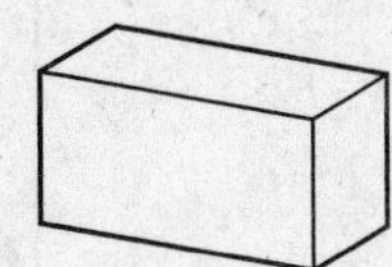

C. 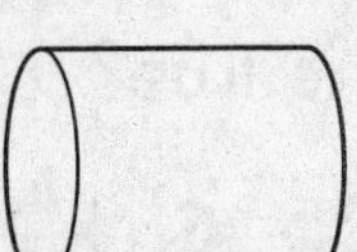

D. 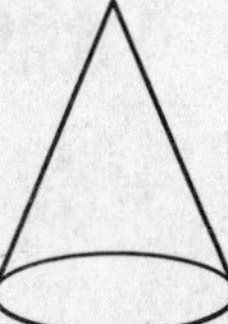

Name Date

Building on Numbers You Know

Larger Targets

Family Connection

Students continue playing **The Digits Game,** this time with five-digit target numbers. Encourage your child to use a variety of subtraction strategies to find the differences.

Use the digits to find the number closest to the target.

Target number: 40,000 Digits: 4 6 1 0 2 9

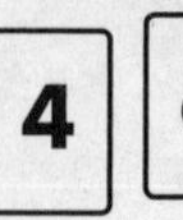

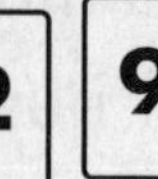

1. Which number is closest to the target number? ________
2. How close is it? ________

Target number: 28,000 Digits: 7 5 0 8 3 4

3. Which number is closest to the target number? ________
4. How close is it? ________

Target number: 32,700 Digits: 8 2 3 9 6 5

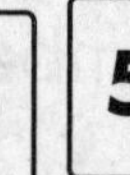

5. Which number is closest to the target number? ________
6. How close is it? ________
7. On another sheet of paper, explain your strategy for finding one of the three target numbers above.

Mixed Review and Test Prep

8. Use the drawing to help you. Which equation is true?

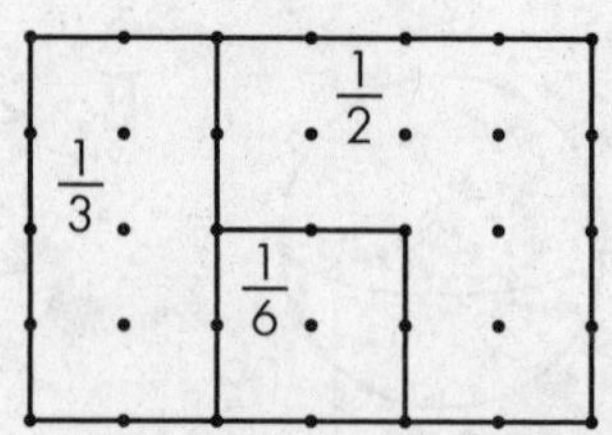

A. $\frac{1}{3} + \frac{1}{6} = \frac{1}{2}$ **C.** $\frac{1}{6} + \frac{1}{6} = \frac{1}{2}$

B. $\frac{1}{2} + \frac{1}{6} = \frac{1}{3}$ **D.** $\frac{1}{2} + \frac{1}{3} = \frac{1}{6}$

Name Date

Building on Numbers You Know

The New Coins

Make up your own name for each coin. Use division strategies to find how many whole coins there would be in each amount.

Family Connection

Students have been learning division strategies based on number sense. For example, they may use doubling or multiples of ten. Encourage your child to solve division problems in more than one way.

Interesting Tidbit

A two cent coin was produced in the United States from 1864–1873.

This coin is worth 31 cents. Its name is ______________.

1. 1 dollar ______ 2. 2 dollars ______ 3. 5 dollars ______

This coin is worth 6 cents. Its name is ______________.

4. 1 dollar ______ 5. 2 dollars ______ 6. 5 dollars ______

This coin is worth 17 cents. Its name is ______________.

7. 1 dollar ______ 8. 2 dollars ______ 9. 5 dollars ______

This coin is worth 48 cents. Its name is ______________.

10. 1 dollar ______ 11. 2 dollars ______ 12. 5 dollars ______

Mixed Review and Test Prep

13. Which shows how a sudden stop would look on a graph that shows a bicycle's speed?

A. 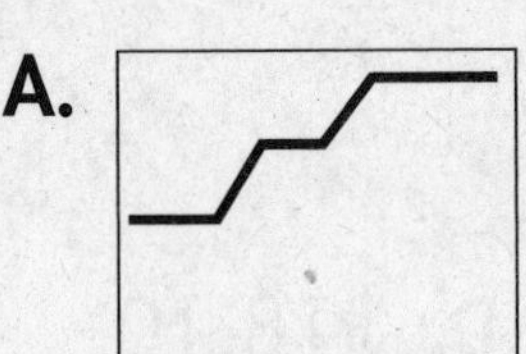

B.

C. 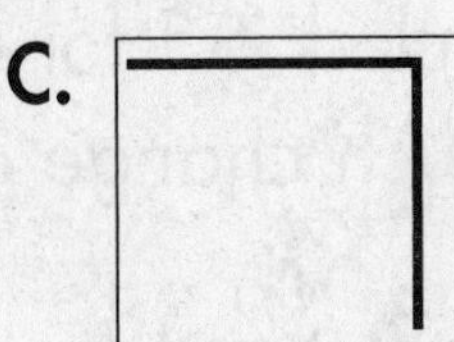

D.

Name Date

Building on Numbers You Know

Sharing Equally

Share the supplies equally among the students in each class.

Family Connection

Students continue using number sense to solve division problems. In these questions, the number of items left over does not matter. Students will learn to deal with remainders later in the unit.

Students in Ellen's class: 24 Stickers on each roll: 80

1. The class has 1 roll. Each student gets _____ stickers.
2. The class has 2 rolls. Each student gets _____ stickers.
3. The class has 5 rolls. Each student gets _____ stickers.

Students in Ami's class: 32 Counting cubes in each bucket: 120

4. The class has 1 bucket. Each student gets _____ cubes.
5. The class has 2 buckets. Each student gets _____ cubes.
6. The class has 5 buckets. Each student gets _____ cubes.

Students in Matteo's class: 22 Pens in each box: 240

7. The class has 1 box. Each student gets _____ pens.
8. The class has 2 boxes. Each student gets _____ pens.
9. The class has 5 boxes. Each student gets _____ pens.

Mixed Review and Test Prep

10. Violet gave the clerk $5 for a $3.62 bag of grapes. How much change did she get back?

A. $1.38 **B.** $2.38 **C.** $8.62 **D.** $18.10

Name Date

Building on Numbers You Know

Division Notations

Write the answer to each problem using a fraction for the remainder.

Family Connection

Students have been learning to write division problems in different ways. Fractions are another way to show division. For example, $\frac{8}{2} = 8 \div 2$.
Questions you might ask your child: "In how many ways can you show 60 divided by 9?" "What are they?"

1 $35\overline{)193}$ = 5 R 18 ________

2 $18\overline{)205}$ = 11 R 7 ________

Complete the situation for each division problem.

3 140 ÷ 6 is 23 R 2 A group of _____ people shared _____ postcards equally. Each person got _____ postcards and there were _____ left over.

4 $43\overline{)700}$ = 16 R 12 A group of _____ people shared _____ stamps equally. Each person got _____ stamps and there were _____ left over.

Circle the two problems in each row that have the same meaning.

5 $\frac{94}{8}$ $94\overline{)8}$ 94 ÷ 8

6 138 ÷ 24 $\frac{138}{24}$ $138\overline{)24}$

7 $\frac{15}{224}$ $15\overline{)224}$ 224 ÷ 15

Mixed Review and Test Prep

8 If you start at 0 and skip count by 5's, what is the 32nd number?

A. 37 **B.** 80 **C.** 130 **D.** 160

Name Date

Building on Numbers You Know

Dividing 500 by 16

Family Connection

Students have been learning how to interpret remainders in division problems. This page illustrates some of the different situations. Ask your child to create a problem involving the division of money in which the answer is shown as a decimal.

Find the quotient and remainder for Problem 1. Use your answer to solve the other problems.

1. 500 ÷ 16 is ______ and a remainder of ______.

2. Vicky needs 500 paper plates. There are 16 plates in a bag. How many bags should she buy? ______

3. Sean has 500 pounds of apples for 16 horses. How many pounds can each horse have? ______

4. Ed has 500 tomato plants. He is putting 16 plants in each box. How many boxes can he fill? ______

5. Sharon is shipping 500 wind-up toy cows. She will put 16 or 17 cows in a box. Describe the shipment of cows.

   _____ boxes with 16 cows and _____ boxes with 17 cows

Mixed Review and Test Prep

6. Which set of multiples are shaded in the table?

   A. multiples of 2 **C.** multiples of 4

   B. multiples of 3 **D.** multiples of 5

2	4	6	8
3	6	9	12
4	8	12	16
5	10	15	20

Name Date

Building on Numbers You Know

Related Problems

Write a multiplication or division problem for each situation. Use ? to show the number to find. The first one is done for you.

Family Connection

Students are writing problem situations for related multiplication and division situations. Have your child write two situations like problems 1 and 2 using something at home or in a store. For example, students might use 10 pencils in a box or 8 slices of cheese in a package.

There are 8 melons in a carton.

1. How many melons are there in 42 cartons? $8 \times 42 = ?$
2. How many cartons do you need for 336 melons?

____

Tickets for the baseball game cost $18.

3. Pam spent $756. How many tickets did she buy?

____

4. How much do 42 tickets cost? _______________
5. Choose one multiplication and one division problem to solve. Show your strategies on another sheet of paper.

Mixed Review and Test Prep

6. A cube building looks like this from the right side. What does the building look like from the left side?

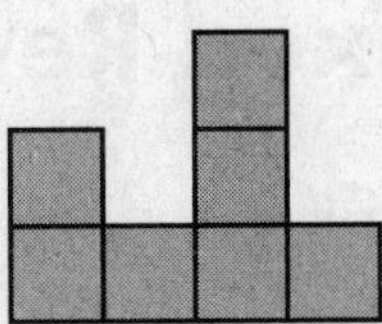

A. 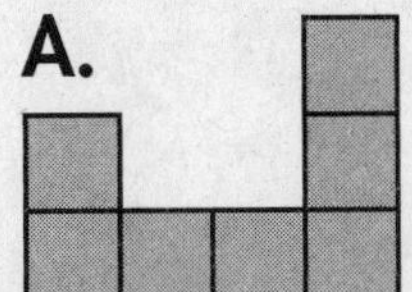

B. 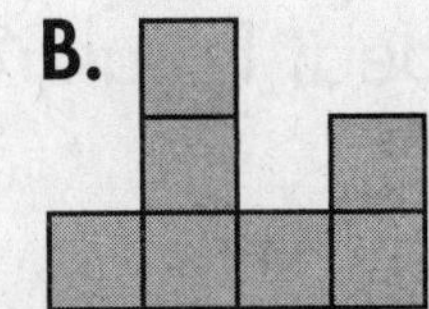

C. 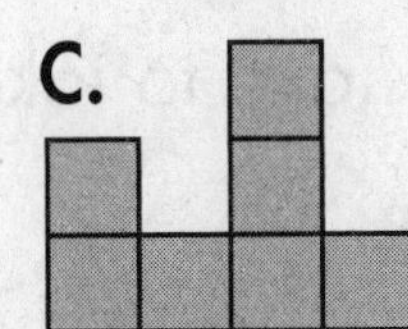

D. 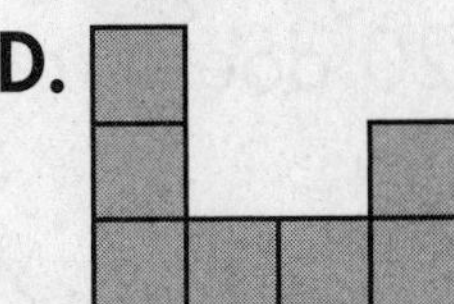

Name Date

Building on Numbers You Know

Mystery Towers

One number in each multiple tower is circled. Write one multiplication sentence and two division sentences using the circled number.

Family Connection

Students continue their work with related multiplication and division problems. Tell your child a multiplication sentence, such as $42 \times 15 = 630$. Ask him or her to tell you the two related division sentences: $630 \div 42 = 15$ and $630 \div 15 = 42$.

1. 455, (442), 429, 416, 403

   ______

   ______

   ______

2. 918, 901, (884), 867, 850

   ______

   ______

   ______

3. 962, 936, 910, 884, (858)

   ______

   ______

   ______

4. 768, (720), 672, 624, 576

   ______

   ______

   ______

5. (627), 608, 589, 570, 551

   ______

   ______

   ______

6. 664, 656, (648), 640, 632

   ______

   ______

   ______

Mixed Review and Test Prep

7. Freaky Frog took 13 jumps of 10. Frogurt Frog decided to take jumps of 20. How many jumps of 20 does Frogurt have to take to beat Freaky?

   A. 7 **B.** 8 **C.** 14 **D.** 30

Name Date

Building on Numbers You Know

Tea Time

Mrs. Jackson measured one box of tea bags. Use her measurements to solve these problems.

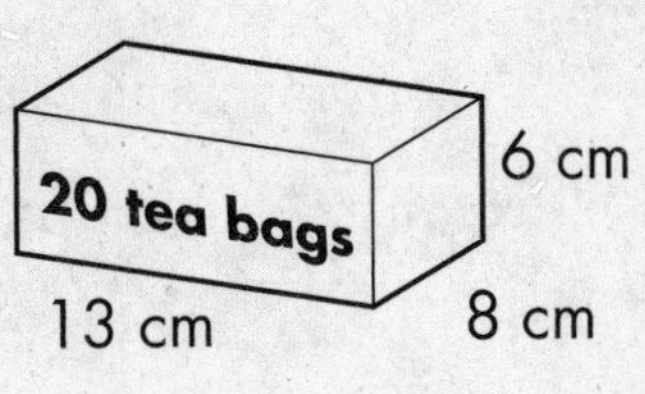

Family Connection

Students have been solving problems about school supplies that come in large quantities. Their solutions used multiplication, division, estimation, and measurement. Measure a box of items with your child. Then find out how tall a stack of 10 boxes would be.

1. A store has 64 boxes of tea bags. How many tea bags are there in all of these boxes? ________
2. The 64 boxes of tea bags are arranged in 4 stacks. How many boxes are there in each stack? ________
3. How high is a stack of 10 boxes? ________
4. How high is a stack of 16 boxes? ________
5. The tea company made 3000 bags of mint tea. How many boxes did they need for this many bags? ________
6. If you placed the small boxes end-to-end, how many would you need to make a row 1000 centimeters long? Show your work on another sheet of paper. ________

Mixed Review and Test Prep

7. Which shapes are rectangles?

A. T and Z **C.** X and O

B. T and O **D.** O and H

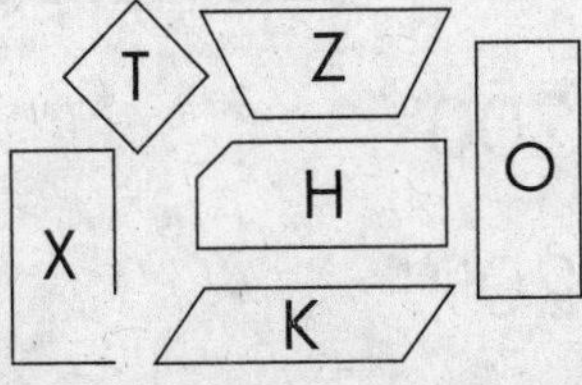

Name Date

Building on Numbers You Know

Using Multiples of 10

Use the closest multiple of 10 to make each estimate.

Family Connection
Students have learned previously how to round to the nearest ten. They round up if the ones digit is 5 or more; down if the ones digit is less than 5. Now your child will use this skill to estimate products.

1. Problem: 38 × 5

   _____ × 5 = _____

2. Problem: 52 × 7

   _____ × 7 = _____

3. Problem: 61 × 8

   _____ × 8 = _____

4. Problem: 79 × 4

   _____ × 4 = _____

Complete two estimates for each problem. Circle the one that is larger.

5. 41 × 62 — 40 × 62 = _____ ; 41 × 60 = _____

6. 31 × 91 — 30 × 91 = _____ ; 31 × 90 = _____

7. 62 × 18 — 60 × 18 = _____ ; 62 × 20 = _____

8. 82 × 63 — 80 × 63 = _____ ; 82 × 60 = _____

9. 57 × 71 — 60 × 71 = _____ ; 57 × 70 = _____

10. 79 × 27 — 80 × 27 = _____ ; 79 × 30 = _____

Mixed Review and Test Prep

11. Use the related problem set to find 139 + 82.

    130 + 70 = 200
    139 + 70 = 209
    130 + 80 = 210

    A. 200
    B. 209
    C. 211
    D. 221

Name Date

Building on Numbers You Know

Estimating Products

Family Connection

Students use number sense and logical reasoning to choose the closer of two estimates. Rather than computing, students learn to think about how far away an estimate is from an exact product. The sample answer for Problem 4 illustrates this strategy.

Circle the closer estimate.

1. Problem: 36×73

   30×73 or 40×73

2. Problem: 43×69

   40×69 or 50×69

3. Problem: 238×64

   230×64 or 240×64

Compare each estimate to the problem. Circle the closer estimate.

4. Problem: 57×81

   60×81 Three 81's away from the answer

   57×80 ______

5. Problem: 77×32

   80×32 ______

   77×30 ______

6. Problem: 93×51

   90×51 ______

   93×50 ______

Mixed Review and Test Prep

7. Which is the next multiple in the list?

   8, 16, 24, 32, 40, ____

   A. 42 **B.** 48 **C.** 50 **D.** 72

Name Date

Building on Numbers You Know

Multiplication Clusters

Family Connection

Students have been breaking larger products into smaller parts. For example, 48 × 24 can be broken into 40 × 24 and 8 × 24. There are lots of different ways to combine the smaller products. Ask your child to show you more than one way for one or two problems.

Use the cluster problems to help you solve each problem. Circle the problems in the cluster you use.

1. 48 × 24 = __________

2 × 24	5 × 24	10 × 24	20 × 24
4 × 24	8 × 24	40 × 24	50 × 24

2. 73 × 31 = __________

2 × 31	3 × 31	10 × 31	20 × 31
7 × 31	8 × 31	70 × 31	80 × 31

3. 312 × 45 = __________

2 × 45	10 × 45	12 × 45	100 × 45
3 × 45	30 × 45	200 × 45	300 × 45

4. 58 × 17 = __________

2 × 17	10 × 17	5 × 17	50 × 17
4 × 17	8 × 17	20 × 17	60 × 17

Mixed Review and Test Prep

5. What is a typical height for this group of people?

A. 52 inches

B. 54 inches

C. 56 inches

D. 58 inches

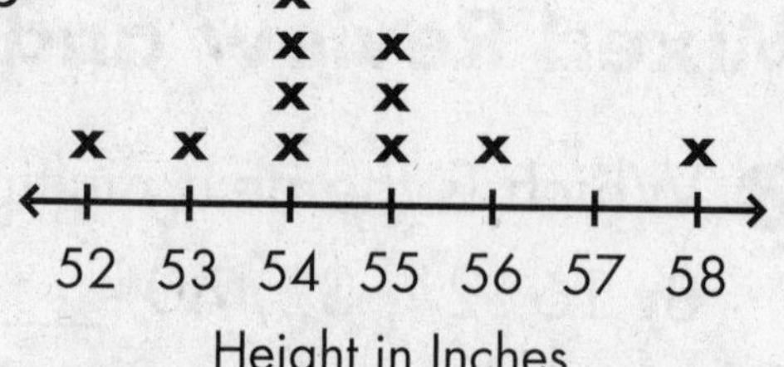

Name Date

Building on Numbers You Know

Estimating Quotients

Complete each estimate. Then tell whether it is larger or smaller than the exact answer.

Family Connection

Students use familiar division fact pairs to help them estimate quotients with larger numbers. Practice division facts with your child by saying a fact such as 8 × 7. Your child gives the product and the two related division facts.

1. Problem: $435 \div 6$

   $420 \div 6 =$ ____ ________

   $480 \div 6 =$ ____ ________

2. Problem: $251 \div 3$

   $270 \div 3 =$ ____ ________

   $240 \div 3 =$ ____ ________

3. Problem: $719 \div 8$

   $640 \div 8 =$ ____ ________

   $720 \div 8 =$ ____ ________

4. Problem: $410 \div 9$

   $450 \div 9 =$ ____ ________

   $360 \div 9 =$ ____ ________

5. Problem: $300 \div 27$

   $270 \div 27 =$ ____ ________

   $300 \div 30 =$ ____ ________

6. Problem: $620 \div 16$

   $640 \div 16 =$ ____ ________

   $620 \div 20 =$ ____ ________

7. Make two estimates for $900 \div 12$, one with a larger quotient and one with a smaller quotient.

____

Mixed Review and Test Prep

8. Which number on the fraction strip is greater than $\frac{1}{2}$?

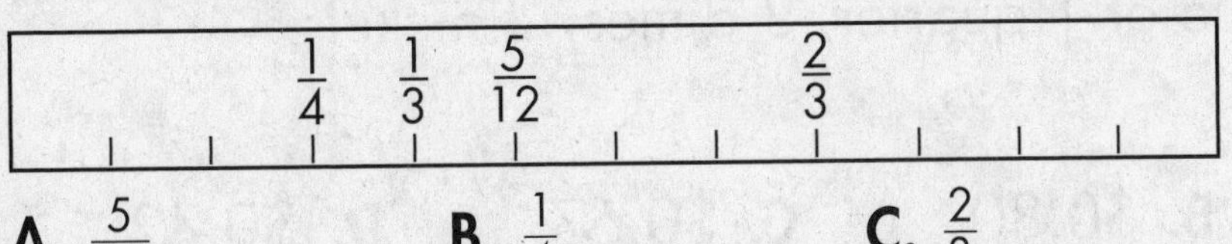

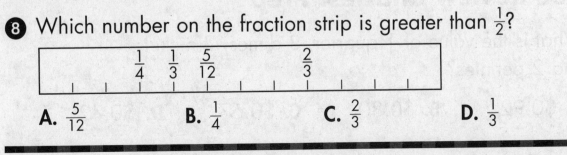

A. $\frac{5}{12}$ **B.** $\frac{1}{4}$ **C.** $\frac{2}{3}$ **D.** $\frac{1}{3}$

Name Date

Building on Numbers You Know

Division Clusters

Solve the cluster problems. Then use them to help you divide.

Family Connection

Students have been using cluster problems to help them divide. For example, 364 ÷ 8 is the sum of 320 ÷ 8 and 44 ÷ 8. Ask your child to make and explain an estimate for one problem on this page.

1

32 ÷ 8 = ______ 320 ÷ 8 = ______

40 ÷ 8 = ______ 44 ÷ 8 = ______

364 ÷ 8 = ______

2

30 ÷ 15 = ______ 300 ÷ 15 = ______

45 ÷ 15 = ______ 50 ÷ 15 = ______

350 ÷ 15 = ______

3

70 ÷ 7 = ______ 140 ÷ 7 = ______

63 ÷ 7 = ______ 67 ÷ 7 = ______

137 ÷ 7 = ______

4

120 ÷ 12 = ______ 252 ÷ 12 = ______

240 ÷ 12 = ______ 264 ÷ 12 = ______

259 ÷ 12 = ______

5

320 ÷ 40 = ______ 328 ÷ 41 = ______

360 ÷ 40 = ______ 369 ÷ 41 = ______

340 ÷ 41 = ______

Mixed Review and Test Prep

6 What is the value of 1 quarter, 3 dimes, 2 nickels, and 2 pennies?

A. \$0.92 **B.** \$0.80 **C.** \$0.67 **D.** \$0.42

Name Date

Building on Numbers You Know

Multiplying to Divide

Do the multiplication problems.
Then use them to divide.

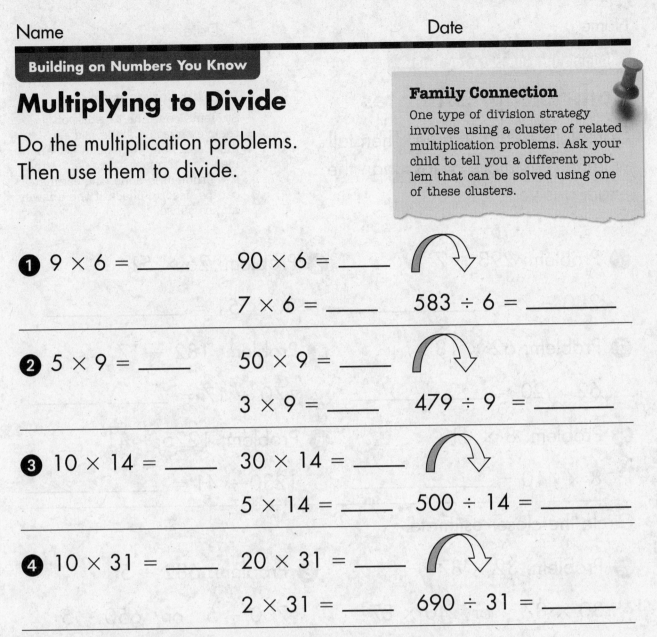

Family Connection

One type of division strategy involves using a cluster of related multiplication problems. Ask your child to tell you a different problem that can be solved using one of these clusters.

1. $9 \times 6 =$ ____ $90 \times 6 =$ ____ 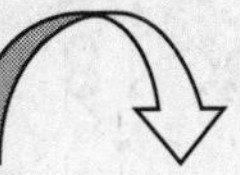
   $7 \times 6 =$ ____ $583 \div 6 =$ ____

2. $5 \times 9 =$ ____ $50 \times 9 =$ ____ 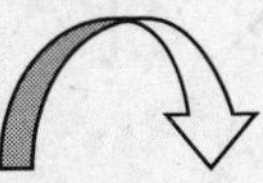
   $3 \times 9 =$ ____ $479 \div 9 =$ ____

3. $10 \times 14 =$ ____ $30 \times 14 =$ ____ 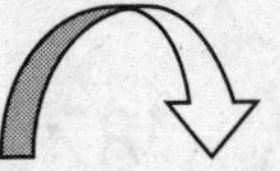
   $5 \times 14 =$ ____ $500 \div 14 =$ ____

4. $10 \times 31 =$ ____ $20 \times 31 =$ ____
   $2 \times 31 =$ ____ $690 \div 31 =$ ____

5. Choose one division problem on this page. On another sheet of paper, write a situation that uses this problem.

Mixed Review and Test Prep

6. Which rectangle is divided into thirds?

A. 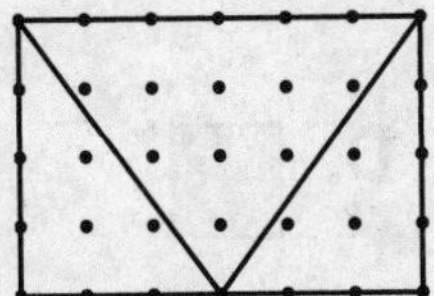 **B.** 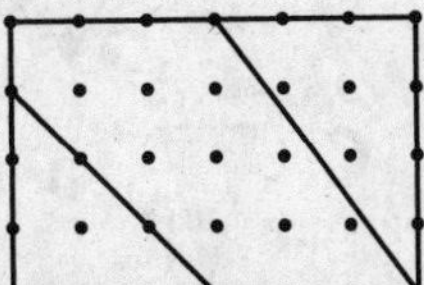 **C.** 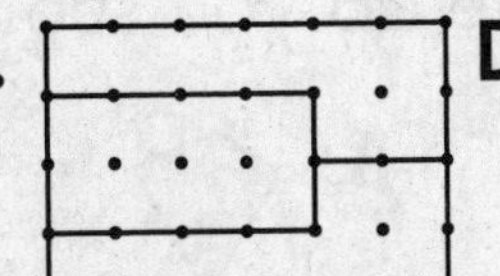 **D.** 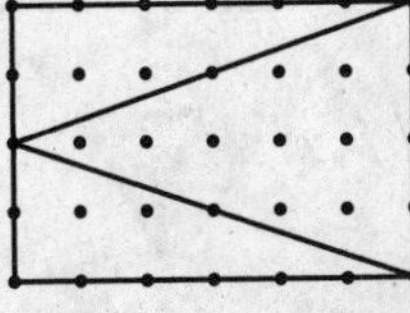

Name Date

Comparing Estimates

Complete each estimate. Then tell whether it is more or less than the exact answer.

Family Connection
Students continue to work on their estimating skills. An estimate can help your child get an idea how to start a problem. When the problem is done, the estimate can be used to check if the answer makes sense.

1. Problem: $293 \div 7$

   $280 \div 7 =$ ______ ______

2. Problem: 26×51

   $30 \times 51 =$ ______ ______

3. Problem: 62×18

   $62 \times 20 =$ ______ ______

4. Problem: $182 \div 17$

   $170 \div 17 =$ ______ ______

5. Problem: 8×417

   $8 \times 410 =$ ______ ______

6. Problem: $1225 \div 41$

   $1230 \div 41 =$ ______ ______

Circle the closer estimate.

7. Problem: 32×87

   30×87 or 40×87

8. Problem: $682 \div 5$

   $700 \div 5$ or $650 \div 5$

9. Problem: $410 \div 15$

   $450 \div 15$ or $300 \div 15$

10. Problem: 48×32

    48×30 or 50×32

Mixed Review and Test Prep

11. If you look at this solid from the top, what silhouette do you see?

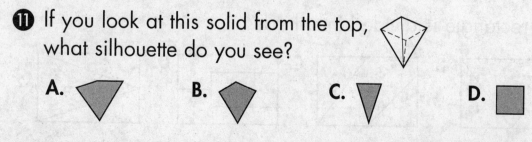

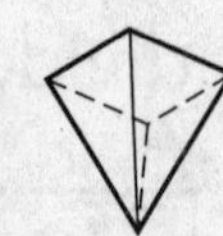

A.  **B.**  **C.** 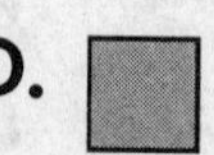 **D.** ■

Name Date

Finish It Up!

You are given the first step for solving each problem. Use this step to find the solution. Show your work on another sheet of paper.

Family Connection
Students have been creating solution strategies using a given first step. Ask your child to tell you a different first step for one or two of these problems.

1. Find 53×6 by first solving 50×6. $53 \times 6 =$ ______
2. Find 401×13 by first solving 400×10. $401 \times 13 =$ ______
3. Find 74×23 by first solving 2×74. $74 \times 23 =$ ______
4. Find 58×14 by first solving 58×10. $58 \times 14 =$ ______
5. Find 8×643 by first solving 8×40. $8 \times 643 =$ ______
6. Find $93 \div 11$ by first solving $88 \div 11$. $93 \div 11 =$ ______
7. Find $158 \div 7$ by first solving $140 \div 7$. $158 \div 7 =$ ______
8. Find $342 \div 5$ by first solving 5×70. $342 \div 5 =$ ______
9. Find $871 \div 16$ by first solving 5×16. $871 \div 16 =$ ______
10. Find $755 \div 22$ by first solving $66 \div 22$. $755 \div 22 =$ ______

Mixed Review and Test Prep

11. Each square on the grid shows 1 square block. What is the shortest distance from the square to the triangle?

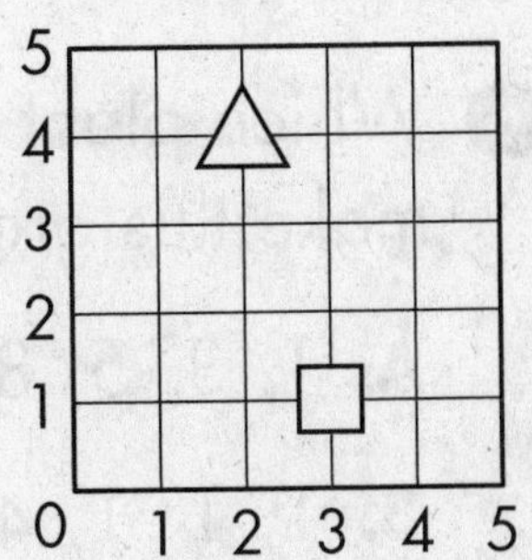

A. 3 blocks **C.** 5 blocks

B. 4 blocks **D.** 7 blocks

Name Date

Building on Numbers You Know

Different First Steps

Tell two different first steps you could use to do each problem. Choose one of your first steps and find the solution. Show your work on another sheet of paper.

Family Connection

Students have been solving the same problem in two or more different ways. Your child is starting to learn that the choice of strategy depends on the numbers in the problem as well as the types of computation he or she prefers.

1. To find 73 × 29, I could start with ________ or ________.

   The answer is ________.

2. To find 87 ÷ 15, I could start with ________ or ________.

   The answer is ________.

3. To find 578 ÷ 4, I could start with ________ or ________.

   The answer is ________.

4. To find 482 × 7, I could start with ________ or ________.

   The answer is ________.

5. To find 318 ÷ 26, I could start with ________ or ________.

   The answer is ________.

Mixed Review and Test Prep

6. Which plant height measurements would make this graph?

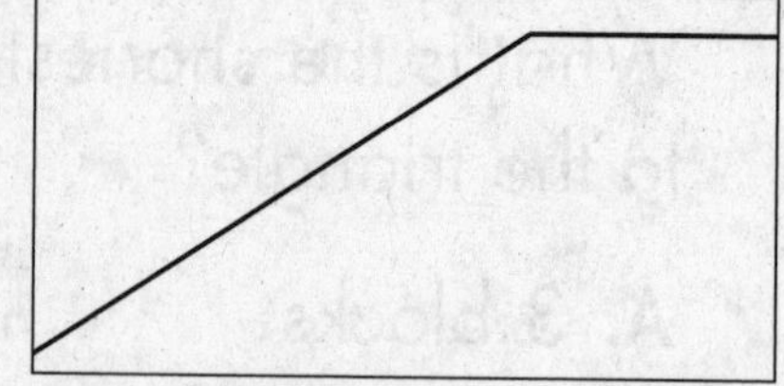

   A. 1, 3, 5, 8, 8 **C.** 1, 3, 3, 5, 7

   B. 1, 1, 1, 4, 4 **D.** 1, 5, 6, 6, 8

Name Date

Building on Numbers You Know

The Picnic Puzzle

Use the clues in the story to find the missing numbers.

Family Connection

Students can apply their logical reasoning skills in this puzzle. If your child needs help getting started, show him or her how to use the last several sentences to find the number of children at the picnic: divide the number of pony rides by 2.

The day of the big school picnic was finally here. There were 408 children coming on buses and

1. ______ coming in cars. Each bus held
2. 34 children, so they needed ______ buses.
3. If 4 children rode in each car, they used ______ cars.

The eighth grade had made 1600 cookies.

4. Each child got ______ cookies and there were
5. ______ left over. The paper plates came in packages of 36. They bought 15 packages so they
6. had plenty of paper plates. There were ______ in all. They used even more paper cups—13 bags
7. of ______, or 624 in all. The pony ride was a big success. Everyone got to ride twice. That was 1040 rides! I bet those ponies were tired.

Mixed Review and Test Prep

8. The scale on a map is 1 inch = 0.5 mile. If the map shows 3.5 inches between the post office and the school, what is the actual distance?

A. 1.75 mi **B.** 3.5 mi **C.** 7 mi **D.** 17.5 mi

Name Date

Building on Numbers You Know

Ways to Make 10,000

Family Connection

Students have made rectangles that contain 10,000 dots. The rectangles have blocks of 100 dots, so your child used 100 blocks. Ask your child to tell you how the blocks were arranged—10 rows of 10, 4 groups of 25, or some other way.

Complete each situation to show a way to make 10,000.

1. Two hundred runners sign up for a charity race. To raise 10,000 dollars, each runner must pay a fee of __________ dollars.

2. The Better Banana Company packs 25 bananas in a box. To ship 10,000 bananas, they need __________ boxes.

3. The library needs some more computers. If 20 people each donate __________ dollars, they will have 10,000 dollars to spend.

4. A square tile tabletop has 25 rows of tiles, with 25 in each row. A carton of 10,000 tiles will make __________ of these tabletops.

Follow the patterns. Count up to reach 10,000.

5. 7000, 7500, 8000, 8500, ________, ________, ________

6. 8800, 9000, 9200, 9400, ________, ________, ________

Mixed Review and Test Prep

7. Which is **not** a factor of 100?

A. 5 **B.** 15 **C.** 20 **D.** 25

Name Date

Building on Numbers You Know

Reaching One Million

Family Connection

Your child's class has been working on a display of 1 million dots! They are using sheets of paper that each show 5000 dots. Ask your child to explain why there are 5000 dots on each sheet. (There are 50 blocks of 100 dots. They are in 10 rows of 5 blocks each.)

A class is counting by 5000's up to one million. Write the next number each person should say.

1. Carla: 230,000 235,000 240,000 ________
2. Jonas: 385,000 390,000 395,000 ________
3. Bill: 510,000 515,000 520,000 ________
4. Emily: 795,000 800,000 805,000 ________

Complete each situation to show a way to make one million.

5. There were 20,000 people at a rock concert.

   At this rate, the rock group will need ________ concerts to sell one million tickets.

6. Sidney plans to save 2500 dollars per year. At this rate, it will take him ________ years to save a million dollars.

Mixed Review and Test Prep

7. Which shows the graph of a plant that grew slowly at first and then faster and faster?

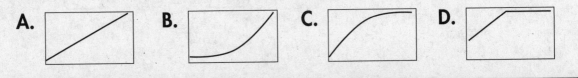

A.  **B.** 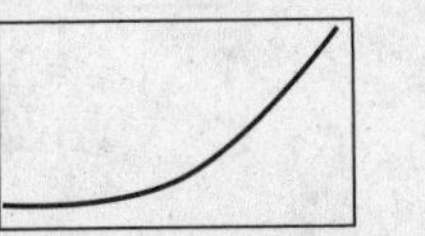 **C.** **D.**

Name Date

Making Estimates

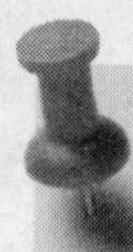

Family Connection

Students have been practicing estimates for more difficult multiplication and division problems. Your child may use multiples of 10, familiar facts, or doubling strategies. Ask your child to explain one or two estimates on this page.

Complete the estimate for each problem.

1. Problem: 34×62

   $30 \times 62 =$ ________

2. Problem: $843 \div 8$

   $840 \div 8 =$ ________

3. Problem: 79×61

   $80 \times 61 =$ ________

4. Problem: $2764 \div 7$

   $2800 \div 7 =$ ________

5. Problem: 29×58

   $30 \times 60 =$ ________

6. Problem: $719 \div 19$

   $720 \div 20 =$ ________

7. Problem: 32×418

   $32 \times 400 =$ ________

8. Problem: $463 \div 82$

   $480 \div 80 =$ ________

9. Problem: 673×76

   $700 \times 80 =$ ________

10. Problem: $3128 \div 64$

    $3000 \div 60 =$ ________

Mixed Review and Test Prep

11. What does this shape look like after a right turn of 90 degrees?

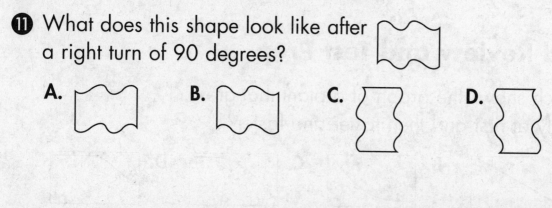

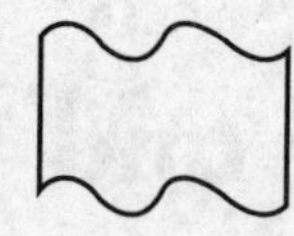

A. 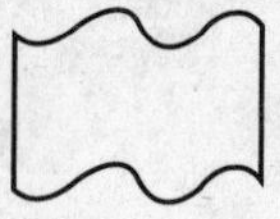

B. 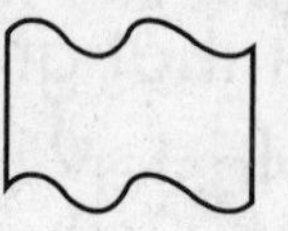

C. 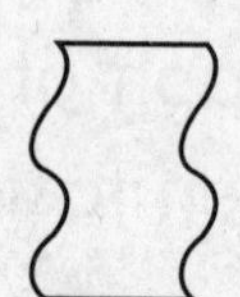

D. 

Name Date

Building on Numbers You Know

Comparing Estimates

Find the difference between the exact answer and the estimate.

Family Connection
Students have been playing an estimation game in which they compare products or quotients to estimates they make in 30 seconds. The activities on this page are similar to what your child does during the game.

1. Problem: 76×39

   $75 \times 40 =$ ________

   Exact answer: ________

   Difference: ________

2. Problem: $386 \div 9$

   $360 \div 9 =$ ________

   Exact answer: ________

   Difference: ________

3. Problem: 62×85

   $61 \times 80 =$ ________

   Exact answer: ________

   Difference: ________

4. Problem: $643 \div 28$

   $630 \div 30 =$ ________

   Exact answer: ________

   Difference: ________

5. Problem: 428×64

   $430 \times 60 =$ ________

   Exact answer: ________

   Difference: ________

6. Problem: $851 \div 46$

   $850 \div 50 =$ ________

   Exact answer: ________

   Difference: ________

Mixed Review and Test Prep

7. Which shape is a pyramid?

A. 

B. 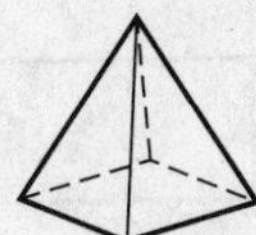

C. 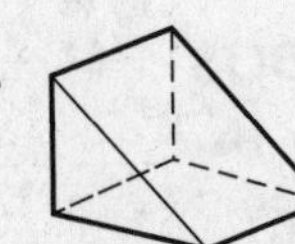

D. 

Name Date

Building on Numbers You Know

Large and Small Hunt

In each row, circle the largest product or quotient. Then underline the smallest.

> **Family Connection**
> Students have been developing strategies for solving multiplication and division problems without using a calculator or a standard algorithm. They can practice using these strategies with these problems.

1	46×77	67×51	39×86
2	23×97	36×58	69×33
3	152×93	84×168	71×194
4	72×807	714×82	62×924
5	$468 \div 26$	$68 \div 34$	$114 \div 6$
6	$2150 \div 43$	$624 \div 13$	$960 \div 24$
7	$1120 \div 14$	$1680 \div 24$	$3400 \div 34$
8	$225 \div 15$	$905 \div 5$	$224 \div 16$

Mixed Review and Test Prep

9. What might this data show?

   A. the heights of first graders

   B. the heights of houses

   C. the heights of basketball players

   D. the heights of dogs

Individual	Inches
A	78
B	84
C	80
D	75
E	82
F	84

Name Date

Building on Numbers You Know

Using What You Know

Find the first answer mentally. Then use it to solve the second problem. Show your work on another sheet of paper.

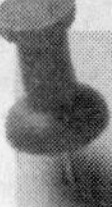

Family Connection

Students have been creating solution strategies using a given first step. Use the problems on this page to talk to your child about the kinds of strategies that work best for him or her.

1. $53 \times 10 =$ ______ ⟹ $53 \times 67 =$ ______
2. $40 \times 90 =$ ______ ⟹ $48 \times 92 =$ ______
3. $100 \times 79 =$ ______ ⟹ $356 \times 79 =$ ______
4. $100 \times 6 =$ ______ ⟹ $845 \div 6 =$ ______
5. $380 \div 38 =$ ______ ⟹ $756 \div 38 =$ ______
6. $54 \times 10 =$ ______ ⟹ $921 \div 54 =$ ______
7. Choose one of the above problems. Use a different first step and solve it another way. Show your work on another sheet of paper.

Mixed Review and Test Prep

8. Which of these is true for the data in the graph?

   A. Less than $\frac{1}{4}$ chose cats.

   B. More than $\frac{1}{4}$ chose cats.

   C. Less than $\frac{1}{3}$ chose dogs.

   D. More than $\frac{1}{2}$ chose birds.

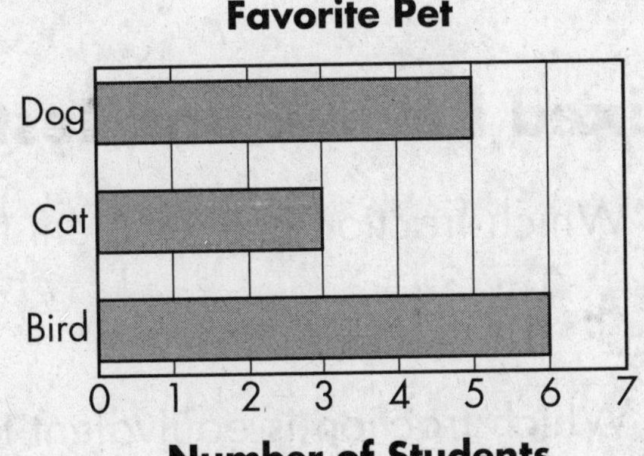

Name Date

Building on Numbers You Know

Two-Part Problems

Each problem has two parts. You'll need the first answer to solve the second problem.

Family Connection
Students have used multiplication and division to solve word problem situations. Some of these problems have remainders. Ask your child to tell you what should be done with the "extras."

1. **PART 1** Suppose there are 48 balloons in a bag. If you buy 10 bags, how many balloons will you have? ______

   PART 2 There are 37 people coming to your party. How many balloons can each person have? ______

2. **PART 1** A factory made 1800 yellow duck buttons. They put four on each card. How many cards were filled? ______

   PART 2 The factory put 24 cards in each box. How many boxes were filled? ______

3. **PART 1** You and eight friends wash 57 cars. Suppose you charge \$12 per car. How much will you earn? ______

   PART 2 If you share what you earn with your eight friends, how much will each person get? ______

Mixed Review and Test Prep

4. Which fraction is equivalent to $\frac{1}{2}$?

   A. $\frac{1}{4}$ **B.** $\frac{2}{8}$ **C.** $\frac{4}{16}$ **D.** $\frac{4}{8}$

5. Which fraction is equivalent to $\frac{3}{4}$?

   A. $\frac{6}{6}$ **B.** $\frac{6}{8}$ **C.** $\frac{6}{12}$ **D.** $\frac{3}{9}$

Name Date

Building on Numbers You Know

Getting to 10,000

Each problem shows a different way to get to 10,000. Find the missing numbers. The computation is done in order from left to right.

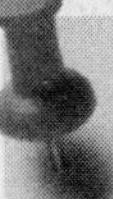

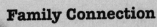

Family Connection

Students have been playing a number game that uses multiplication, division, and other operations. The goal is to form a string of problems that end up with an answer of 10,000. Have your child pick one problem and find a different way to get to 10,000 using the same starting number.

1. 794 × 8 + ________ = 10,000
2. 6000 ÷ 3 + ________ = 10,000
3. 4375 ÷ 7 × ________ = 10,000
4. 26 × 487 − ________ = 10,000
5. 4800 ÷ 12 × ________ = 10,000
6. 7200 ÷ 9 + ________ = 10,000
7. 5120 ÷ 64 × ________ = 10,000
8. 249 × 38 + ________ = 10,000
9. 8000 ÷ 16 + ________ = 10,000
10. For the exercise on the right side of this page, start with any number you like, but you must end on 10,000.

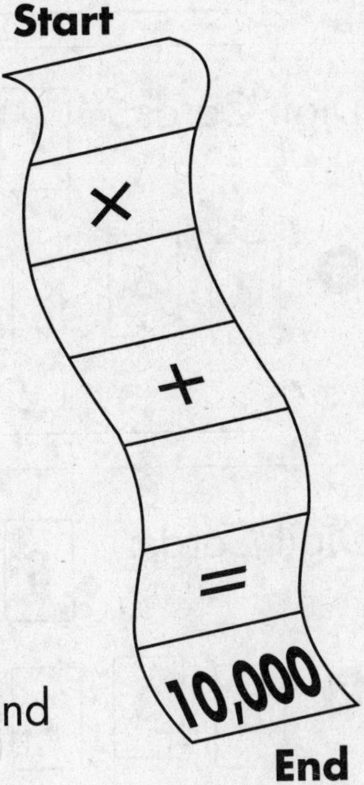

Mixed Review and Test Prep

11. Which three amounts total $1.00?

A. 27¢, 23¢, 40¢

B. 18¢, 47¢, 25¢

C. 15¢, 53¢, 32¢

D. 14¢, 37¢, 59¢

Name Date

Building on Numbers You Know

Digit Mix Up

Find the largest product and the smallest quotient for each set of cards.

> **Family Connection**
>
> Students have learned to solve difficult multiplication and division problems without using a calculator. They can show you their skills as they solve these digit puzzles.

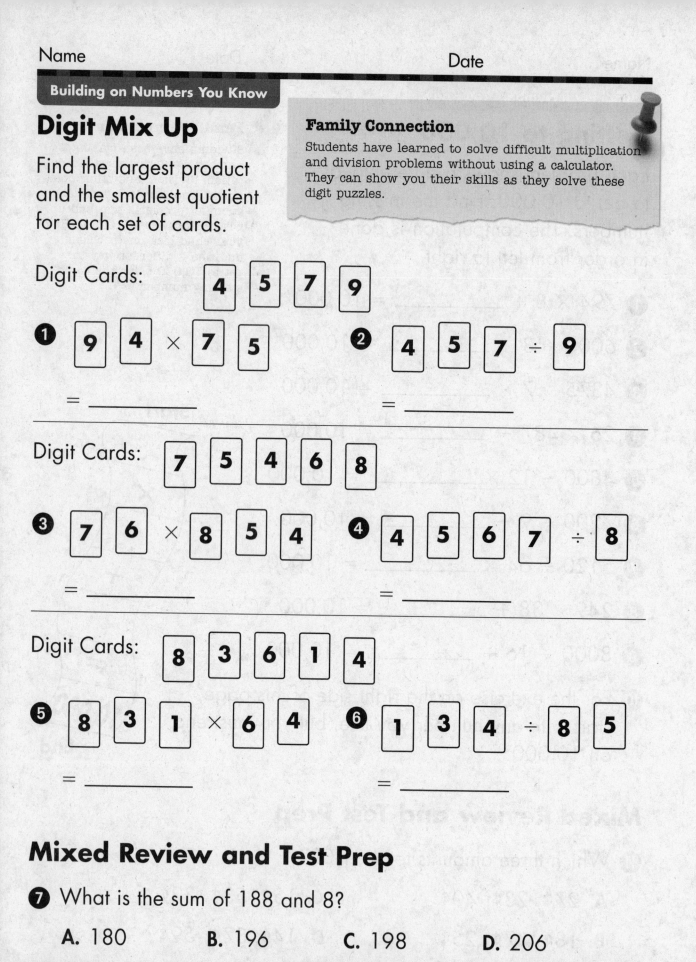

Digit Cards: 4 5 7 9

❶ 9 4 × 7 5 = ______

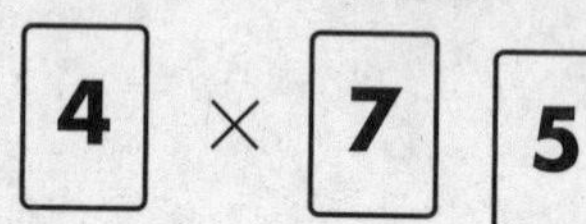

❷ 4 5 7 ÷ 9 = ______

Digit Cards: 7 5 4 6 8

❸ 7 6 × 8 5 4 = ______

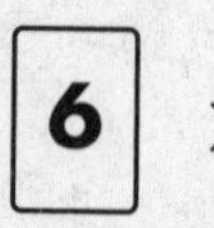

❹ 4 5 6 7 ÷ 8 = ______

Digit Cards: 8 3 6 1 4

❺ 8 3 1 × 6 4 = ______

❻ 1 3 4 ÷ 8 5 = ______

Mixed Review and Test Prep

❼ What is the sum of 188 and 8?

A. 180 **B.** 196 **C.** 198 **D.** 206

Name Date

Measurement Benchmarks

Unit Match Up

Family Connection

Students measured a variety of objects looking for objects that measured 1 unit: 1 centimeter, 1 meter, 1 foot, 1 minute, 1 pound, 1 kilogram, 1 cup, and 1 liter. Later students will use these measures as benchmarks to help them find other measures. You might want to help your child find other objects that measure 1 unit.

1 Mary wrote this letter to her friend. Help her fill in the units of measure. Each measure is used only once.

centimeter	foot	meter	minute	pound	kilogram	cup	liter

I measured all sorts of things in school today. It took me 1 ______________ to weigh a couple of books. The larger, my dictionary, weighed 1 ______________. A smaller book weighed 1 ______________.

I measured liquids too. My glass holds 1 ______________ and the whole bottle of water holds 1 ______________.

I measured my fingernail. It was 1 ______________ long. And believe it or not, my shoe is almost 1 ______________ long! I went looking for something longer and found that my bat is 1 ______________ long. And I found out something more—measuring is fun.

Mixed Review and Test Prep

2 Which set of multiples is shaded in the table?

2	4	6	8
3	6	9	12
4	8	12	16
5	10	15	20

A. multiples of 2 **C.** multiples of 4

B. multiples of 3 **D.** multiples of 5

Name Date

Measurement Benchmarks

Handy Measure

If you spread out your hand, the length from your little finger to your thumb is your **hand span.** It is a handy measuring tool.

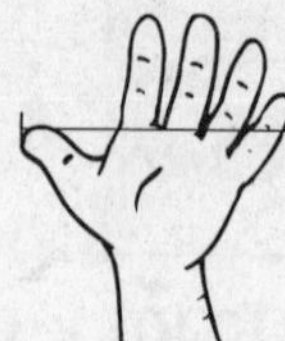

Family Connection

Students have been learning how to estimate length using benchmarks. A benchmark is something of a known measure that helps you estimate the measure of other objects.

Interesting Tidbit

At arm's length, a hand span appears to be about the length of the Big Dipper.

1 Use your hand span to measure four items. List the items and the length of each in spans.

Item	Number of Spans

2 How can you estimate length in inches if you know the length of your hand span in inches?

____

____

Mixed Review and Test Prep

3 Which shape is at (4, 3)?

A. 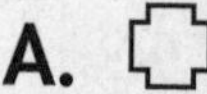

B. △

C. ○

D. ⬠

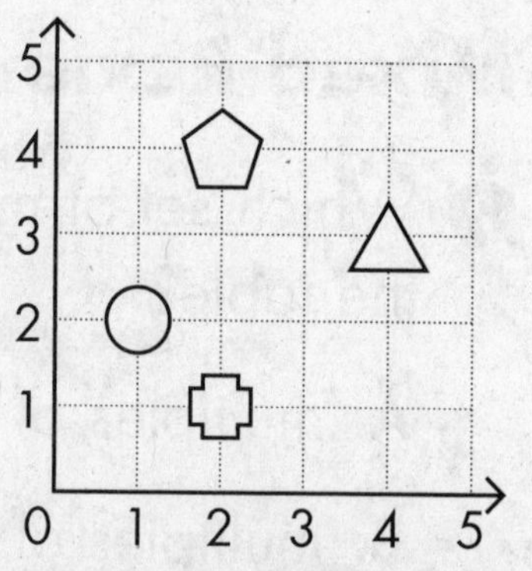

Name Date

Measurement Benchmarks

E and E Measuring Services

Eva makes exact measurements;
Esther estimates.

Family Connection
Students are learning to identify situations in which an estimated length is enough and situations that require an exact measurement. Have your child tell you which category each of these jobs falls into.

Who should do each job?

1. **Job:** find the size of the opening for the new window.

 ____

2. **Job:** figure out if we can get the mirror through the door.

 ____

3. **Job:** find a box to ship Brian's birthday gift in.

 ____

4. **Job:** figure out whether it takes more than a minute to walk from the house to the barn.

 ____

5. **Job:** make pattern for building a planter box.

 ____

6. **Job:** label wing spans in butterfly collection.

 ____

Mixed Review and Test Prep

7. What is the total value of 2 quarters, 2 dimes, 3 nickels, and 1 penny?

A. 8¢ **B.** 61¢ **C.** 81¢ **D.** 86¢

Name Date

Measurement Benchmarks

Long and Longer

Compare these measurements for Harry and Kevin. For each measurement, circle the greater length.

Family Connection

Students have been comparing measurements they made with those their classmates made. They learned how to compare measurements, like those in this activity, that are expressed in different ways. They also discussed reasons why everyone did not get the same length when they measured. Have your child tell you about possible reasons for differences in the measurements.

1. Harry's head is **56 centimeters** around.
   Kevin's is **0.5 meter** around.

2. Harry's arm span is **1.5 meters.**
   Kevin's is **163 centimeters.**

3. Harry is **1 meter and 70 centimeters** tall.
   Kevin is **$1\frac{75}{100}$ meters** tall.

4. Harry's foot is **0.3 meter** long.
   Kevin's foot is **26 centimeters** long.

5. Harry's walking stride is **0.9 meter** long.
   Kevin's is **85 centimeters** long.

Mixed Review and Test Prep

6. What is the next number in this pattern?
   11, 22, 33, 44, ___

   A. 33 **B.** 45 **C.** 55 **D.** 77

Name Date

Measurement Benchmarks

100-Meter Mark

On another sheet of paper, tell how each person can mark a path 100 meters long.

Family Connection

To help them understand how far 100 meters is, students measured out a path 100 meters long. Have your child tell you how his or her group did it.

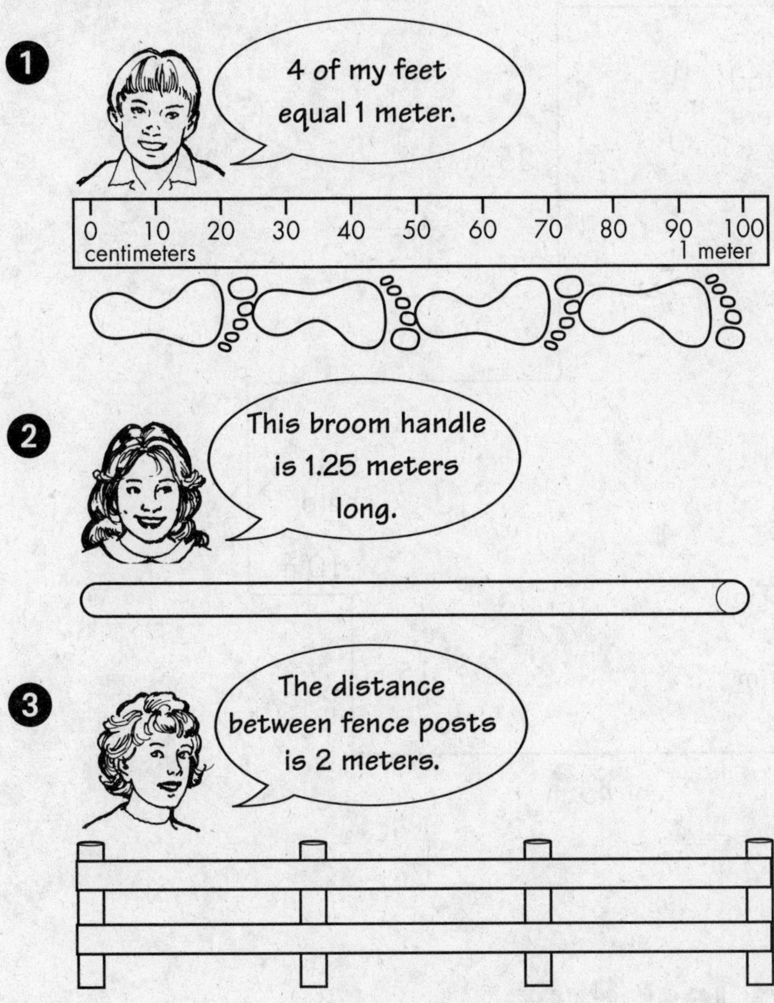

1
4 of my feet equal 1 meter.
0 10 20 30 40 50 60 70 80 90 100
centimeters
1 meter
2
This broom handle is 1.25 meters long.
3
The distance between fence posts is 2 meters.

Mixed Review and Test Prep

4 What is the sum of 8204 and 333?

A. 11,537 **B.** 11,534 **C.** 8537 **D.** 8534

Name Date

Measurement Benchmarks

Walk Around

Family Connection

In class, students made presentations showing drawings of their 100-meter paths and describing their measuring strategies. Ask your child to tell you about some of the measuring strategies used by the groups in his or her class.

1 From each starting point, mark a 100-meter path.

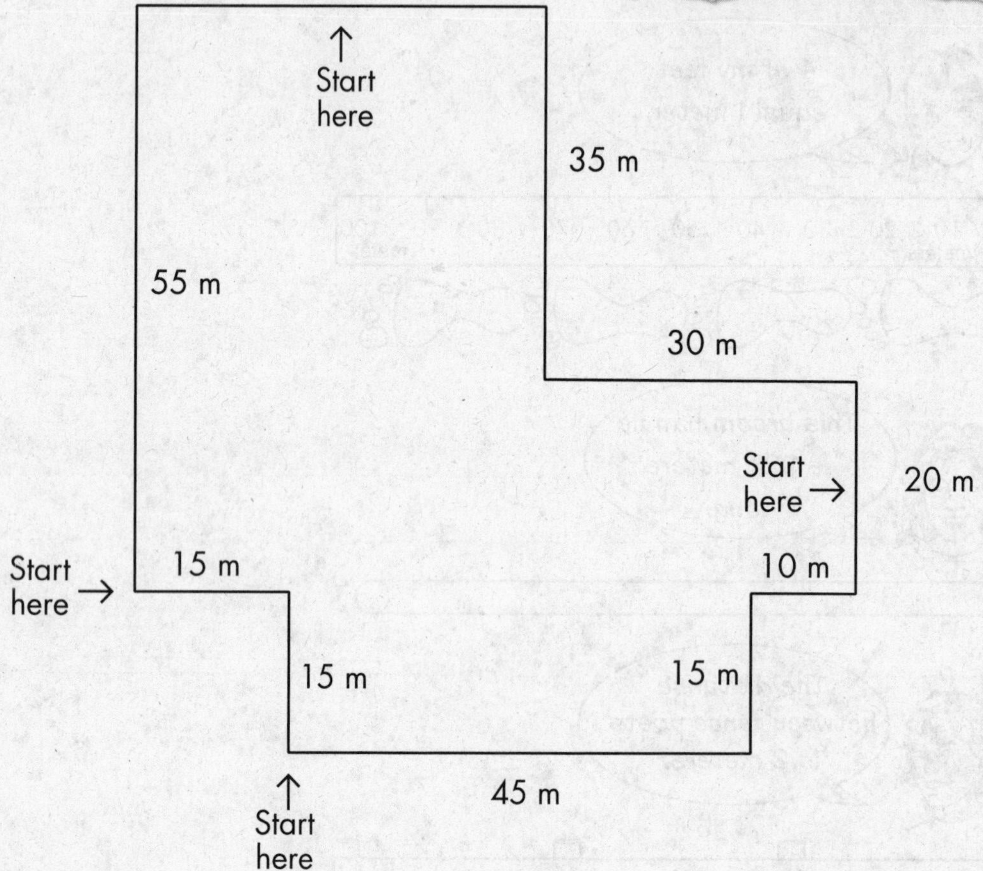

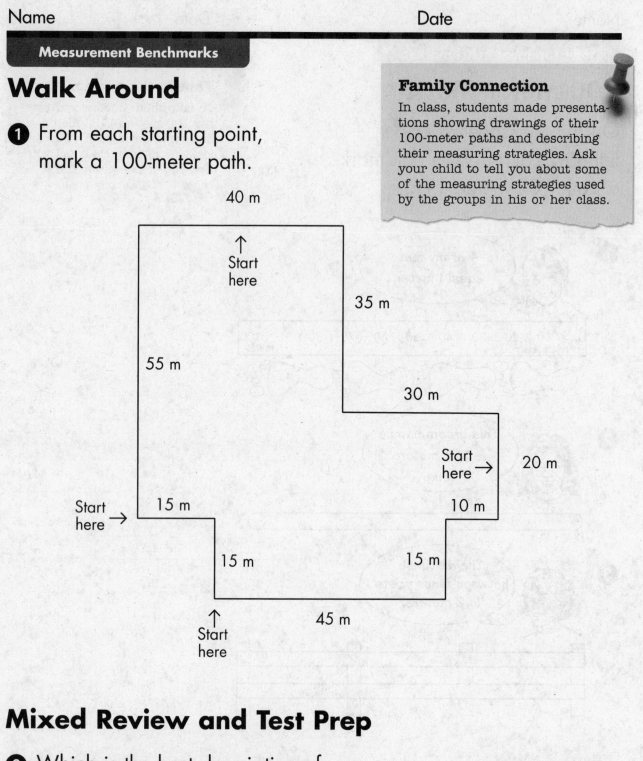

Mixed Review and Test Prep

2 Which is the best description of this design?

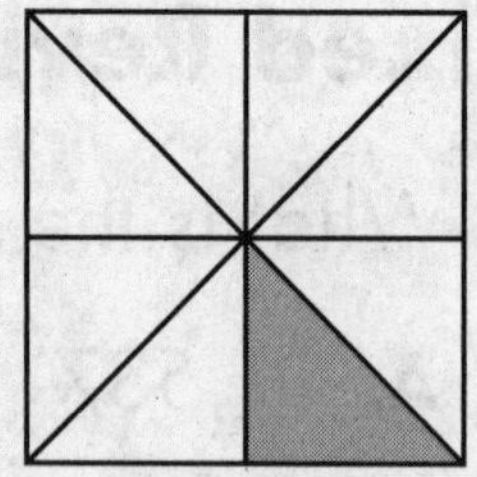

A. $\frac{1}{8}$ shaded

B. $\frac{1}{7}$ shaded

C. $\frac{1}{6}$ shaded

D. $\frac{1}{5}$ shaded

Name Date

Measurement Benchmarks

From There to Here

Mason listed the scale for each map he used and the distance on the map that each product traveled to get to his home in Columbus, Ohio. Help him complete the table to find the actual distance each product traveled.

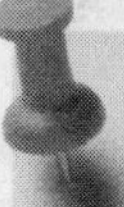

Family Connection

Students are using map scales to find the distances various products traveled from their places of origin to your town. **Questions you might ask your child:** "Which product traveled the farthest? How far did it travel?"

Wisconsin

Michigan

Hawaii

Florida

	Map Scale	Map Distance	Actual Distance
1.	1 in = 200 mi	$2\frac{1}{4}$ in	
2.	$\frac{1}{2}$ in = 60 mi	3 in	
3.	1 in = 1600 mi	$3\frac{1}{8}$ in	
4.	$\frac{1}{2}$ in = 100 mi	4 in	

Mixed Review and Test Prep

5. In Lanya's class, 9 out of 40 students are the oldest child in their family. Which familiar fraction on the strip is closest to $\frac{9}{40}$?

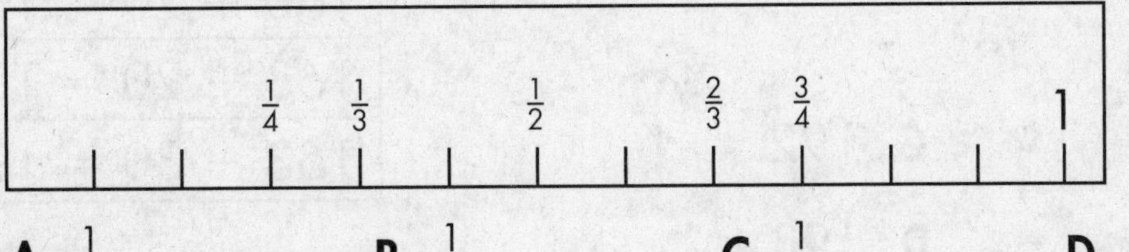

A. $\frac{1}{4}$ **B.** $\frac{1}{3}$ **C.** $\frac{1}{2}$ **D.** $\frac{3}{4}$

Name Date

Measurement Benchmarks

Otto's Organic Apples

Family Connection

Students made a class chart showing their products sorted by distance from place of origin to your town. Ask your child to tell you what distance categories his or her class used for the sort.

1 Otto sorts his apple shipments by distance from his orchard. Sort these shipments for him.

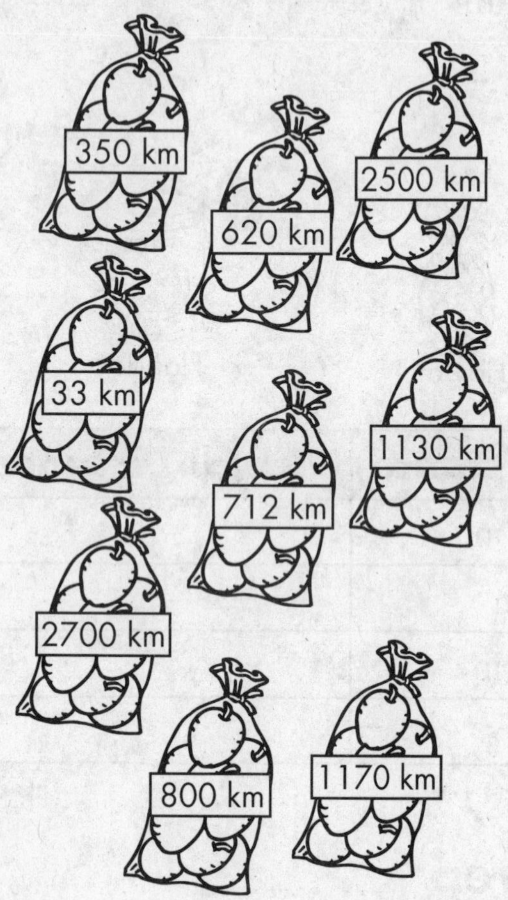

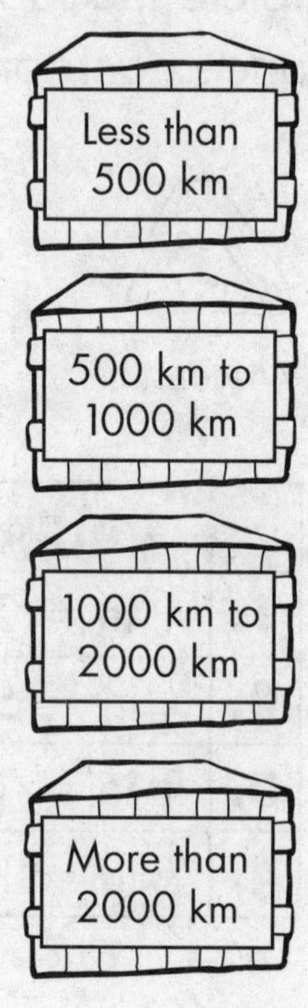

Mixed Review and Test Prep

2 Use the related problem set to find 163 + 29.

160 + 20 = 180
163 + 20 = 183
163 + 30 = 193

A. 180 **C.** 192

B. 183 **D.** 193

Name Date

Measurement Benchmarks

How Is It Measured?

Use the packages shown.

Family Connection

Students are recording measurements from grocery items. They have observed that liquids are measured by capacity, or the amount of space they take up. Solids are measured by weight. Your child may need help remembering what units the abbreviations on the packages represent.

1 Which items are measured by weight?

____

____

2 List some units of weight.

____

____

3 Which items are measured by capacity?

____

4 List some units of capacity.

____

____

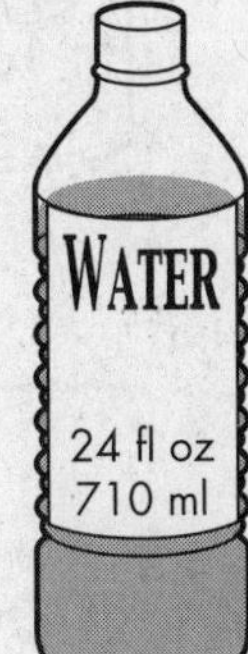

Mixed Review and Test Prep

5 When Alvin got in his car, the odometer read 25,432.1. After he ran an errand, the odometer read 25,435.5. How many miles did he drive?

A. 2.9 **B.** 3.4 **C.** 3.9 **D.** 4.6

Name Date

Measurement Benchmarks

Order Up

Family Connection
Students have been finding both metric and customary capacities of grocery containers and then comparing the metric and customary units. Have your child show you how he or she decided on the order of these containers.

❶ Each package is labeled in both metric and U.S. customary units. Write numbers under the packages to put them in order from least capacity, 1, to greatest capacity, 6.

______

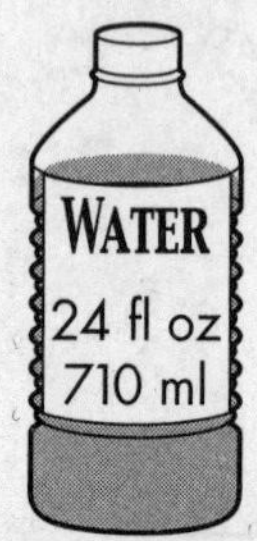
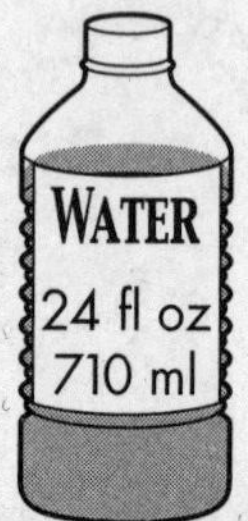

______

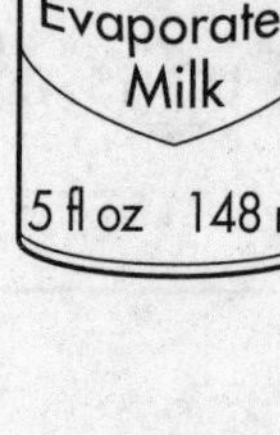

______

JUICE
16.9 fl oz
500 ml

______

______

______

Mixed Review and Test Prep

❷ Which object could have a rectangle for a silhouette?

A. a tennis ball **C.** a light bulb

B. a can of soup **D.** a football

Name Date

Measurement Benchmarks

Prove It!

Write **less than** or **greater than** to complete each statement. Show you are right by matching each statement with the package that proves it.

Family Connection

In class, students worked with balance scales to develop a sense of the weights of 1 kilogram, 500 grams, 100 grams, 1 gram, 1 pound, and 1 ounce and to compare their relationships to one another. Ask your child to list the weights from heaviest to lightest for you.

1. 500 grams is ______________ 1 pound.

2. 1 gram is ______________ 1 ounce.

3. 1 kilogram is ______________ 1 pound.

4. 100 grams is ______________ 1 ounce.

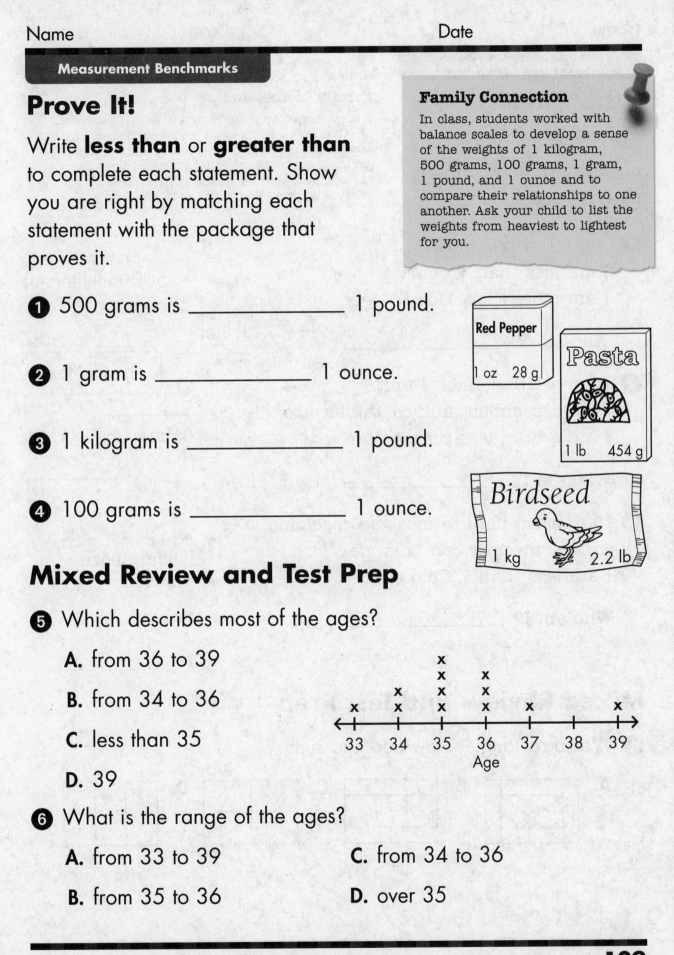

Mixed Review and Test Prep

5. Which describes most of the ages?

A. from 36 to 39

B. from 34 to 36

C. less than 35

D. 39

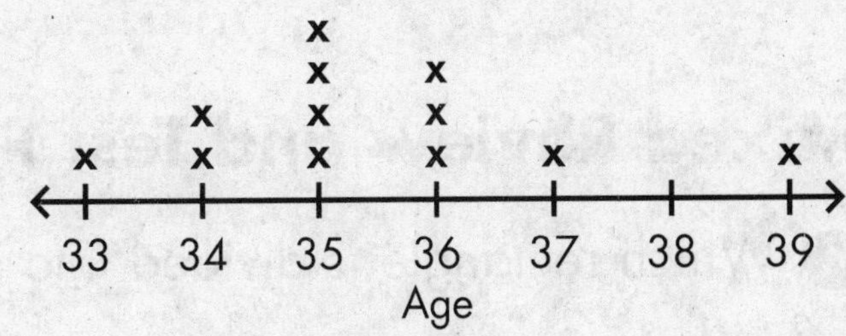

6. What is the range of the ages?

A. from 33 to 39

B. from 35 to 36

C. from 34 to 36

D. over 35

Name Date

Who Am I?

Identify which of the units shown is described by each set of clues.

Family Connection

Students have been developing a sense of the size of 1 liter, 500 milliliters, 1 milliliter, 1 quart, 1 cup, and 1 fluid ounce measures and of the relationships among these metric and U.S. standard units of capacity. Ask your child which of the measures given below is greatest and which is least.

500 milliliters

1 liter

1 milliliter

1 quart

1 cup

1 fluid ounce

1. I am a metric unit.
I am less than 1 quart.
I am more than 1 cup.

Who am I? ______________

2. I am a U.S. standard unit.
I am a common milk container size.
I am a little less than a liter.

Who am I? ______________

3. I am often used to measure medicine.
An eye dropper can hold me.
I am less than 1 fluid ounce.

Who am I? ______________

Mixed Review and Test Prep

4. Which rectangle is divided into sixths?

A. 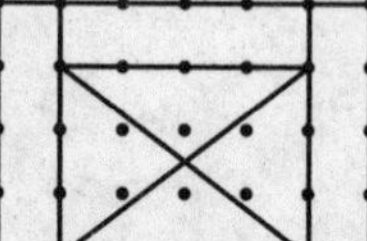
B. 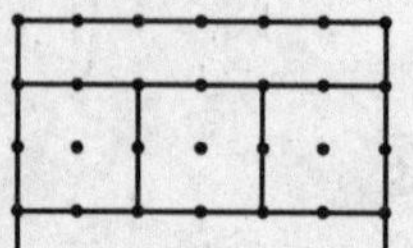
C. 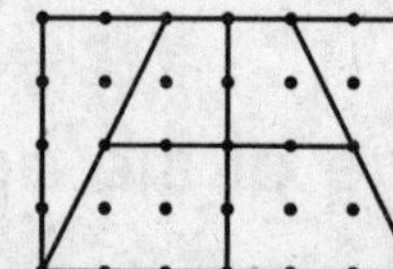
D. 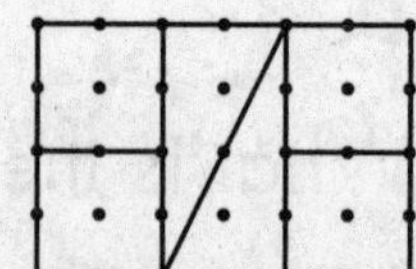

Name Date

Measurement Benchmarks

Dense Decisions

Use the information from the pictures to make each comparison.

Family Connection

Students have been comparing weight and quantity and learning to distinguish between them. They have been introduced to the concept of density, the relationship between size and weight. The sand is denser than the cereal. Ask your child if the paint or water is the denser of the two.

1. Does it look like there is the same amount of cereal and sand?

____

2. Compare the weights of the cereal and sand.

____

____

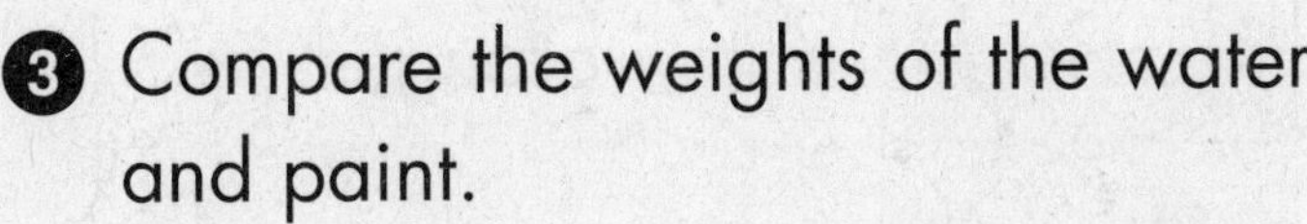

3. Compare the weights of the water and paint.

____

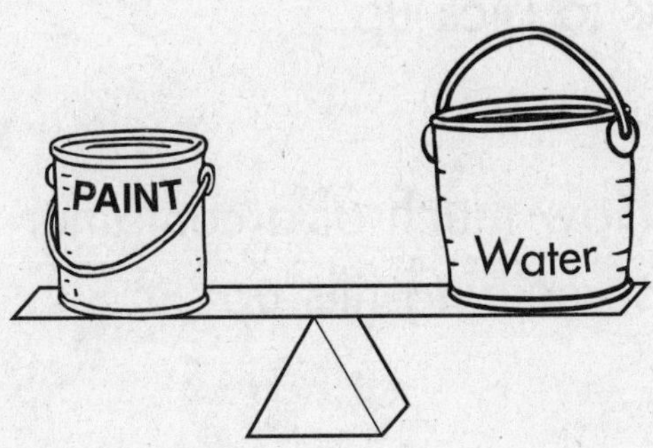

4. Compare the quantities of water and paint.

____

Mixed Review and Test Prep

5. Which array will use the most blocks?

A. 3 rows of 6 blocks each

B. 5 rows of 4 blocks each

C. 2 rows of 9 blocks each

D. 4 rows of 4 blocks each

Name Date

Tell Me About It

Family Connection

In class, students wrote lists of what they know about weight and liquid measure. Ask your child if his or her list included different points than those named here.

1 Connect each description to **Weight** or **Liquid measure**.

How much space something fills up

Measured in units such as pounds, grams, kilograms, and ounces

How hard something is to pick up

How much of a container something fills up

How heavy something is

Measured in units such as milliliters, quarts, liters, and fluid ounces

Used to measure oranges

Used to measure orange juice

Mixed Review and Test Prep

2 The graph shows a boat's speed over time. What could be happening when the speed is at its lowest point?

A. It is low tide.

B. The boat is slowing down.

C. The driver is stopping for gas.

D. Another boat is passing by.

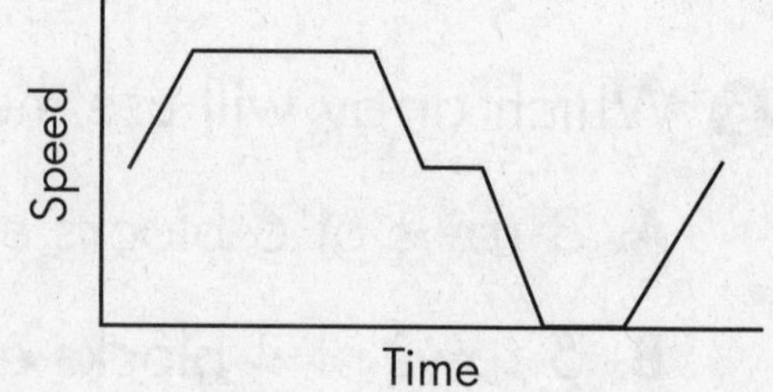

Name Date

Measurement Benchmarks

By the Bag

Zora weighed each of the apples in a bag. Use her line plot to answer these questions.

Family Connection

Groups of students organized and analyzed the data the class gathered about vegetable weights. **Questions you might ask your child:** "What vegetables did your group analyze?" "How did your group organize the weights and determine the typical weight?"

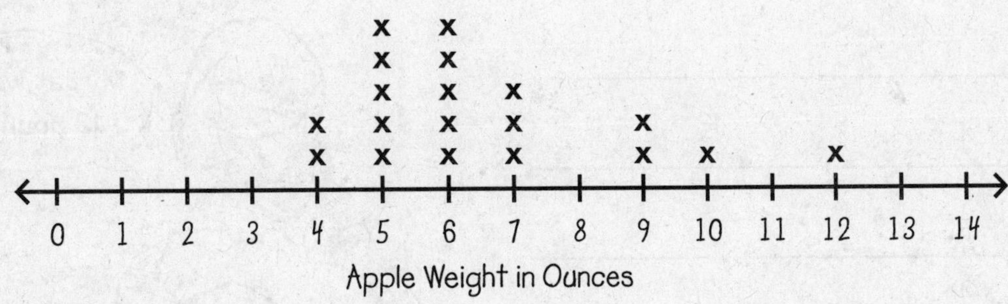

1. What is the range of the apple weights? ____________
2. What is the middle weight? ____________
3. Describe the weights of most of the apples. ____________
4. What is the most common weight? ____________
5. What is the typical weight of an apple from Zora's bag? ____________

Mixed Review and Test Prep

6. Which shapes are rectangles?

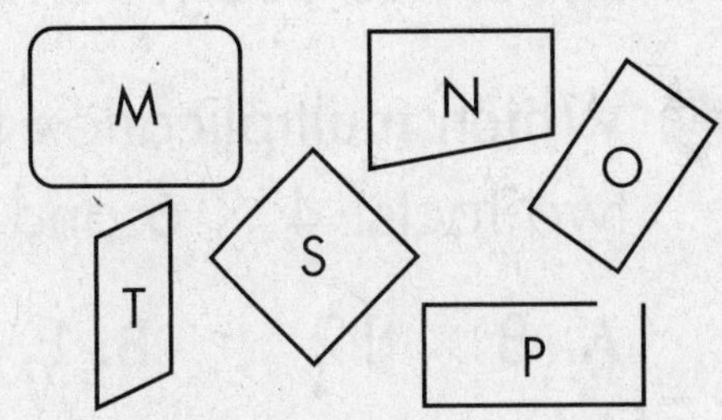

A. M and N **C.** S and O

B. T and S **D.** O and P

Name Date

Use What You Carry

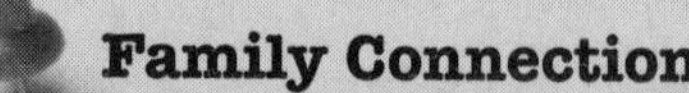

Family Connection

Students are using the record-breaking weights of vegetables to develop benchmarks for large numbers of pounds. Help your child develop a sense of greater weights by pointing out weights of common items, for example, a 25-pound bag of dog food, or a 50-pound bag of topsoil.

1. Explain how each of these people could use the weight he or she knows to develop benchmarks for 25 lb, 50 lb, and 100 lb.

My cat weighs 12 pounds.

My backpack weighs 26 pounds.

Mixed Review and Test Prep

2. Which multiplication fact can you find using these two facts: 4×6 and 2×6

A. 8×12 **B.** 8×4 **C.** 10×8 **D.** 6×6

Name Date

Measurement Benchmarks

Stop!

Family Connection

Students are building a sense of time. In class, they estimated how long 30 seconds is. Work with your child to find some activities that take about 30 seconds.

Tammy timed Héctor as he estimated 30 seconds. The second hand was on 12 each time Tammy said "Go." The clocks show where the second hand was when Héctor said "Stop." What were Héctor's estimates?

____

2

____

3

____

4 How did Héctor's estimates for 30 seconds change with practice?

____

____

Mixed Review and Test Prep

5 Which equation is true?

A. $1 = \frac{1}{2} + \frac{1}{4}$

B. $1 = \frac{1}{4} + \frac{1}{4} + \frac{1}{2}$

C. $1 = \frac{2}{4} + \frac{2}{8}$

D. $1 = \frac{1}{2} + \frac{2}{4} + \frac{4}{8}$

Name Date

April Ads

Sandra's class decided that for each half hour of television, the typical time spent watching commercials is 9 minutes. Help Sandra figure out how many hours of commercials she will watch in April.

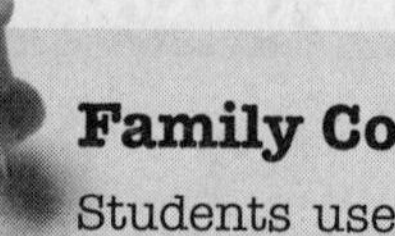

Family Connection

Students used their data on the number of minutes of commercials in $\frac{1}{2}$ hour of television to estimate how much time an average fifth grader spends watching commercials in a year. Work with your child to figure out how many hours of commercials he or she watches in a month.

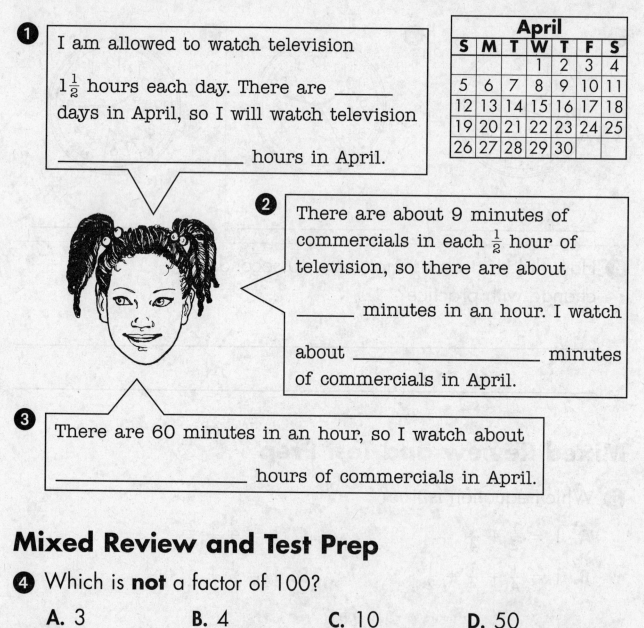

April						
S	M	T	W	T	F	S
			1	2	3	4
5	6	7	8	9	10	11
12	13	14	15	16	17	18
19	20	21	22	23	24	25
26	27	28	29	30		

1 I am allowed to watch television $1\frac{1}{2}$ hours each day. There are ______ days in April, so I will watch television ________________ hours in April.

2 There are about 9 minutes of commercials in each $\frac{1}{2}$ hour of television, so there are about ______ minutes in an hour. I watch about ________________ minutes of commercials in April.

3 There are 60 minutes in an hour, so I watch about ________________ hours of commercials in April.

Mixed Review and Test Prep

4 Which is **not** a factor of 100?

A. 3 **B.** 4 **C.** 10 **D.** 50

 Use after Investigation 3 (It's About Time), Session 2.

Name Date

Measurement Benchmarks

Times Change

Family Connection

Students are learning to understand time using their ages as benchmarks. Have your child tell you how his or her age compares to the ages of family members in terms of difference in years and number of times older.

Naomi is 10.
Her father is 35.

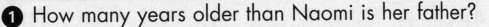

Naomi: □□□□□□□□□□

Dad: □□□□□□□□□□□□□□□□□□□□□□□□□□□□□□□□□□□

1 How many years older than Naomi is her father? _____

2 Find how old Naomi's father would be when Naomi is each age shown on the table.

Naomi's Age	1	10	20	25	30
Father's Age	26	35			
Number of Times Older	26				

3 For each age, find how many times older Naomi's father is than Naomi. How does it change as they get older?

____

Mixed Review and Test Prep

4 Diane gave the clerk $1 to pay for a 38¢ item. Which shows the change she got back?

A.

B.

C.

D.

Name Date

Build a Pattern

The first four steps in each pattern are shown. Draw the tiles for Steps 5 and 6. Then complete the table.

Family Connection

Students have been using square tiles to make patterns that grow in a regular way. They keep track of the number of tiles added at each step and the number of tiles in all.

1

1	2	3	4		
1	2	3	4		
1	2	3	4		

2

Step number	New tiles (step size)	Total so far
1	3	3
2	3	6
3	3	
4		
5		
6		

3

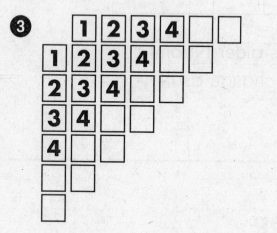

1	2	3	4		
1	2	3	4		
2	3	4			
3	4				
4					

4

Step number	New tiles (step size)	Total so far
1	2	2
2	3	5
3	4	
4		
5		
6		

Mixed Review and Test Prep

5 Thomas has 3 dollar bills, 3 quarters, 1 dime, and 4 pennies. How much money does he have?

A. \$3.89 **B.** \$3.84 **C.** \$3.79 **D.** \$3.64

 Use during Investigation 1 (Number Patterns in Changing Shapes), Sessions 1 and 2.

Name Date

Growing Patterns

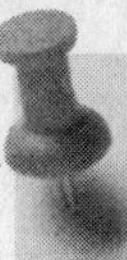

Family Connection

Students are learning to analyze the way in which patterns grow. Your child has made patterns with square tiles and then has shown the growth using tables and graphs.

❶ Continue the pattern. Then complete the table and the two graphs.

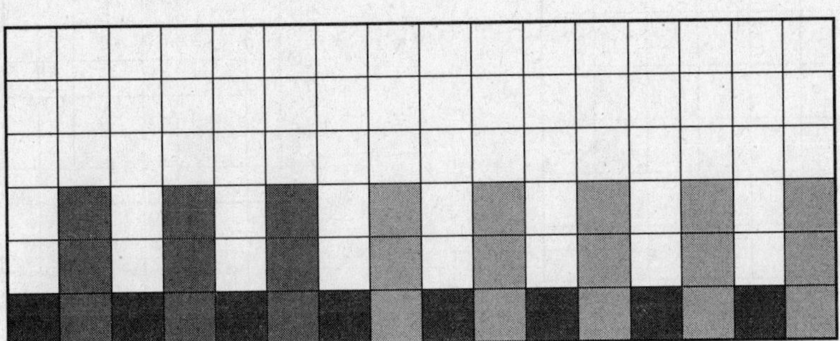

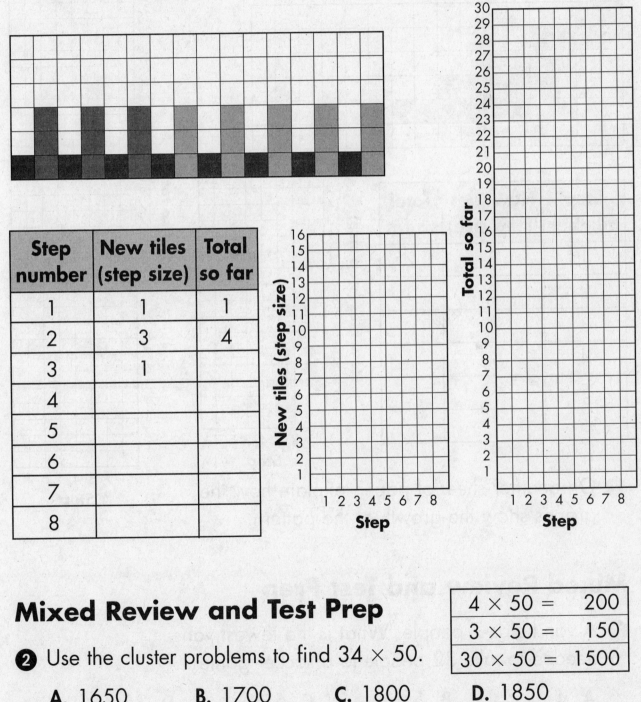

Step number	New tiles (step size)	Total so far
1	1	1
2	3	4
3	1	
4		
5		
6		
7		
8		

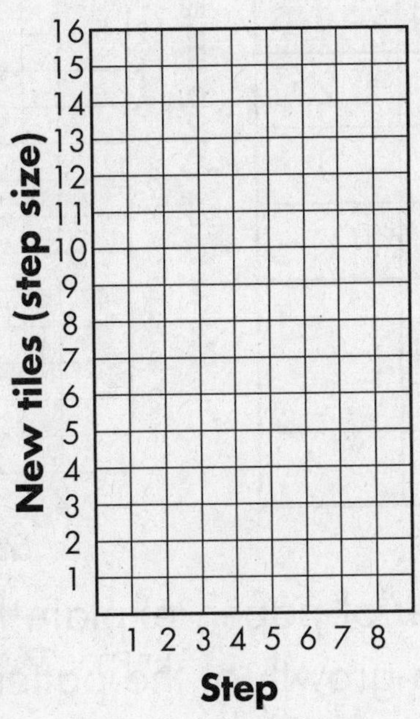

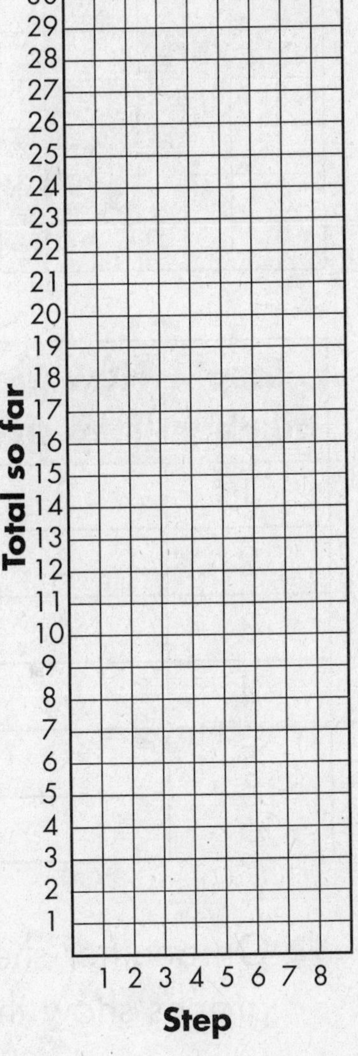

Mixed Review and Test Prep

4 × 50 =	200
3 × 50 =	150
30 × 50 =	1500

❷ Use the cluster problems to find 34 × 50.

A. 1650 **B.** 1700 **C.** 1800 **D.** 1850

Name Date

Comparing Graphs

Family Connection

Students are learning that the step size affects the way in which a pattern grows. Some patterns grow at a steady rate; others grow faster and faster.

❶ Draw the next step. Complete the table and graphs.

1	1														
	2	2	2												
		3	3	3	3										
			4	4	4	4	4								
				5	5	5	5	5	5						

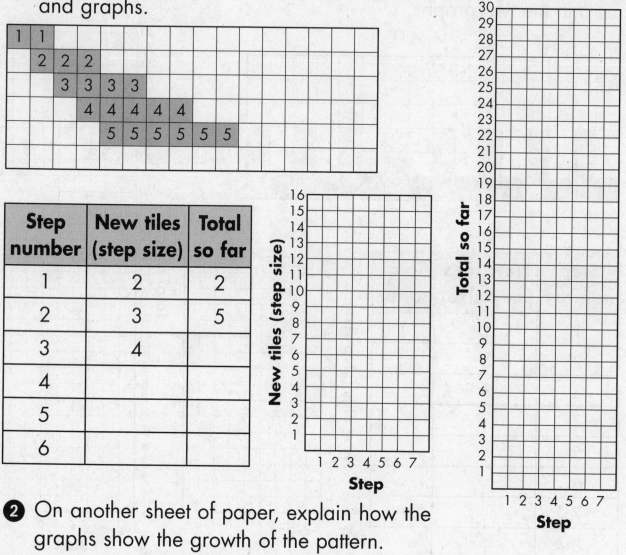

Step number	New tiles (step size)	Total so far
1	2	2
2	3	5
3	4	
4		
5		
6		

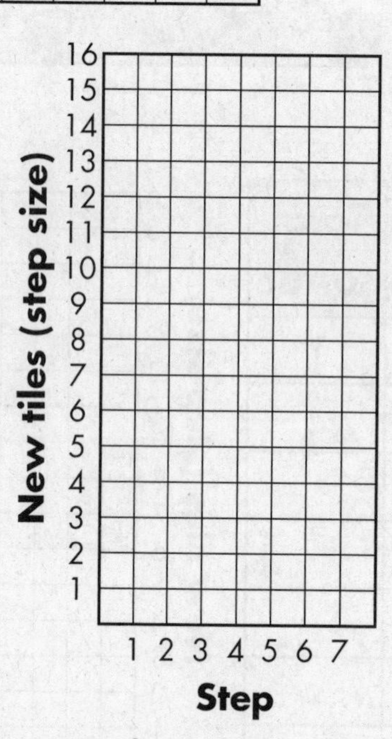

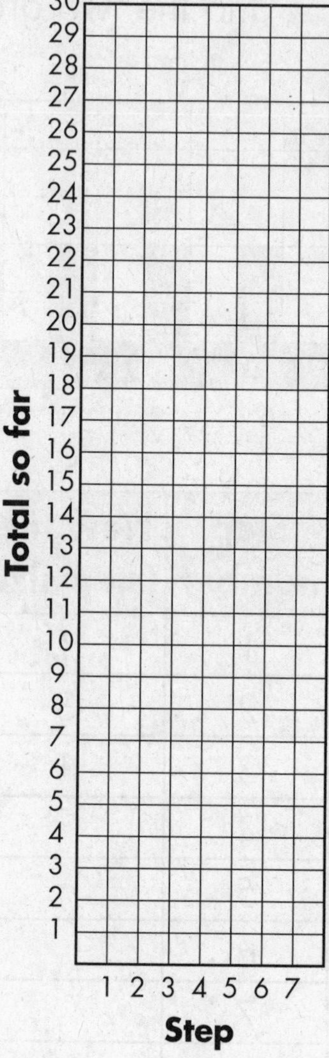

❷ On another sheet of paper, explain how the graphs show the growth of the pattern.

Mixed Review and Test Prep

❸ A van holds 7 people. What is the fewest vans needed to take 32 people to a soccer game?

A. 4 **B.** 5 **C.** 6 **D.** 25

Name Date

Patterns of Change

Predicting Patterns

Draw Step 4 in each pattern. Then find the step size and total for Step 10 for each pattern. You may use tiles, tables, graphs, or a general rule.

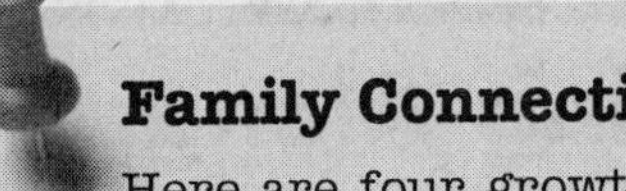

Family Connection

Here are four growth patterns that students have been studying. Your child may know a general rule for a few of the patterns; for example, the total for the **Twos Tower** is twice the step number.

1 Twos Tower

1	1
2	2
3	3

Step 10:
Step size _____

Total _____

2 Squares

1	2	3
2	2	3
3	3	3

Step 10:
Step size _____

Total _____

3 Staircase

1		
2	2	
3	3	3

Step 10:
Step size _____

Total _____

4 In this pattern, the number of tiles doubles at each step. Draw Step 4. Then find the step size and total for Step 6.

			1	1			
		2	2	2	2		
3	3	3	3	3	3	3	3

Step 6: Step size _____

Total _____

Mixed Review and Test Prep

5 Count by 25's. What number comes next?

350, 375, 400, 425, 450, _____

A. 460 **B.** 475 **C.** 500 **D.** 550

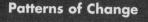

Name Date

Traveling Along the Track

These 12-meter trips are described in words. Invent your own symbols to describe each trip.

Family Connection

Students have used invented symbols to describe trips that vary in speed. Creating their own ways of showing motion helps students appreciate and understand standard line graphs. Ask your child to act out one of these trips.

1. Jana walked slowly about $\frac{1}{3}$ of the way, stopped for 5 seconds, then ran to the end.

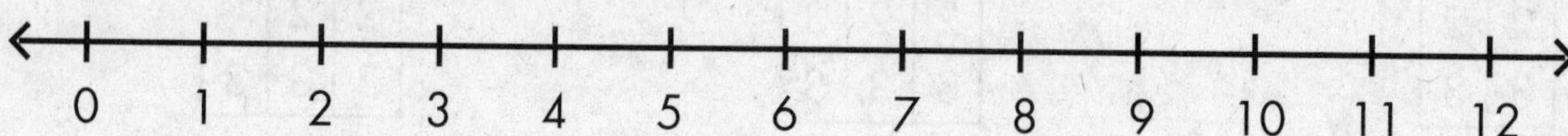

2. Mark ran for 3 steps, stopped for 1 second, then repeated this until he finished.

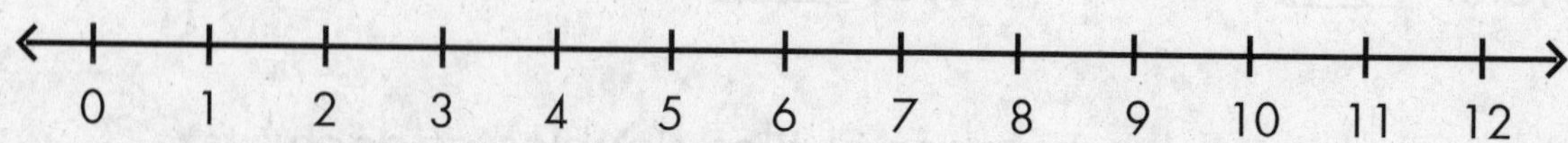

3. Babbie walked forward halfway, then ran back to the beginning. She walked the entire distance, stopping twice for 3 seconds.

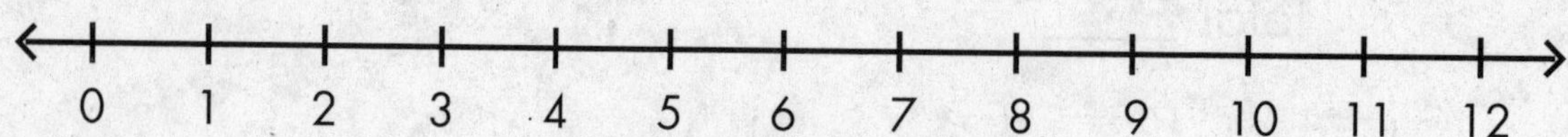

Mixed Review and Test Prep

4. Which is the best estimate of the total?

$$\begin{array}{r} \$2.89 \\ 1.17 \\ 0.55 \\ 0.63 \\ +3.88 \\ \hline \end{array}$$

A. \$5 **C.** \$9

B. \$7 **D.** \$23

Name Date

Comparing Trips

Two students traveled along the same 20-foot track. Fill in the tables for their trips. Then answer the questions.

Family Connection

Students have made tables for trips that vary in speed. In these tables, Rumi starts out walking more than twice as fast as Trudy. Have your child explain how each person's speed changes.

1 **Trudy's Trip**

Time	Total distance	Distance per second
1 sec	2 ft	2 ft
2 sec	4 ft	2 ft
3 sec	4 ft	
4 sec	8 ft	
5 sec	12 ft	
6 sec	16 ft	

2 **Rumi's Trip**

Time	Total distance	Distance per second
1 sec	5 ft	5 ft
2 sec	10 ft	
3 sec	10 ft	
4 sec	10 ft	
5 sec	12 ft	
6 sec	14 ft	

3 Who went fast and then slow? ________

4 Who traveled farther? ________

5 Who stopped for 2 seconds? ________

6 Who went slow and then fast? ________

Mixed Review and Test Prep

7 In which shape is the dotted line a line of symmetry?

A. 

B. 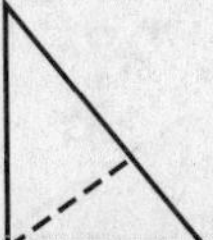

C. 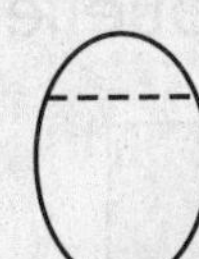

D. 

Name Date

Tables for Trips

Family Connection

Students have represented motion stories in two ways: with number lines and dots for beanbags, and with tables showing total distances. In these trips, Melinda starts out faster than Vinnie but they finish at the same time.

Two students traveled along the same 12-meter track. They dropped beanbags every 2 seconds. Use the pictures of their trips to complete the tables.

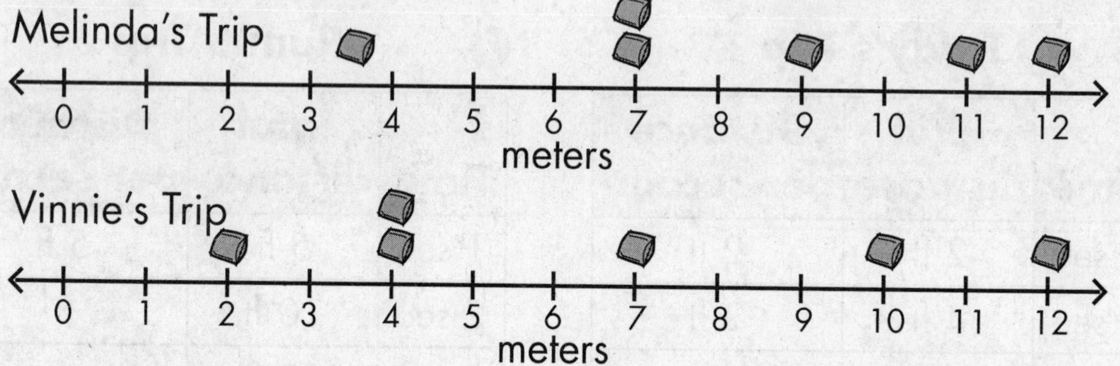

❶ **Melinda's Trip**

Time	Total distance
2 sec	3.5 m
4 sec	7 m
6 sec	
8 sec	

❷ **Vinnie's Trip**

Time	Total distance
2 sec	
4 sec	
6 sec	

❸ On separate paper, describe each trip in words.

Mixed Review and Test Prep

❹ Which shows the silhouette of the bottom of this shape?

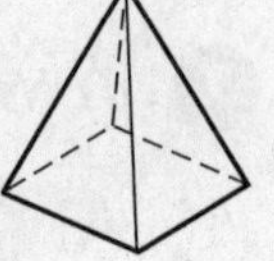

A.  **B.**  **C.** 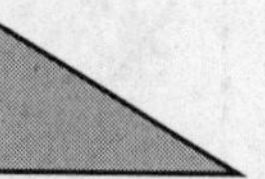 **D.** 

 Use after Investigation 2 (Motion Stories, Graphs, and Tables), Session 3.

Name Date

Graphs from Tables

Family Connection

Your child is learning to make line graphs to show motion that varies in speed. In this type of graph, a flat section shows that the moving object has stopped. A line going down would show something going backward.

Graph each trip. Label each part of your graph with one of these words: **fast, slow,** or **stop.**

1

Time (seconds)	Total distance (meters)
2	4
4	8
6	8
8	8
10	9
12	10

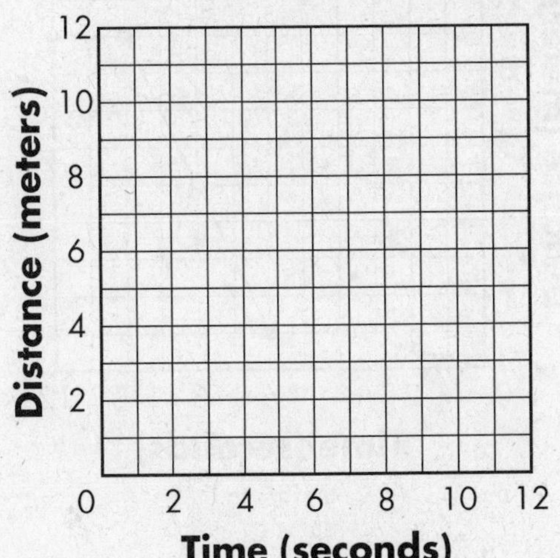

2

Time (seconds)	Total distance (meters)
2	1
4	2
6	2
8	2
10	2
12	12

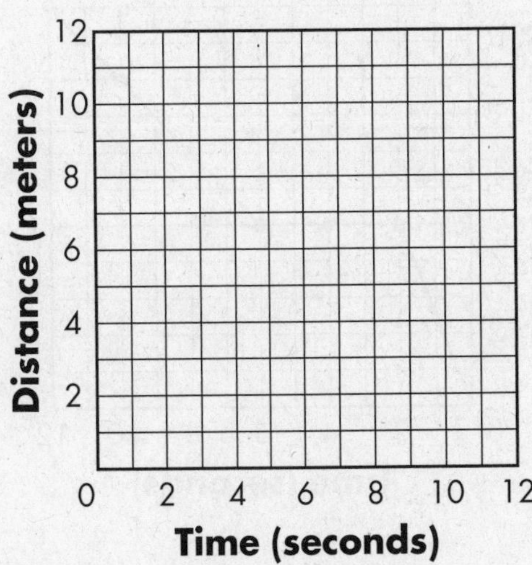

Mixed Review and Test Prep

3 Which fraction is greater than 1?

A. $\frac{2}{3}$ **B.** $\frac{7}{8}$ **C.** $\frac{4}{3}$ **D.** $\frac{2}{2}$

Name Date

Patterns of Change

Tables from Graphs

Use the graphs to make tables. Then label the parts of the graphs.

Family Connection

Students have been learning to relate graphs, tables, and verbal stories. Translating a graph to a table helps students interpret graphed data. Have your child draw a second trip on each grid and then tell you a matching story.

1

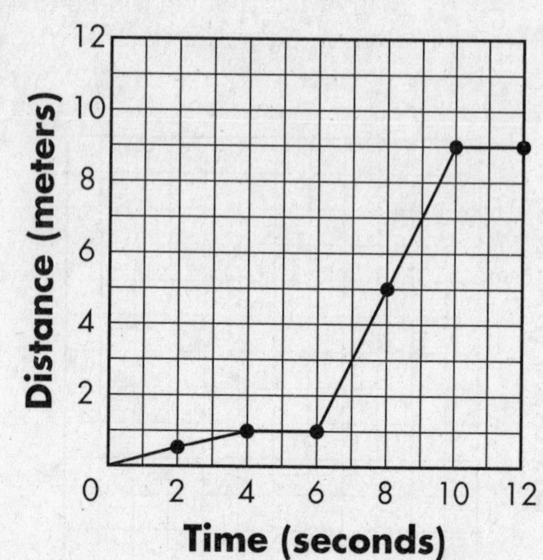

Time (seconds)	Total distance (meters)
2	0.5
4	1

2

Distance (meters)

12 10 8 6 4 2 0

2 4 6 8 10 12

Time (seconds)

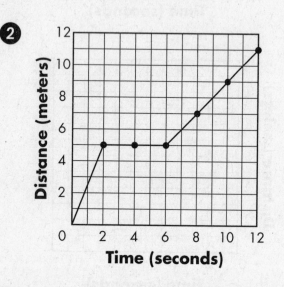

Time (seconds)	Total distance (meters)

Mixed Review and Test Prep

3 In Bertie's class, 10 out of 31 students play football. Which familiar fraction is closest to $\frac{10}{31}$?

A. $\frac{1}{31}$ **B.** $\frac{1}{10}$ **C.** $\frac{1}{3}$ **D.** $\frac{1}{6}$

Name Date

Patterns of Change

Who Won?

Graph each race to find the winner.

Family Connection

Students have been using a computer program called **Trips.** In the program, a boy and girl run a 100-meter race. This page shows the computer commands and resulting graphs. For example, in the first race, the boy runs 10 meters every second. The girl runs 5 meters per second, but has a head start of 30 meters.

1 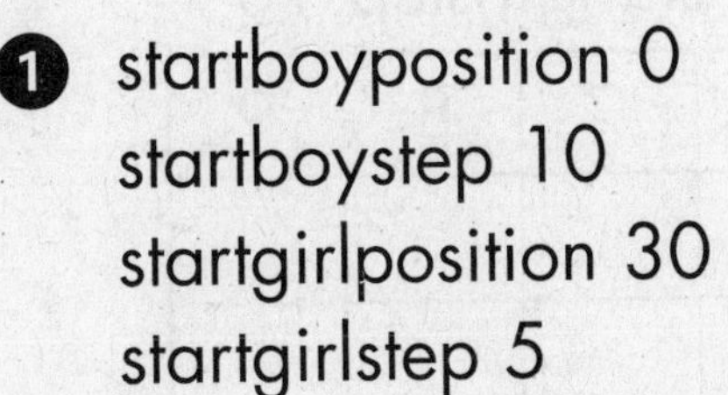
startboyposition 0
startboystep 10
startgirlposition 30
startgirlstep 5

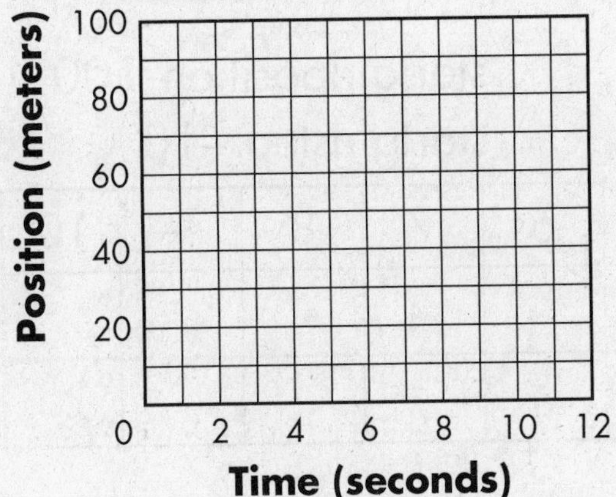

Who won? _________

2 startboyposition 50
startboystep 5
startgirlposition 10
startgirlstep 15

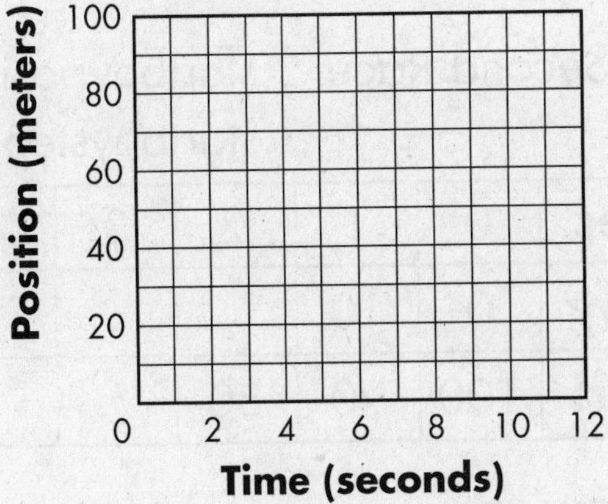

Who won? _________

3 How long did it take the students in the first problem to finish the race?

Boy _________ Girl _________

Mixed Review and Test Prep

4 Skip count by 6's. What is the next number?

60, 66, 72, 78, 84, _____

A. 85 **B.** 86 **C.** 90 **D.** 96

Name Date

Running in Opposite Directions

Family Connection
In these races, the two runners go in opposite directions. Ask your child to tell you when the runners pass each other.

Finish the tables;
then make the graphs.

❶ First Race startboyposition 100 startgirlposition 10
startboystep –5 startgirlstep 10

Sec	0	1	2	3	4	5	6	7	8	9
Boy	100	95								
Girl	10	20								

❷ Second Race startboyposition 0 startgirlposition 100
startboystep 10 startgirlstep –10

Sec	0	1	2	3	4	5	6	7	8	9	10
Boy	0	10									
Girl	100	90	80								

❸ First Race

❹ Second Race

Mixed Review and Test Prep

❺ Which division fact is related to $6 \times 3 = 18$?

A. $6 \div 3 = 2$ **C.** $18 \div 2 = 9$

B. $6 \div 2 = 3$ **D.** $18 \div 6 = 3$

Name Date

Patterns of Change

Changing Speed

Graph each race to find the winner.

Family Connection

Part way through the race, each runner changes speed. **Questions you might ask your child:** "In the first race, what are the boy's speeds?" "What are the girl's speeds?"

First Race

startboyposition 20 startgirlposition 0
startboystep 10 startgirlstep 5
changeboystepto 5 [when boyposition = 60]
changegirlstepto 15 [when girlposition = 30]

Second Race

startboyposition 30 startgirlposition 10
startboystep 5 startgirlstep 15
changeboystepto 20 [when boyposition = 60]
changegirlstepto 5 [when girlposition = 70]

1 First Race

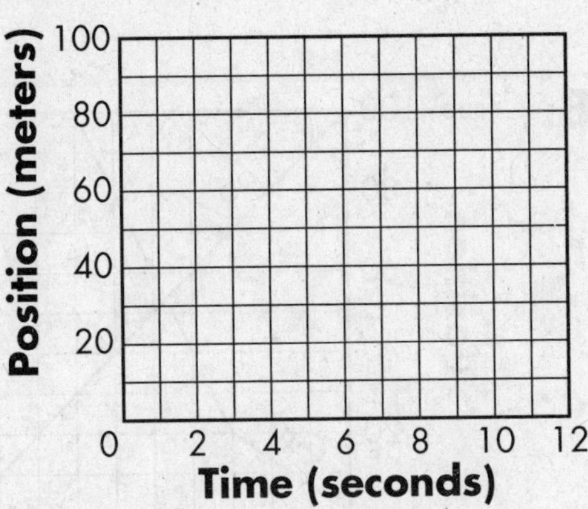

2 Second Race

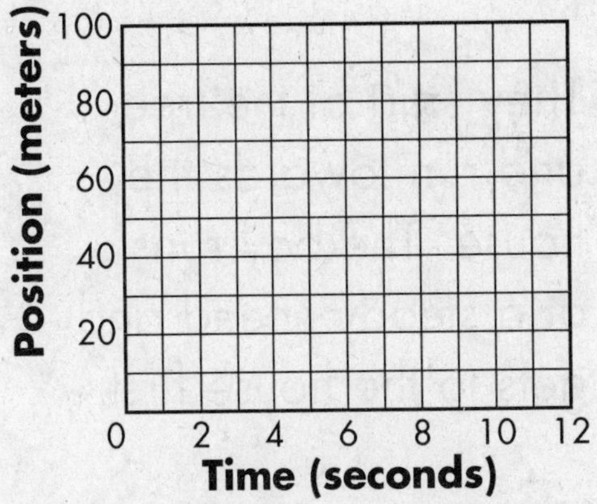

3 First Race

Who won? ________

4 Second Race

Who won? ________

Mixed Review and Test Prep

5 What does the median tell you?

A. How spread out the data is

B. If there are unusual data values

C. The greatest data value

D. The middle of the data

Name Date

Match the Stories

Draw lines to match each story with its graph.

Family Connection

In the stories on this page, a boy and a girl run 100 meters from a house to a tree, or vice versa. In class, your child has been creating races on the computer to match stories like these. Have your child explain how he or she decided which graph belonged with which story.

1. The boy starts at the tree and the girl starts at the house. The girl starts slow, speeds up, and gets to the tree before the boy gets to the house.

A.

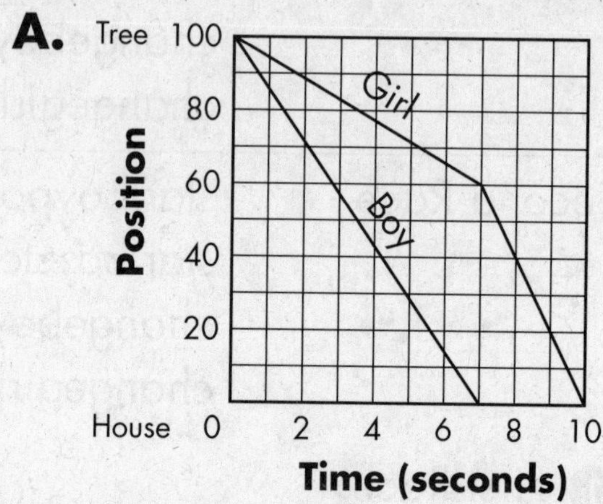

2. They start at the tree and run towards the house. The boy runs at a steady speed and gets to the house first.

B.

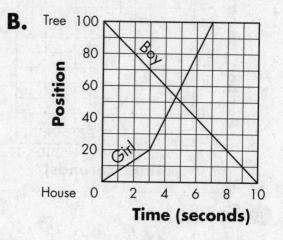

Tree 100
80
60
40
20
House 0
Position
Boy
Girl
2 4 6 8 10
Time (seconds)

Mixed Review and Test Prep

3. A muffin costs $1.29. How much change do you get from $5.00?

A. $3.71 **C.** $4.71

B. $4.29 **D.** $6.29

Name Date

Patterns of Change

Two Types of Graphs

1 Use the position vs. time graph to complete this table.

Time (seconds)	Position	Step size
1	0.5	0.5
2	1	0.5
3	1	
4		
5		
6		
7		
8		
9		
10		

Family Connection

Students have been learning to make a new type of graph, one that uses bars to indicate changes in speed. In the step size vs. time graph, a taller bar represents a faster speed. Have your child point to the section of the graph in which the person is moving fastest.

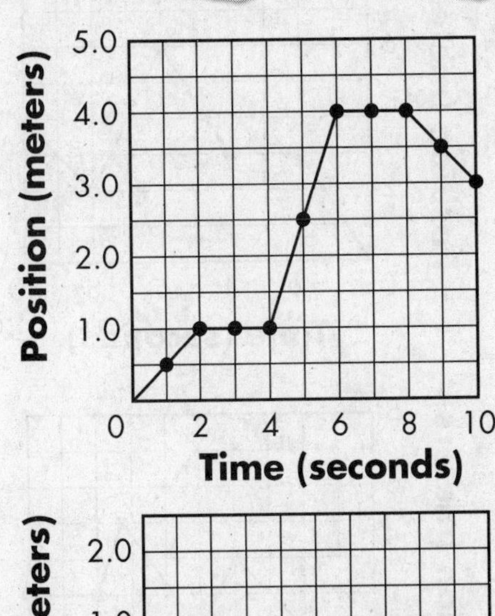

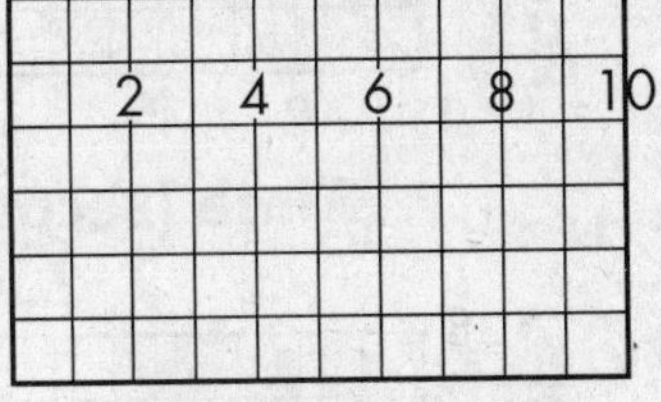

2 Complete the second graph to show step size vs. time.

3 On another sheet of paper, write a story that could go with these graphs.

Mixed Review and Test Prep

4 Which two amounts total $1.00?

A. 17¢ and 73¢

B. 21¢ and 89¢

C. 64¢ and 26¢

D. 73¢ and 27¢

Name Date

Graph Match

Family Connection

Students are learning to relate two types of graphs that show motion. When the person or object has stopped, the line is flat and there is no bar. Have your child point out where this happens.

Draw lines to match the graphs that show the same trip.

❶
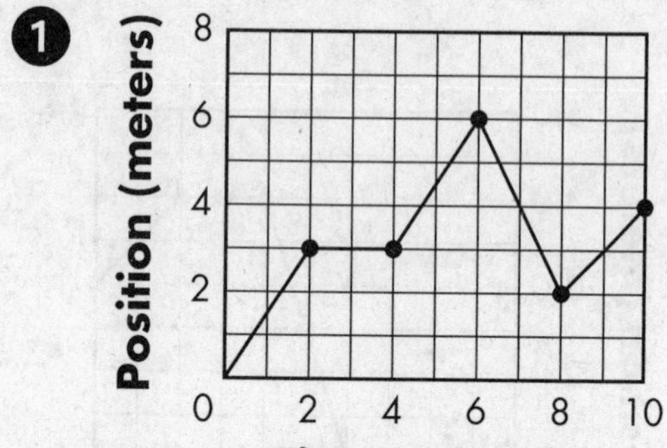

❷
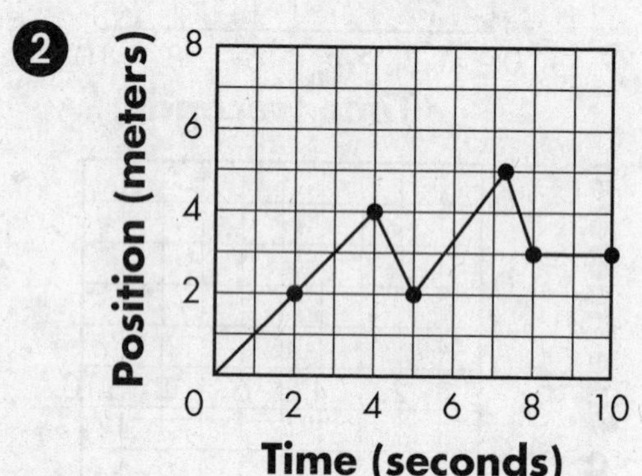

❸
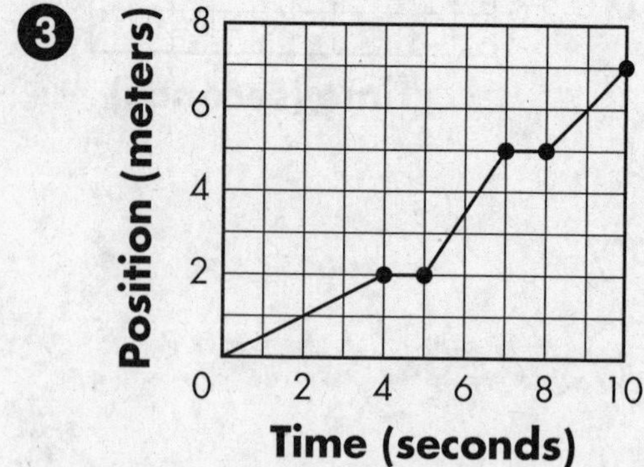

A.
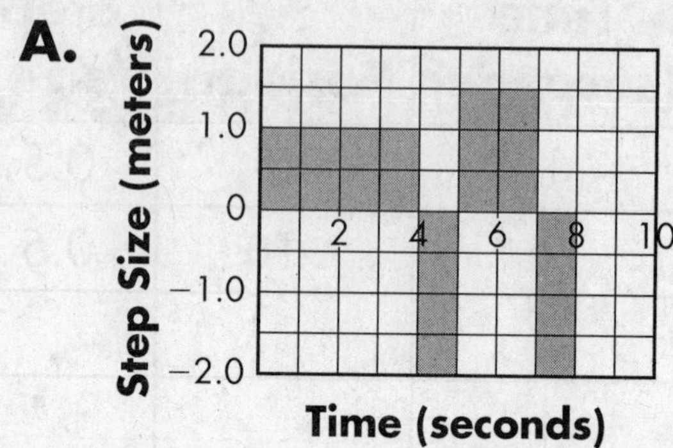

B.
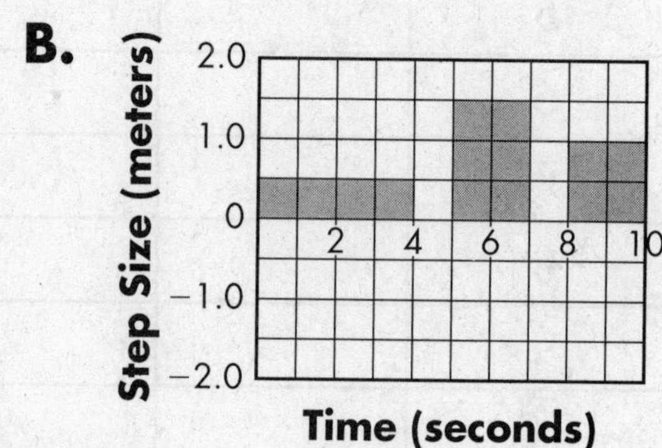

C.
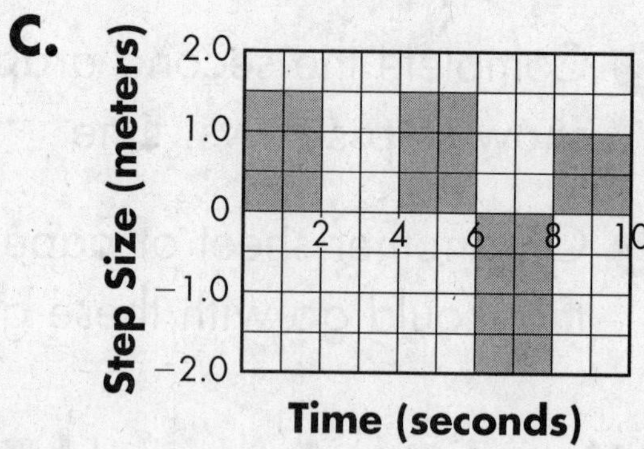

Mixed Review and Test Prep

❹ How many 20's are in 300?

A. 6 **B.** 15 **C.** 50 **D.** 60

Name Date

Making Graphs

Make a step size vs. time graph for each position vs. time graph. If you want to make tables, use another sheet of paper.

Family Connection

Students have been making and interpreting step size vs. time graphs. On this type of graph, bars that go below 0 indicate a backwards motion. Have your child show you where this occurs.

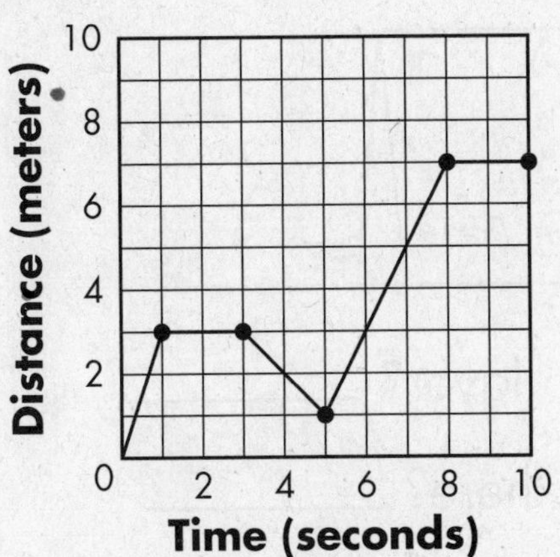

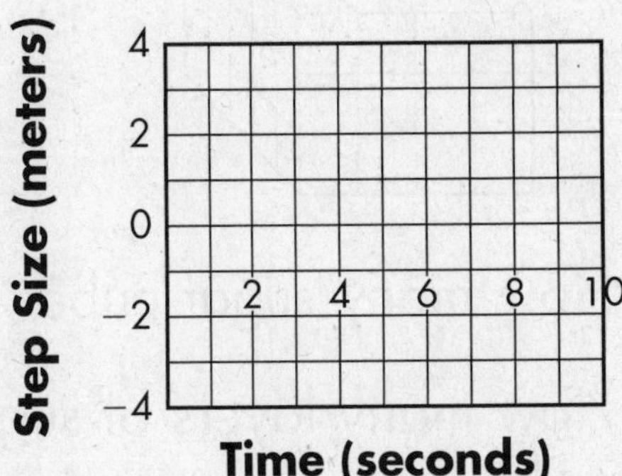

2

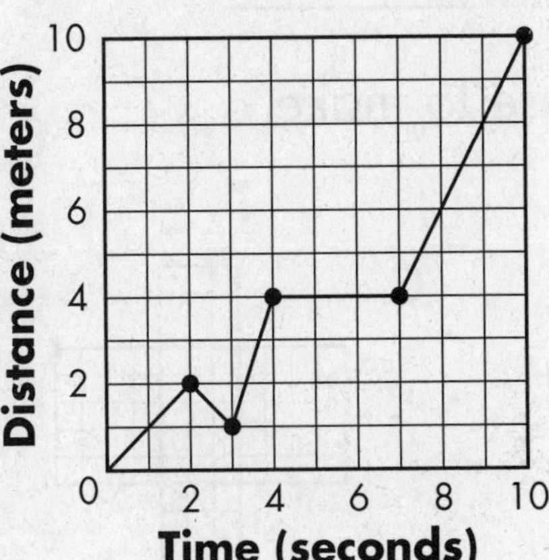

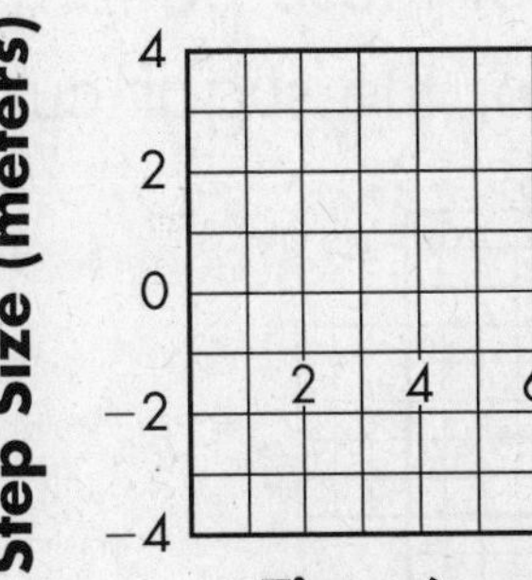

Step Size (meters)

4 2 0 −2 −4

Time (seconds)

Mixed Review and Test Prep

3 Ben wants to graph these numbers: 26, 30, 28, 28, 30, 27. Which line plot should he use?

A. 0 1 2 3 4

B. 26 27 28 30

C. 26 27 28 29 30

D. 26 28 30 32 34

Name Date

Containers and Cubes

Will They Fit?

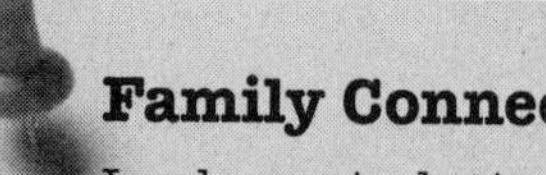

Family Connection

In class, students predicted how many cubes would fit into a box, and then built a box and filled it with cubes to check their predictions. In this activity, your child figures out which of three box patterns to use for packaging some sugar cubes. Encourage your child to show the sugar cubes with blocks or other cubes if he or she has difficulty answering the questions.

These sugar cubes are Amy's birthday gift to her horse, Henrietta.

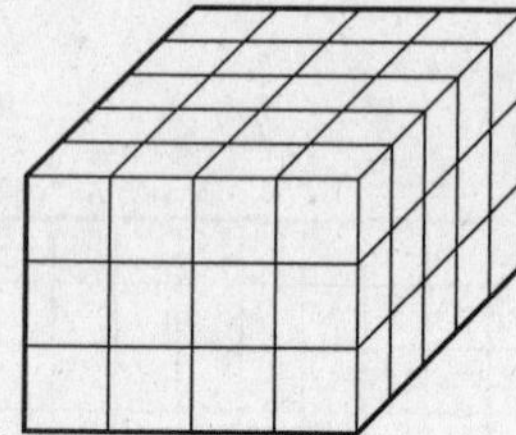

You're Invited to Henrietta's Birthday Party

1. How many sugar cubes are in the top layer? ________
2. How many layers of sugar cubes are there? ________
3. How many sugar cubes are there in all? ________
4. Which of these patterns should Amy use to make a box for the sugar cubes?

A.

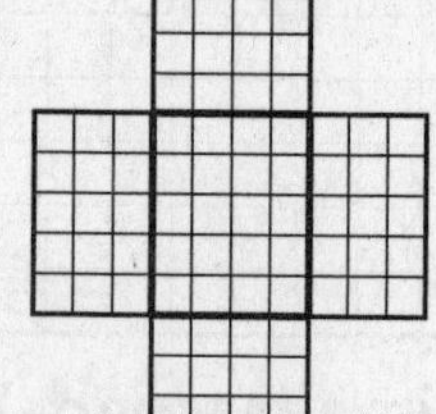

B.

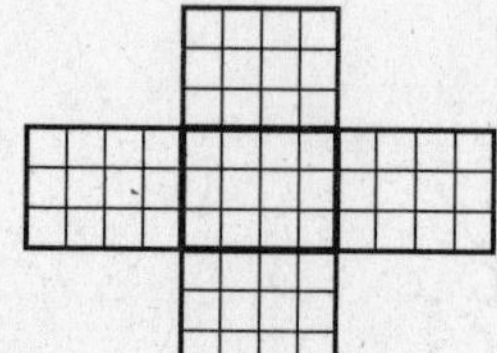

C.

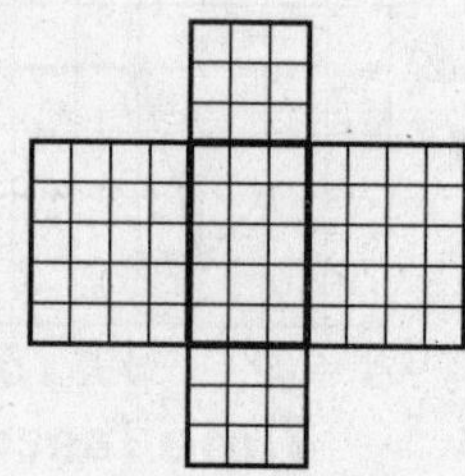

Mixed Review and Test Prep

5. How many 4's are in 200?

   A. 40 B. 50 C. 100 D. 800

6. How many 5's are in 300?

   A. 1500 B. 60 C. 50 D. 6

Name Date

Perfect Fit

Brian is looking for a box to hold 36 blocks.

Brian has boxes with these dimensions:

> **Family Connection**
> Students have been developing strategies for finding the number of cubes that fit in a box.
> **Questions you might ask your child:** "Which box holds the least number of cubes? How many cubes does it hold?"

A. 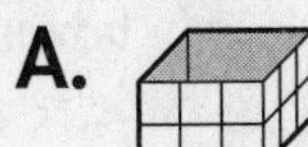
B. 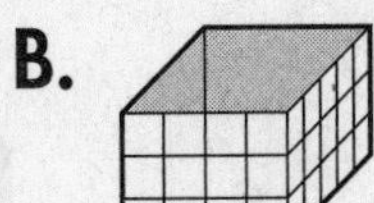
C. 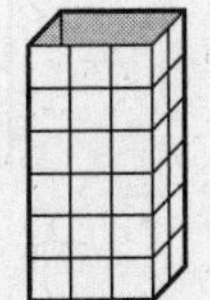
D. 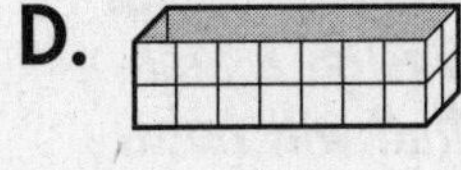

1. Which boxes will hold at least 36 blocks?

   Write the letters. ______________

2. Which box will hold **exactly** 36 blocks? How do you know?

   ____

   ____

3. How many blocks could Brian fit in all 4 boxes?

   Explain. ________________________________

   ____

Mixed Review and Test Prep

4. Three corners of a rectangle are at (−2, −1), (−1, −2), and (1, 2). Where is the fourth corner?

   A. (1, −1) **C.** (2, 1)

   B. (−2, 1) **D.** (2, 2)

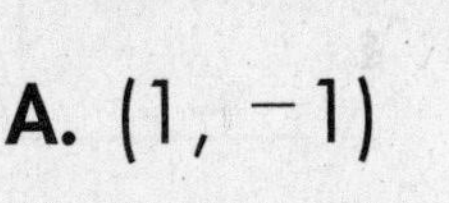

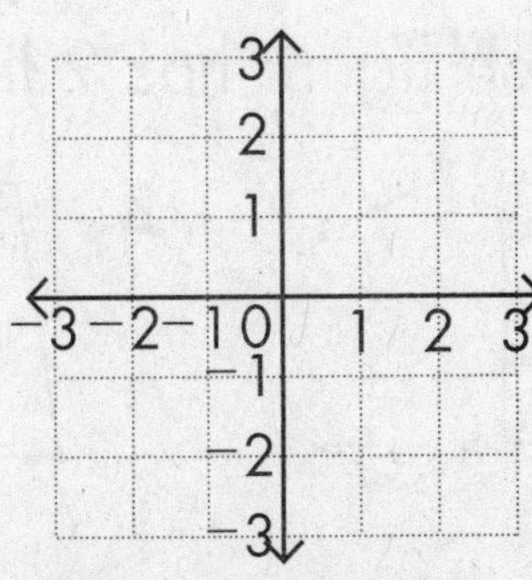

Name Date

Double Design

Family Connection

Students have been discussing ways to describe the dimensions of a box. Some ways are 6 wide, 2 long, 3 high; $6 \times 2 \times 3$; and 6 by 2 by 3. As your child judges the boxes in this contest, encourage him or her to compare the new dimensions to those of the current box to help judge how much each new box will hold.

❶ Who won the contest? Explain your answer.

Contest:

Design a box that will hold twice as many cubes as our current box.

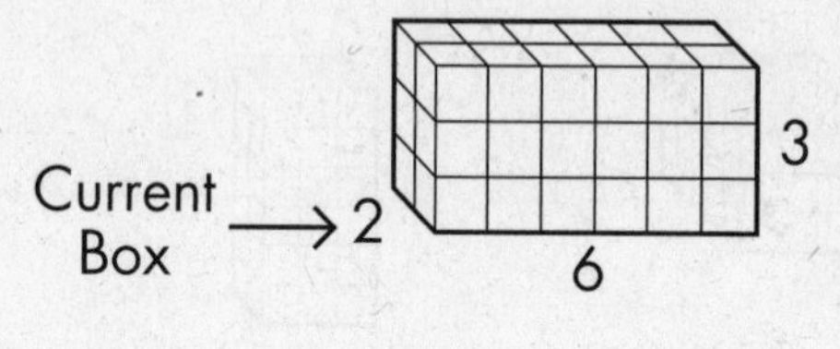
Current Box
2
3
6

My box is
6 × 4 × 3.
Victoria

My box is
6 by 8 by 6.
Ralph

My box is
12 wide by 8 long
by 6 high.
Sandy

AND THE WINNER IS ______________________

____

____

Mixed Review and Test Prep

❷ Which figure has 2 lines of symmetry?

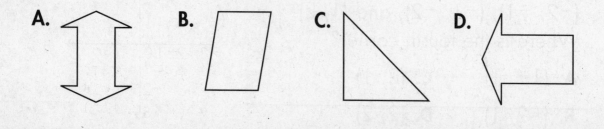

A. 

B. 

C. 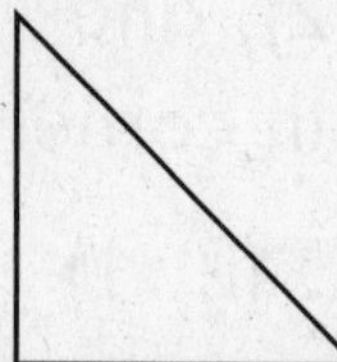

D. 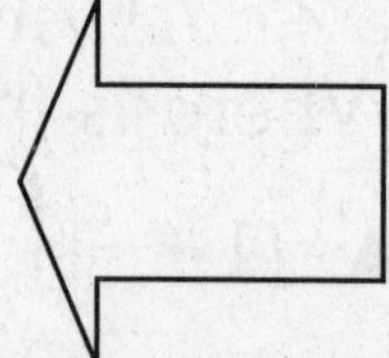

Name Date

Containers and Cubes

Just Plane Half

The planes show three ways to separate an 8-by-4-by-6 package of cubes into halves. What are the dimensions of the halves?

Family Connection

Students have been exploring how to change the dimensions of a box so that it will hold half as many cubes. **Questions you might ask your child:** "How do the dimensions of the original 8-by-4-by-6 package of cubes compare to the dimensions of each half in Exercise 1? in Exercise 2? in Exercise 3?"

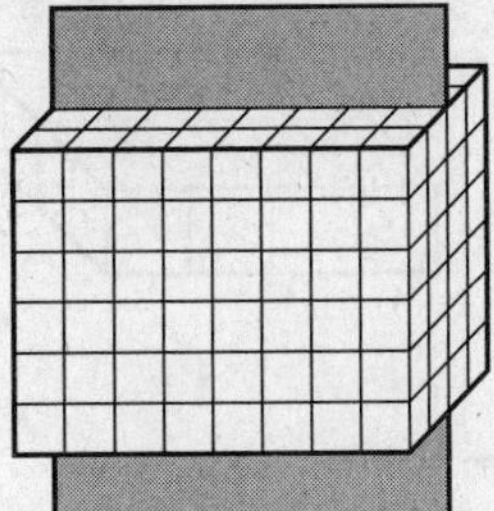

____

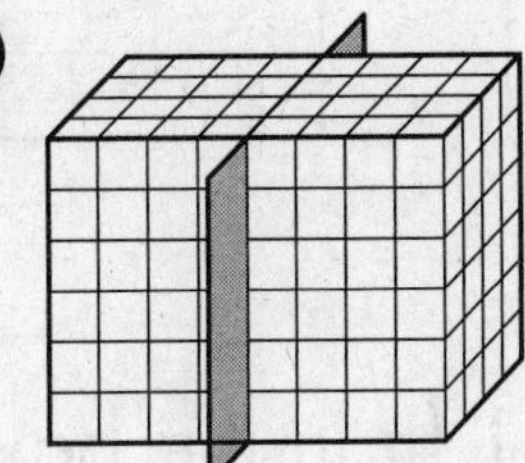

____

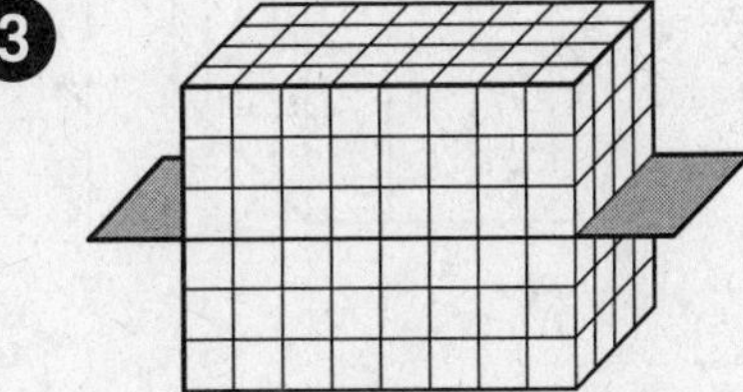

____

4 How can you tell that the planes divide the cubes into halves?

____

____

____

Mixed Review and Test Prep

5 My number is less than 32.
My number is a multiple of 3.
The digits in my number add up to 6.
What is my number?

A. 150 **B.** 42 **C.** 24 **D.** 18

Name Date

Containers and Cubes

Fill It Up!

Figure out how many of each package fit inside the box.

Family Connection
Students are deciding how many packages will fit in a box. Sometimes thinking about layers will help. Ask your child if he or she used another way in class.

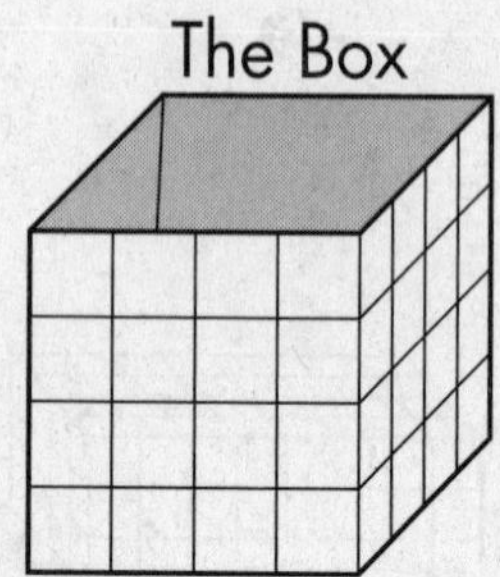

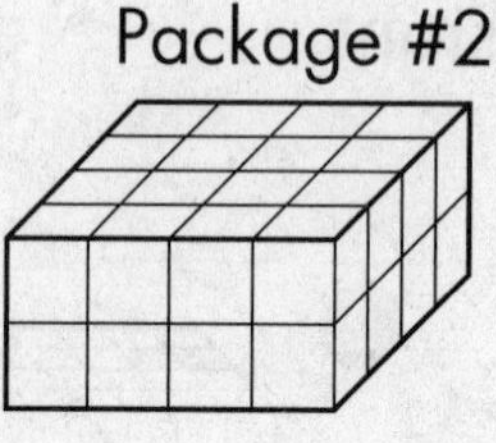

1. How many of package #1 fit in the box? ________
2. How many of package #2 fit in the box? ________
3. How many of package #3 fit in the box? ________
4. How many of package #4? ________
5. Choose two packages to fill the box. How many of each would you use? ________________________

Mixed Review and Test Prep

6. The line plot shows runners' times in seconds. What fraction of runners had times greater than 20 seconds?

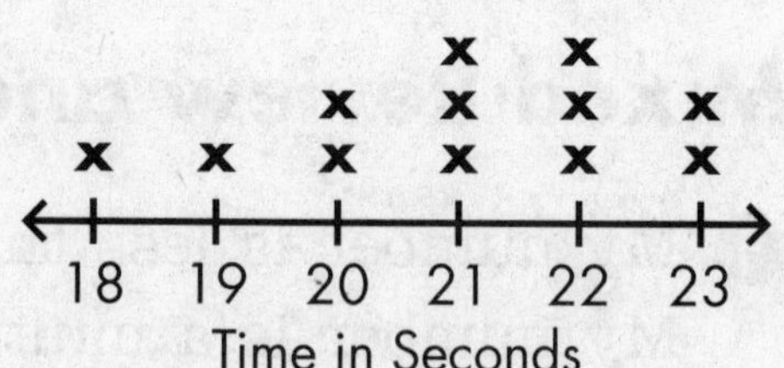

A. $\frac{1}{4}$ **C.** $\frac{1}{2}$

B. $\frac{1}{3}$ **D.** $\frac{2}{3}$

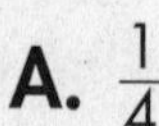

Name Date

Boxes in Boxes

Family Connection

Students are developing strategies for figuring out how many packages can fit in a box. Here your child uses mathematical and visual strategies.

Tanya's Toys ships cars in this package. They put packages in the larger box.

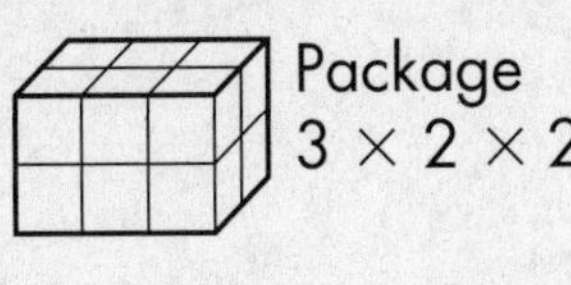

Package
$3 \times 2 \times 2$

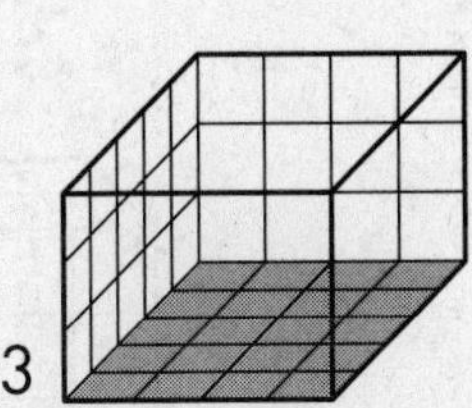

Box
$4 \times 5 \times 3$

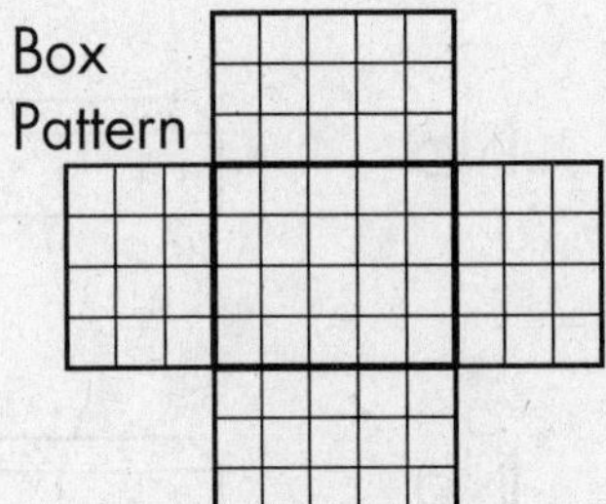

1. What is the most packages that can fit in the box? ________

2. Will the box be full? Tell how you know.

____

____

____

____

Mixed Review and Test Prep

3. What fraction of this design is shaded?

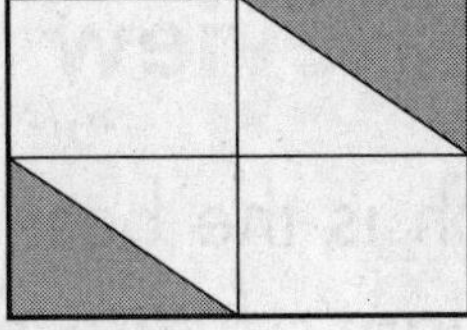

A. $\frac{1}{3}$ C. $\frac{1}{6}$

B. $\frac{1}{4}$ D. $\frac{1}{8}$

4. What fraction of this design is shaded?

A. $\frac{1}{8}$ C. $\frac{1}{3}$

B. $\frac{1}{4}$ D. $\frac{1}{2}$

Name Date

Is It an Exact Fit?

Circle **Yes** or **No** to tell if packages of each type can exactly fill the box.

Family Connection

Students are looking for boxes that can be completely filled with packages of certain dimensions. Ask your child to share some of his or her strategies for choosing packages that will totally fill the box.

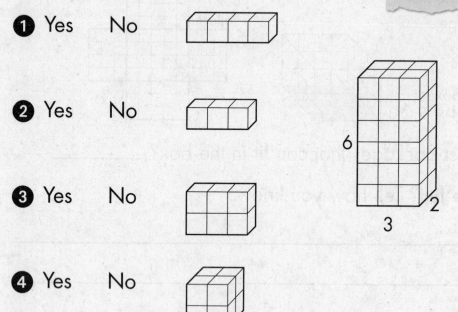

1. Yes No 

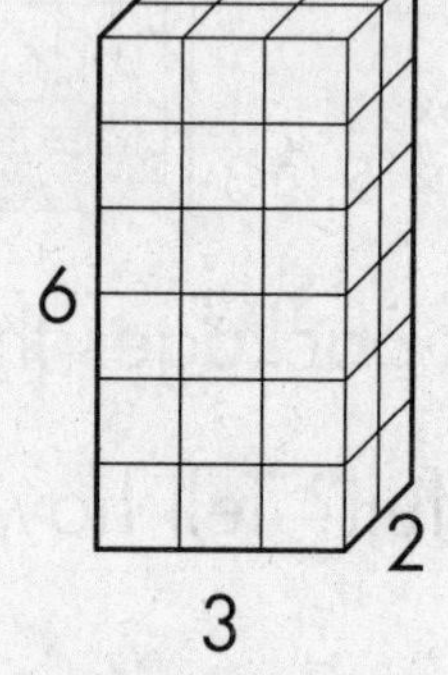

2. Yes No 

3. Yes No 

4. Yes No

5. On another sheet of paper, explain how you decided on your answers for Exercises 1–4.

Mixed Review and Test Prep

6. Which is the best prediction of the plant's future growth?

A. It will grow very fast.

B. It will grow slowly.

C. It will not grow.

D. It will die.

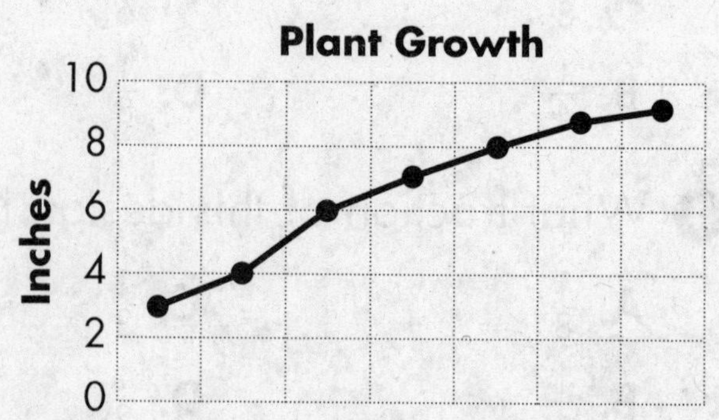

 Use during Investigation 2 (Packing Problems), Sessions 3 and 4.

Name Date

Containers and Cubes

Don't Box Me In!

Family Connection

Students have been finding boxes that can be completely filled by smaller packages. Visualizing three-dimensional packages and boxes is challenging. Ask your child to describe how packages of type B fit into Box 3.

Suppose you are packing these packages into the boxes.

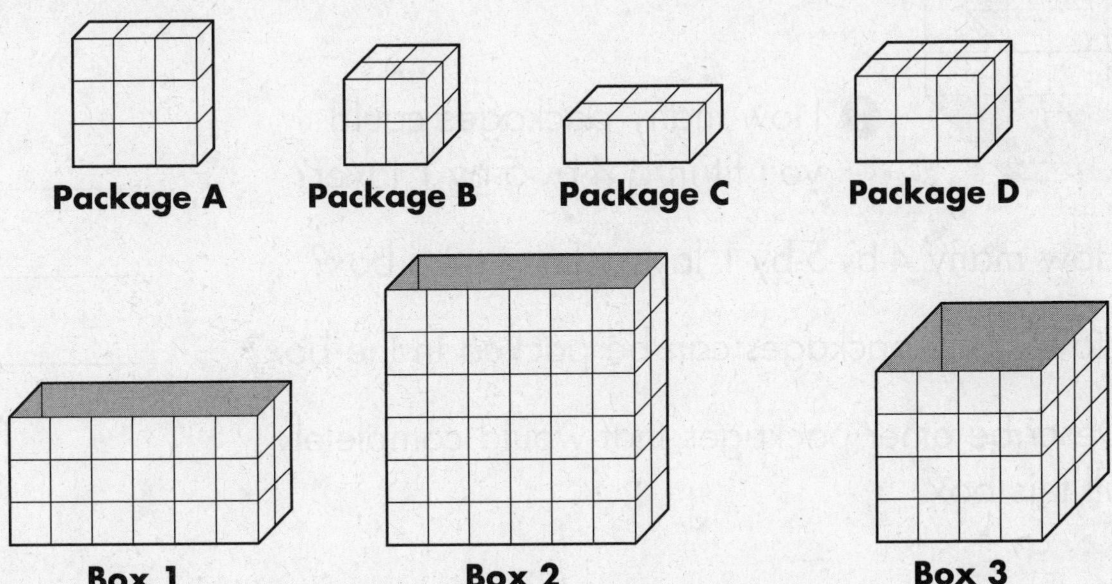

List the boxes that could be completely filled with packages of each type.

1. Package A ______________
2. Package B ______________
3. Package C ______________
2. Package D ______________

Mixed Review and Test Prep

5. In Greg's class, 2 out of 3 students don't know how to play chess. There are 24 students in the class. How many students know how to play chess?

A. 6 **B.** 8 **C.** 12 **D.** 16

Name Date

Building on Numbers You Know

It's a Tight Fit!

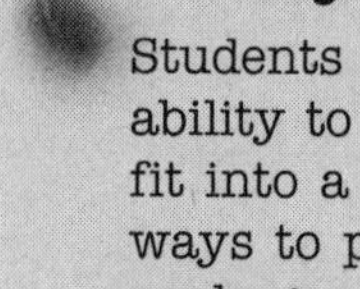

Family Connection

Students are developing their ability to visualize how packages fit into a box. There are many ways to pack the 2-cube packages into the box. You may want to work with your child to find different ways.

Suppose you are packing 2-cube packages in this box.

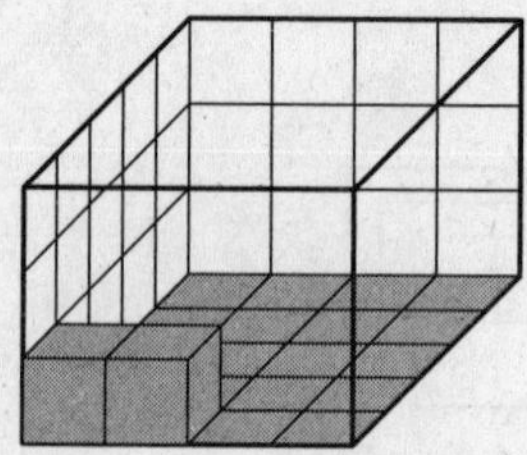

1. How many packages could you fit in a 4-by-5-by-1 layer? ________
2. How many 4-by-5-by-1 layers are in the box? ________
3. How many packages can be packed in the box? ________
4. Describe other packages that would completely fill this box.

____

____

5. How many of the packages you described in Exercise 4 can be packed in the box?

____

Mixed Review and Test Prep

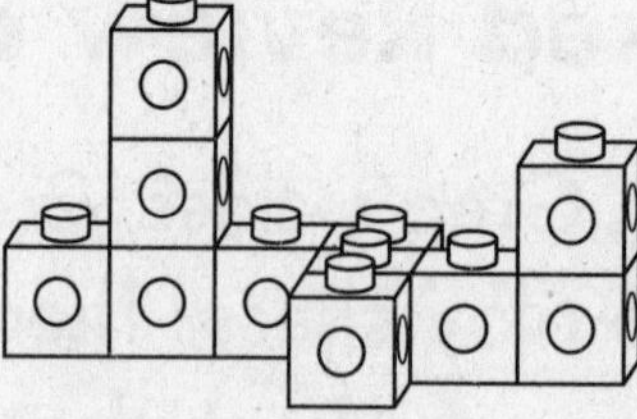

6. How many cubes does it take to make this building?

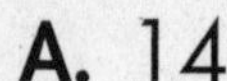

A. 14 **B.** 11 **C.** 10 **D.** 9

Name Date

Containers and Cubes

Picture It

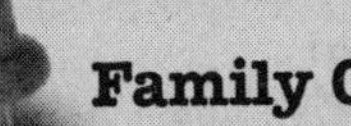

Family Connection

In class, students found the number of cubic centimeters needed to fill a box. A cube that is 1 centimeter on each edge holds a cubic centimeter.

Picture 1-centimeter cubes along the width, length, and height of this box. Write the dimensions of the box.

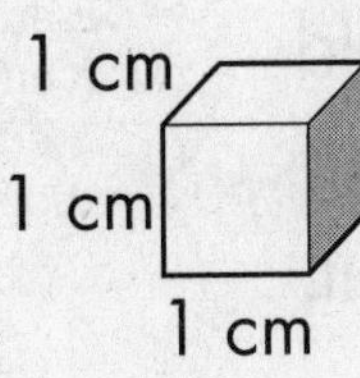

1

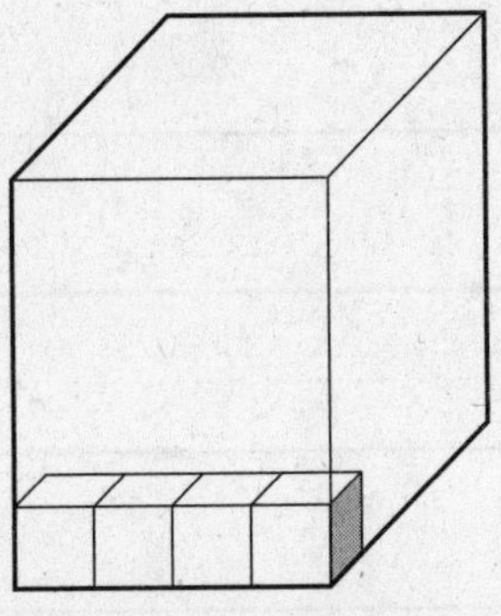

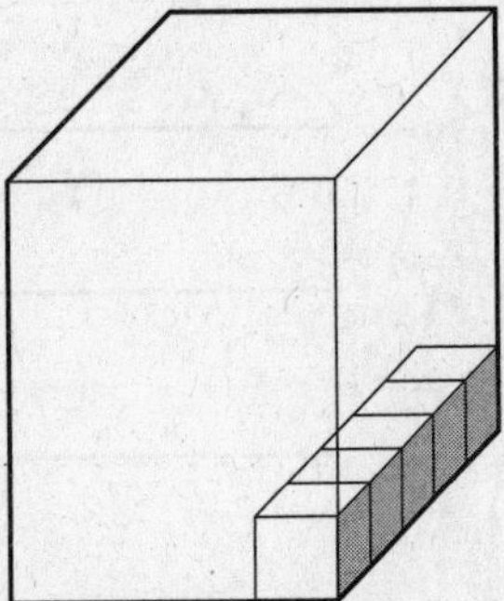

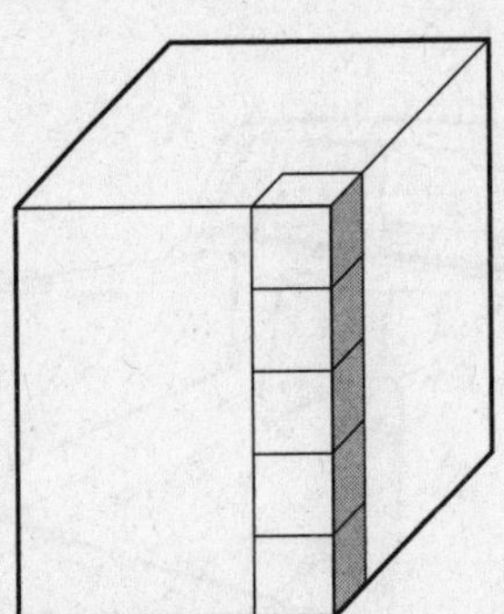

_____ cm wide _____ cm long _____ cm high

2 Figure out how many cubic centimeters will fit in the box. Tell how you do it.

____

____

____

____

Mixed Review and Test Prep

3 The scale on a map is 1 inch = 60 miles. The distance between two cities is $9\frac{1}{2}$ inches on the map. What is the actual distance?

A. 500 miles **B.** 543 miles **C.** 570 miles **D.** 5430 miles

Name Date

Cubic Choice

Family Connection

Students made models to help them visualize 1 cubic centimeter, 1 cubic inch, 1 cubic foot, 1 cubic yard, and 1 cubic meter. These units are used to measure volume. Have your child show you about how much space each takes up.

Decide what unit you would use to measure each volume. Tell why you chose that unit.

❶ The bed of a pick-up truck ______________________

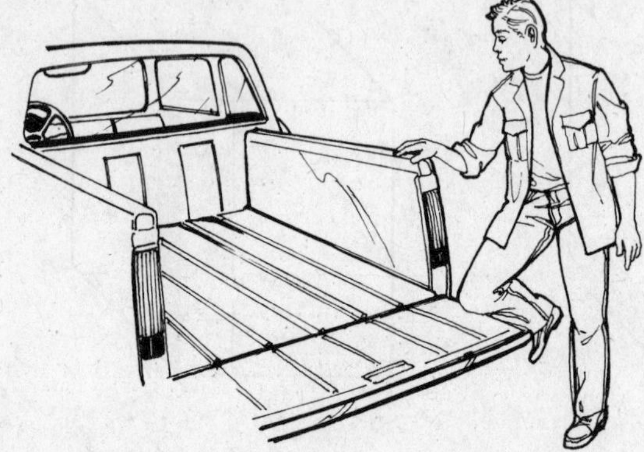

____

____

____

____

____

❷ The inside of a lunch box ______________________

____

____

____

____

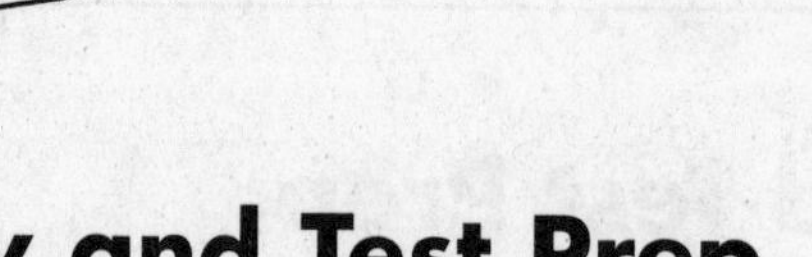

Mixed Review and Test Prep

❸ Which multiplication sentence does this array show?

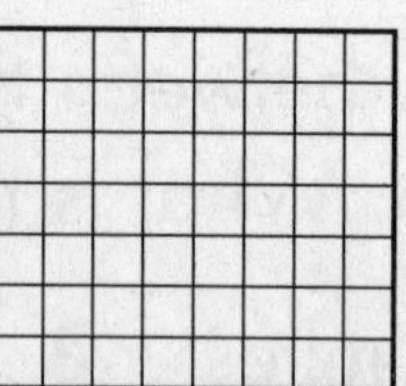

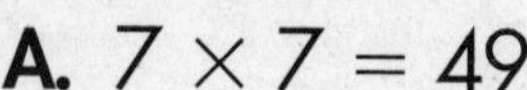

A. $7 \times 7 = 49$ **C.** $7 \times 9 = 63$

B. $7 \times 8 = 56$ **D.** $8 \times 8 = 64$

Name Date

Does It Work?

These people use different ways to find the volume of a room that is 14 feet long, 12 feet wide, and 10 feet tall.

> **Family Connection**
> Students found the volume of their classroom in cubic meters. Ask your child what measurements he or she took and how the class figured out the volume of the room.

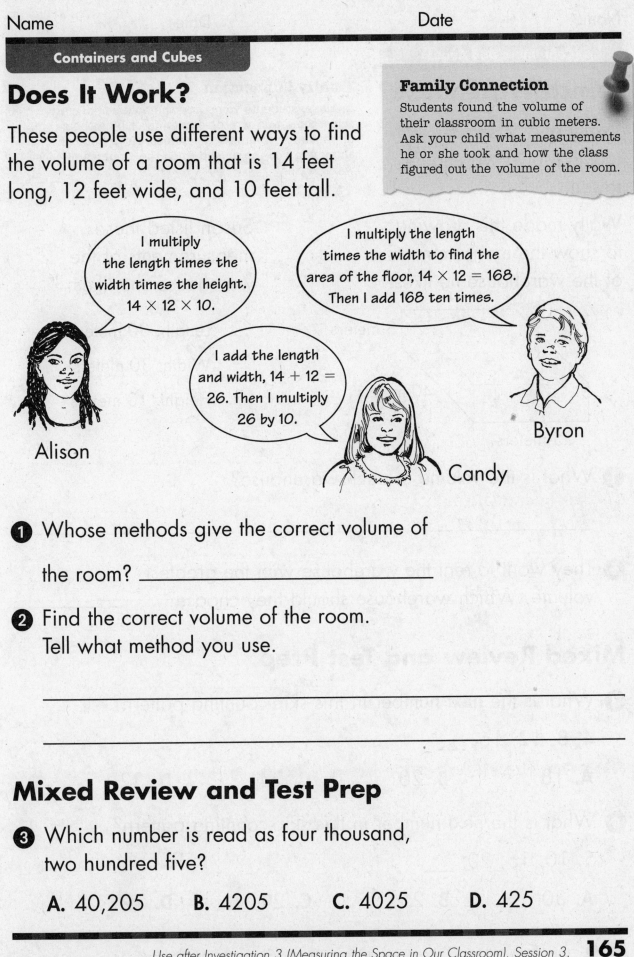

I multiply the length times the width times the height. $14 \times 12 \times 10$.

Alison

I multiply the length times the width to find the area of the floor, $14 \times 12 = 168$. Then I add 168 ten times.

Byron

I add the length and width, $14 + 12 = 26$. Then I multiply 26 by 10.

Candy

1. Whose methods give the correct volume of the room? ______________________

2. Find the correct volume of the room. Tell what method you use.

____

____

Mixed Review and Test Prep

3. Which number is read as four thousand, two hundred five?

A. 40,205 **B.** 4205 **C.** 4025 **D.** 425

Name Date

Which Warehouse?

Family Connection

In class, students compared the volumes of various classrooms and wrote reports describing their methods for finding the volumes. Have your child show you how he or she finds the volumes of these warehouses.

Wally and Susan are looking for a warehouse to rent.

Wally made this drawing to show the measurements of the warehouse he likes:

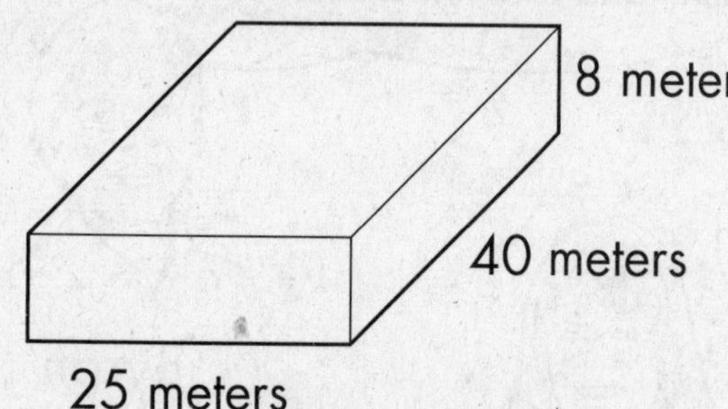

Susan listed these measurements of the warehouse she likes:

Length: 30 meters

Width: 30 meters

Height: 10 meters

1. What is the volume of each warehouse?

____

2. They want to rent the warehouse with the greatest volume. Which warehouse should they choose? ________

Mixed Review and Test Prep

3. What is the next number in this skip-counting pattern?

   4, 8, 12, 16, ___ .

   A. 18 **B.** 20 **C.** 24 **D.** 32

4. What is the next number in this skip-counting pattern?

   5, 10, 15, 20, ___

   A. 30 **B.** 25 **C.** 24 **D.** 22

Name Date

Containers and Cubes

Order, Please!

Family Connection

Students measured how much sand or rice various containers hold and put the containers in order by volume. Have your child tell you how he or she figured out the order.

Use the clues to compare the amounts of sand these containers can hold.

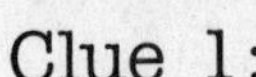

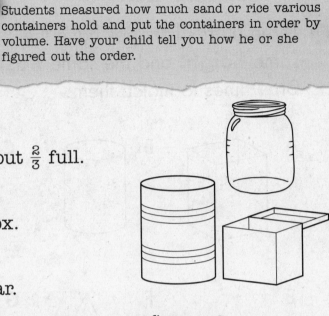

Clue 1:
A box of sand fills the can about $\frac{2}{3}$ full.

Clue 2:
A jar of sand overflows the box.

Clue 3:
A can of sand overflows the jar.

1. Can a jar of sand fit in the can without overflowing? ________

2. Is any container larger than the can? ________

3. List the containers in order from least to greatest volume.

____

Mixed Review and Test Prep

4. What does this shape look like from the right side?

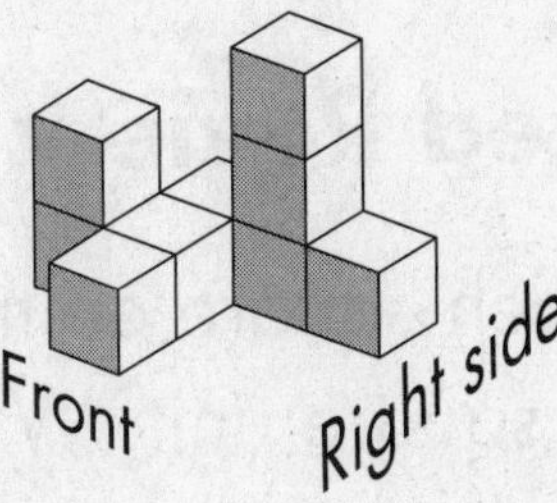

A.

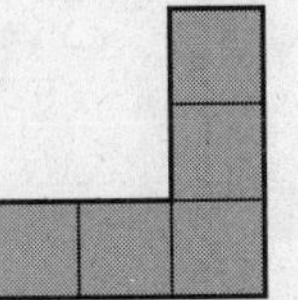

C.

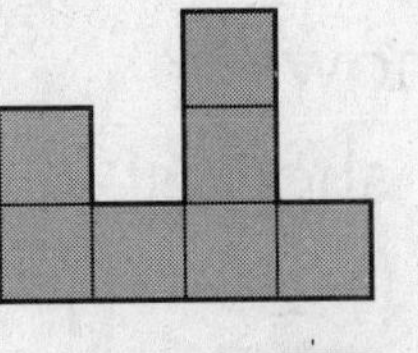

B. **D.**

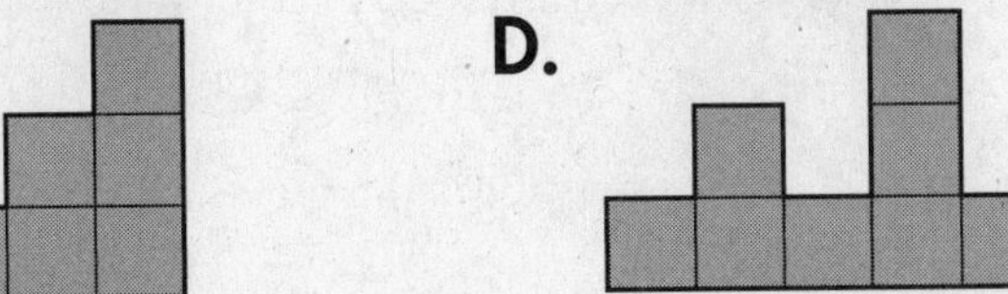

Name Date

Are We Related?

Family Connection
In class, students compared volumes of geometric solids like those shown here. Ask your child what he or she discovered about the volumes of pairs that are related by height and base shape.

1 Three pairs of shapes have the same **height** and the same **base.** Draw lines to match them.

A 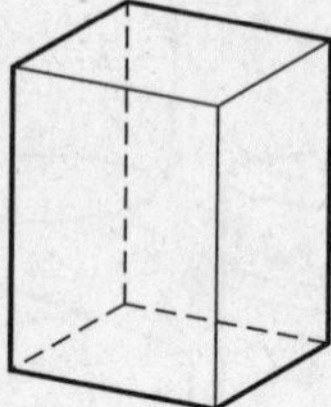 B 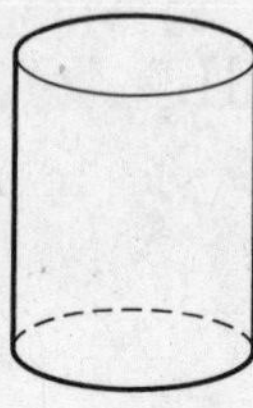 C 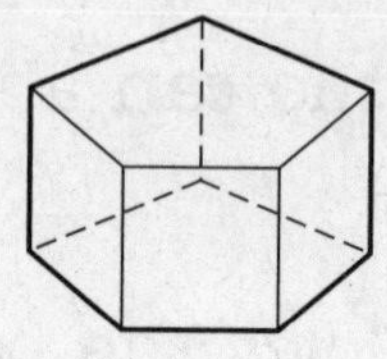 D 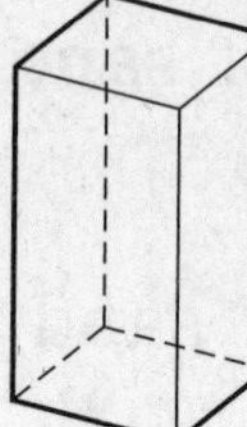

E 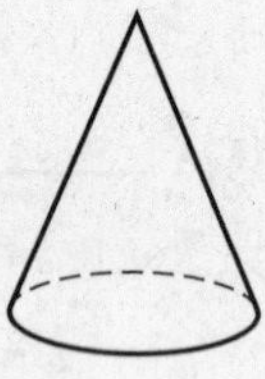 F 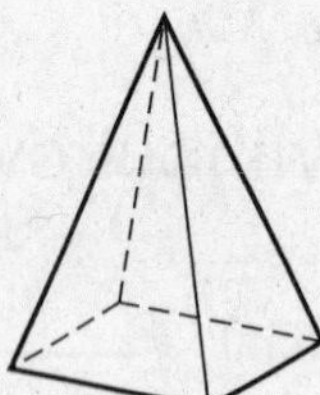 G 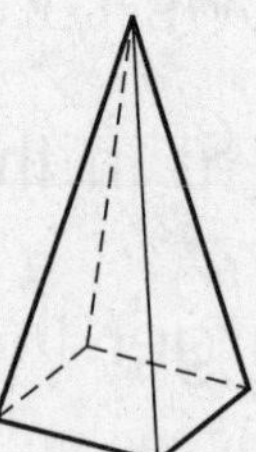 H 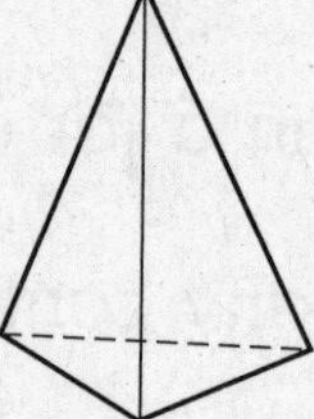

2 For one pair, tell how the two volumes compare.

____

____

Mixed Review and Test Prep

3 Each square on the grid shows 1 square unit. What is the shortest path along grid lines from (−2, −1) to (1, 0)?

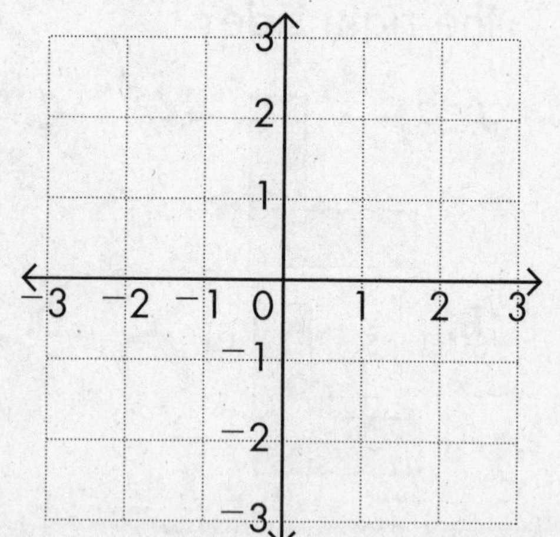

A. −3 units

B. −2 units

C. 3 units

D. 4 units

Name Date

Three Times Three

Family Connection

Students used grid paper to build a prism with three times the volume of a given pyramid. The three boxes (prisms) on this page are all the same box shown in different positions. You might want to use a similarly shaped flat box to help your child visualize the positions.

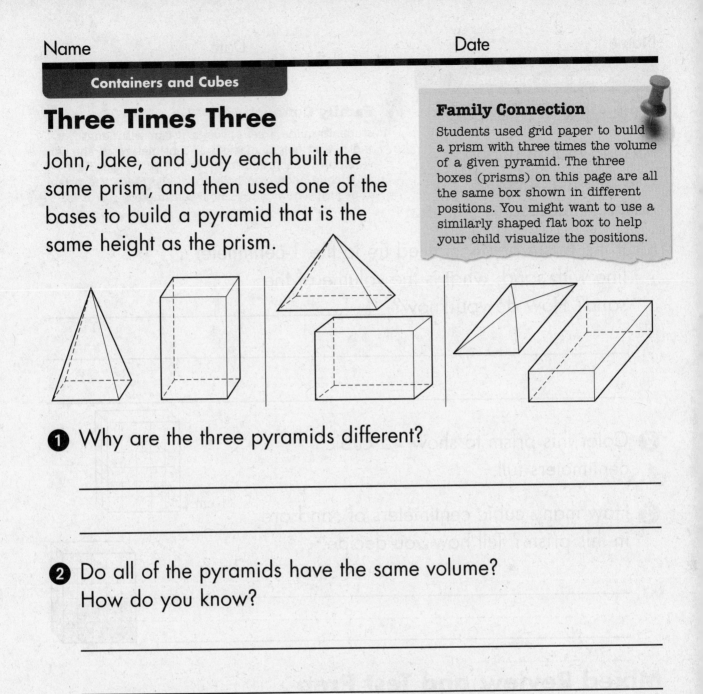

John, Jake, and Judy each built the same prism, and then used one of the bases to build a pyramid that is the same height as the prism.

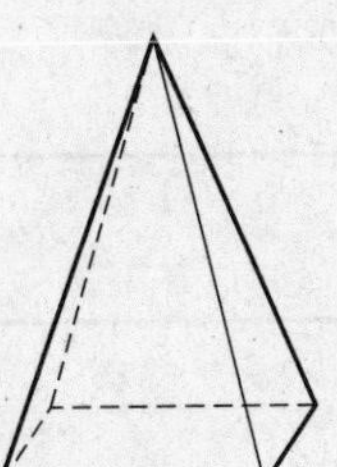
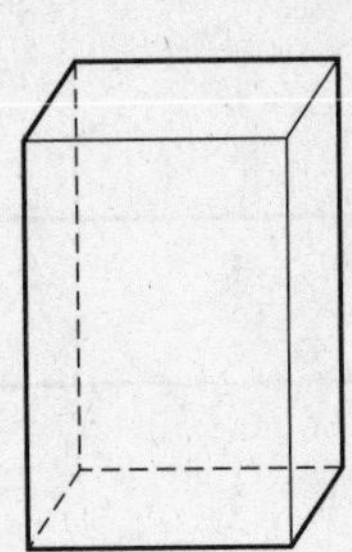
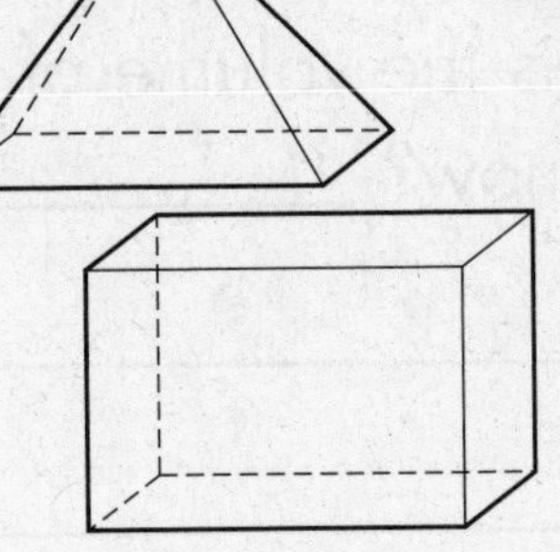
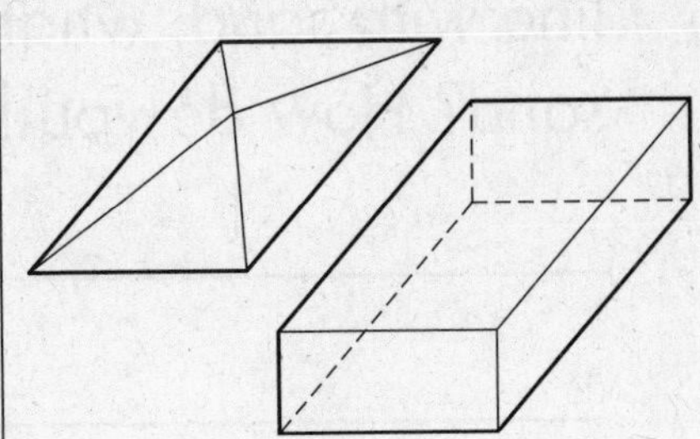

1. Why are the three pyramids different?

____

____

2. Do all of the pyramids have the same volume? How do you know?

____

____

Mixed Review and Test Prep

3. There are 56 notebooks being shared equally by a class of 28 students. Which division sentence shows this situation?

A. $56 \div 28 = 2$ **C.** $28 \div 56 = 2$

B. $56 - 28 = 28$ **D.** $28 \div 2 = 14$

Name Date

Prism Reading

Answer the questions. Use another sheet of paper if necessary.

Family Connection

Students made a see-through prism with length, width, and height marked in centimeters. A shorter version of the prism is shown on this page. Have your child show you how he or she reads the prism to describe how many cubic centimeters full it is.

1. If the prism below is filled up to the 1-centimeter line with sand, what is the volume of the sand? How do you know? ______________________

____

____

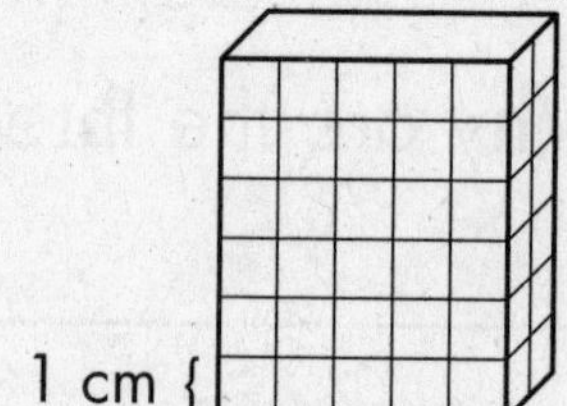

2. Color this prism to show 45 cubic centimeters full.

3. How many cubic centimeters of sand are in this prism? Tell how you decide.

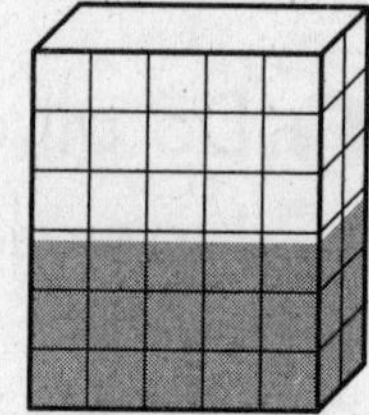

____

____

Mixed Review and Test Prep

4. Between which two times were only Josh and his mother at home?

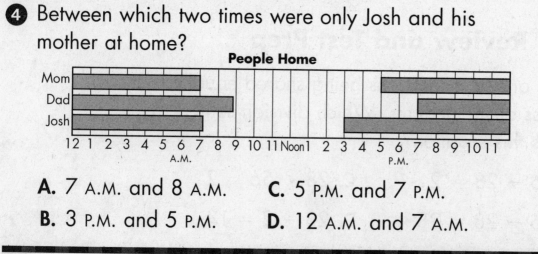

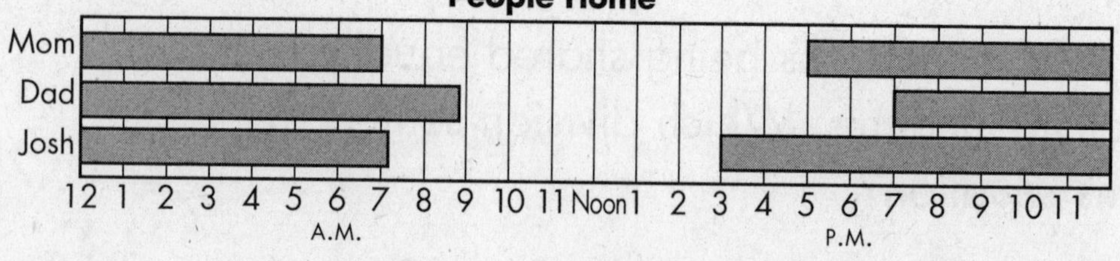

A. 7 A.M. and 8 A.M.
B. 3 P.M. and 5 P.M.
C. 5 P.M. and 7 P.M.
D. 12 A.M. and 7 A.M.

Name Date

Containers and Cubes

Hold It

1 Write the volume in liters below each container. Then put the containers in order from greatest volume to least volume by writing numbers 1–6.

Family Connection

Students have discovered that 1 liter has the same volume as 1000 cubic centimeters. So, 1 milliliter has the same volume as 1 cubic centimeter. Your child will use this relationship to compare the amounts these containers hold.

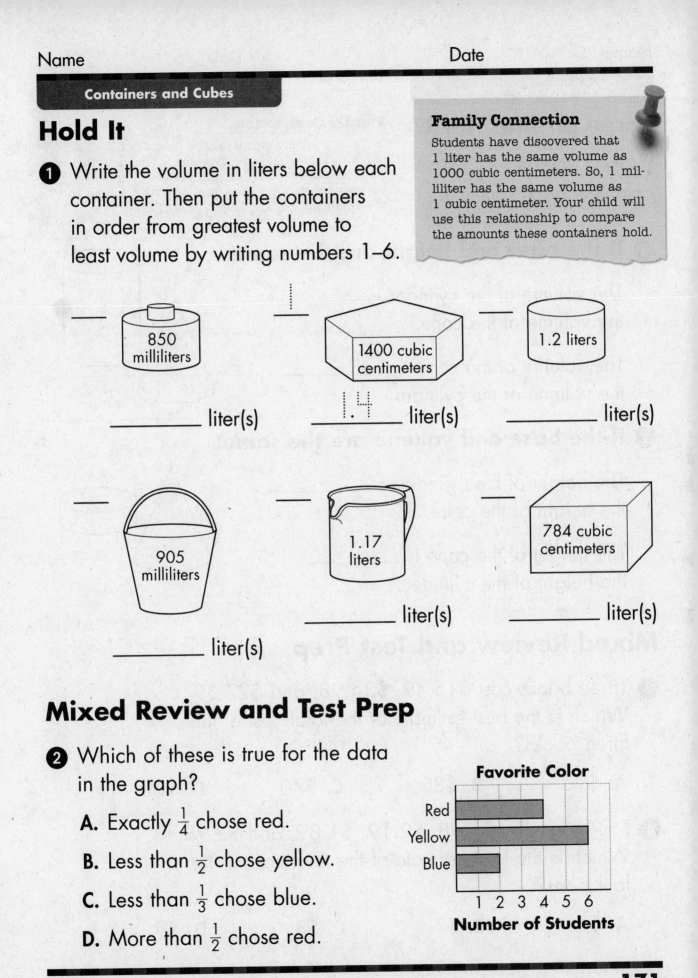

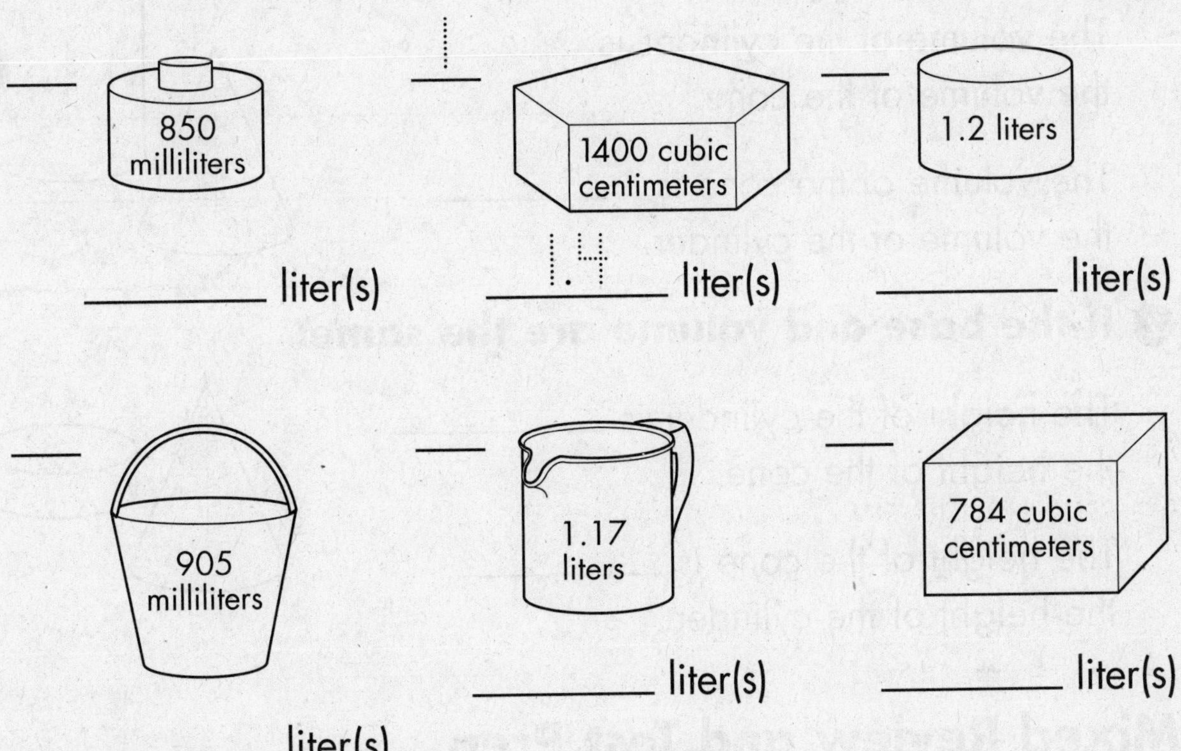

____ liter(s) ____ liter(s) ____ liter(s)

____ liter(s) ____ liter(s) ____ liter(s)

Mixed Review and Test Prep

2 Which of these is true for the data in the graph?

A. Exactly $\frac{1}{4}$ chose red.

B. Less than $\frac{1}{2}$ chose yellow.

C. Less than $\frac{1}{3}$ chose blue.

D. More than $\frac{1}{2}$ chose red.

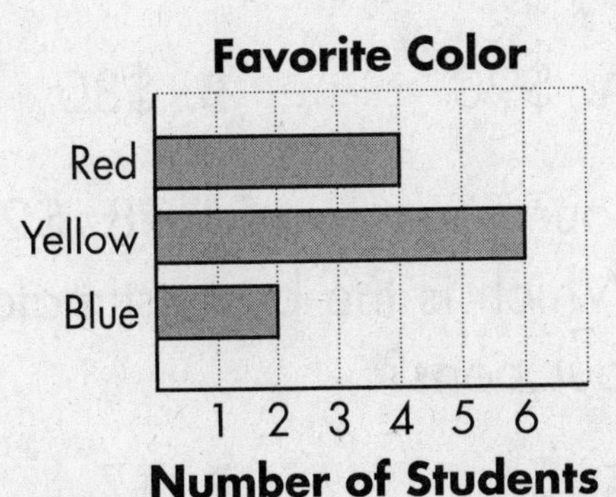

Name Date

Containers and Cubes

Three or One Third?

Write **3 times** or $\frac{1}{3}$ to complete each statement.

> **Family Connection**
> In class, students compared the heights of a cone and a cylinder that have the same volume and the same base. In this activity they will review the relationships between the volume, base, and height of a cone and the volume, base, and height of a cylinder.

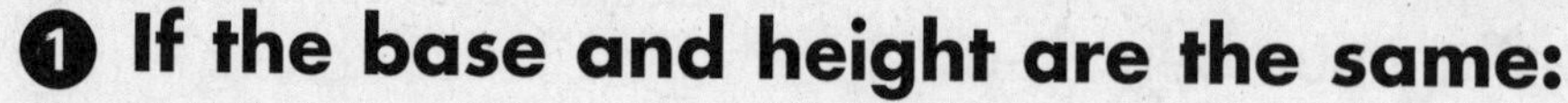

1 If the base and height are the same:

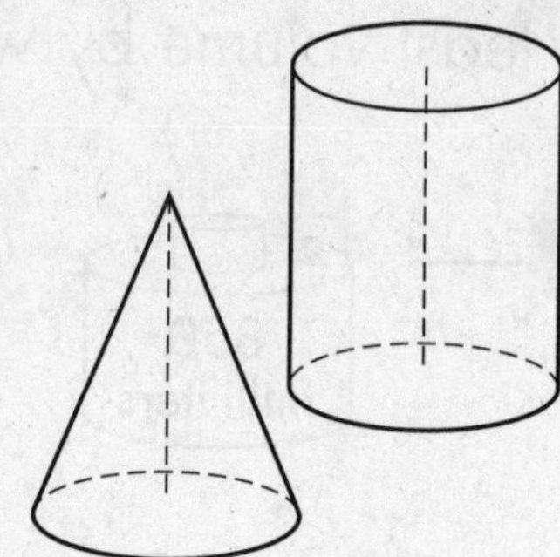

The volume of the cylinder is __________ the volume of the cone.

The volume of the cone is __________ the volume of the cylinder.

2 If the base and volume are the same:

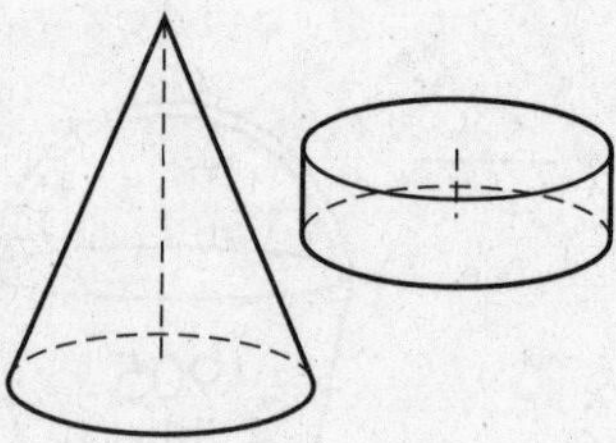

The height of the cylinder is __________ the height of the cone.

The height of the cone is __________ the height of the cylinder.

Mixed Review and Test Prep

3 Three books cost \$15.49, \$34.98, and \$27.39. Which is the best estimate of the total cost of the three books?

A. \$90 **B.** \$80 **C.** \$70 **D.** \$60

4 Four pens cost \$1.98, \$2.19, \$1.89, and \$2.98. Which is the best estimate of the total cost of the four pens?

A. \$6 **B.** \$7 **C.** \$8 **D.** \$9

Name Date

Containers and Cubes

Billy Bird

1 This is a model one group plans to make. Complete the table with the name of each solid in the model.

Family Connection

As a final project, students are designing and building a model made from geometric solids. Ask your child to tell you about the model his or her group plans to make.

Number	Name of Solid
1	Cylinder
2	
3	
4	
5	
6	
7	
8	

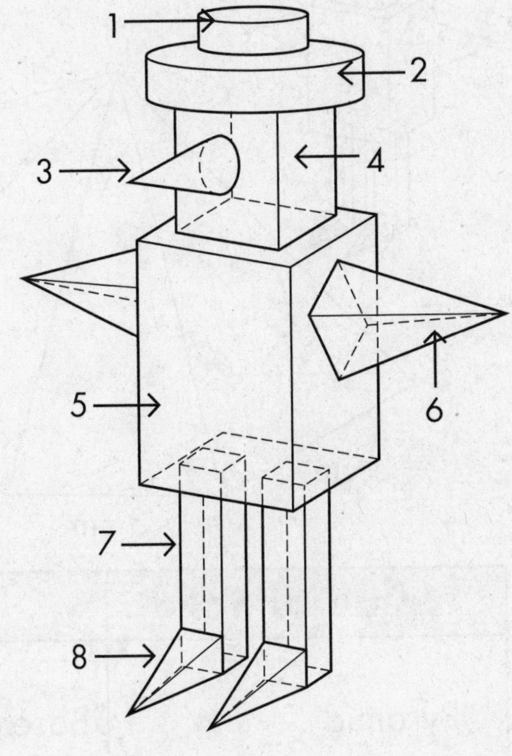

Mixed Review and Test Prep

2 Which fraction is equal to $\frac{1}{4} + \frac{1}{8}$?

A. $\frac{3}{8}$

B. $\frac{2}{8}$

C. $\frac{2}{12}$

D. $\frac{1}{6}$

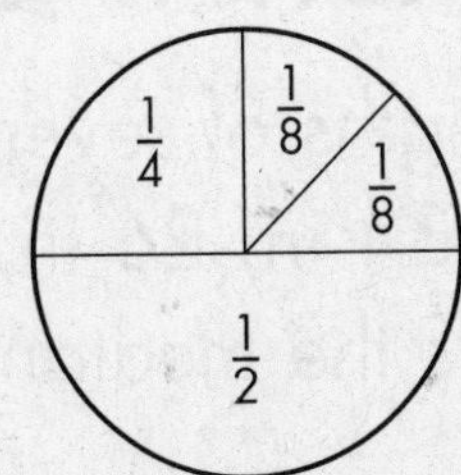

Name Date

Billy Bird's Wings

Family Connection

Students are making patterns and assembling the solids they need to build their model. As they do so, they record the dimensions of each solid and find its volume.

1. The pattern and pyramid for Billy Bird's wings are shown. Record the dimensions and the volume in the table.

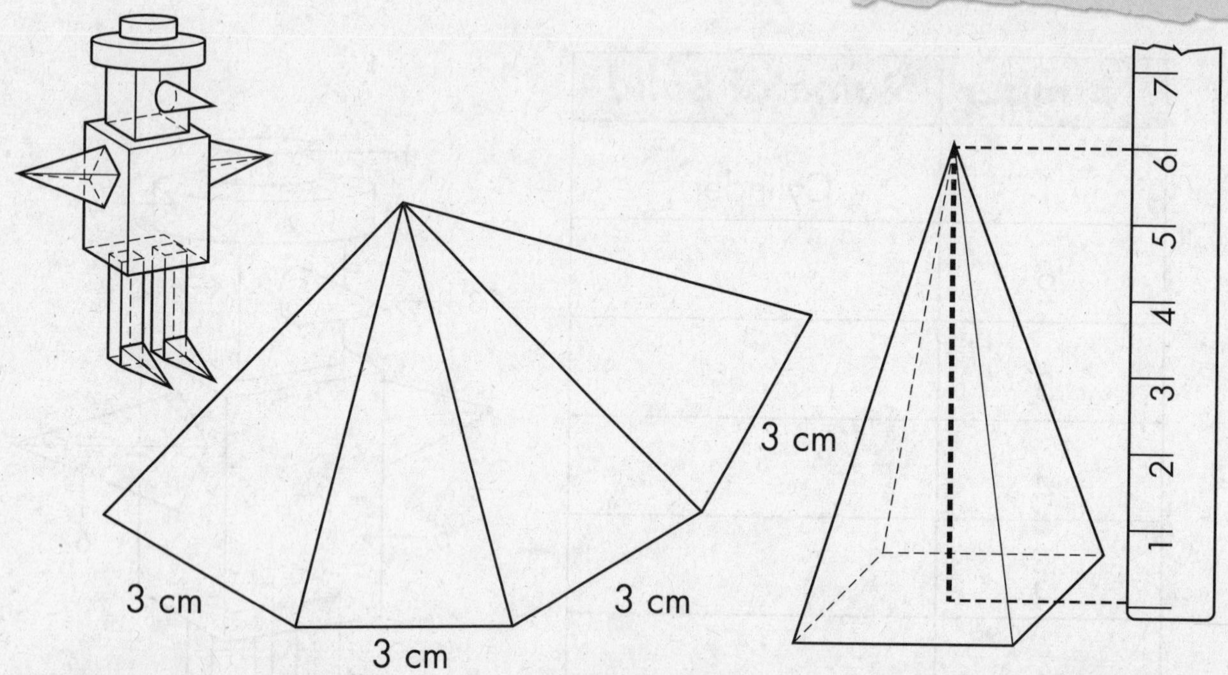

Name of Solid	Dimensions	Volume
Pyramid	Base: Height:	

Mixed Review and Test Prep

2. The lengths of seven garter snakes are: 28 in, 34 in, 26 in, 32 in, 32 in, 30 in, 27 in. What is the median length?

A. 28 in **B.** 30 in **C.** 32 in **D.** 34 in

 Use during Investigation 4 (Prisms and Pyramids, Cylinders and Cones), Sessions 7, 8, and 9.

Name Date

Containers and Cubes

Point It Out

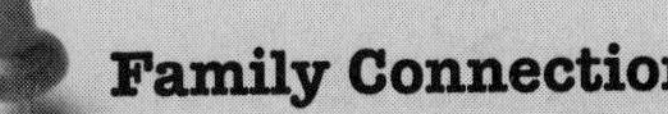

Family Connection

Each group completed their model and found its total volume. They then presented the model and their methods for finding volume to the rest of the class. Ask your child how his or her group found the volume of their model.

1 Draw an arrow to a shape the person could have been pointing to as he or she spoke.

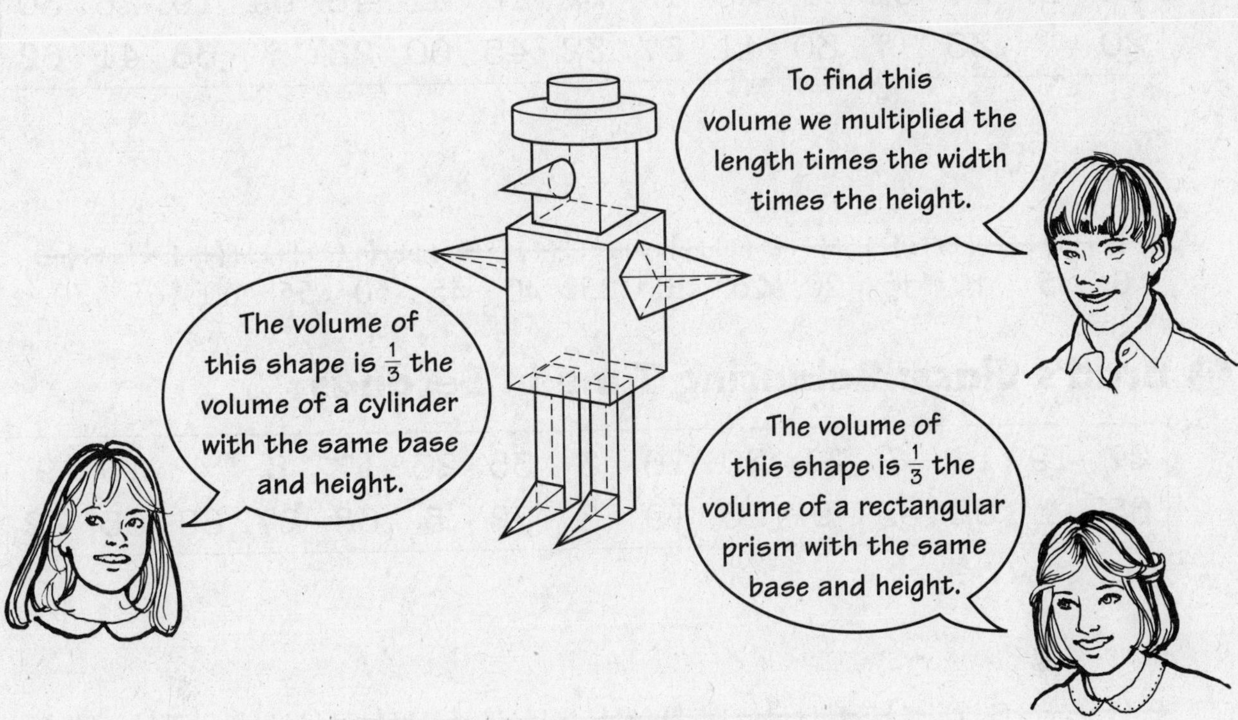

To find this volume we multiplied the length times the width times the height.
The volume of this shape is $\frac{1}{3}$ the volume of a cylinder with the same base and height.
The volume of this shape is $\frac{1}{3}$ the volume of a rectangular prism with the same base and height.

Mixed Review and Test Prep

2 Carlos shared 36 balloons among 4 friends. How many balloons did each person get?

A. 40 **B.** 12 **C.** 9 **D.** 6

3 Hannah can put 6 jars in a box. How many boxes does she need for 30 jars?

A. 5 **B.** 6 **C.** 36 **D.** 180

Name Date

Data: Kids, Cats, and Ads

Making Line Plots

Make a line plot for each data set.

Family Connection

Students have been collecting data about how long they can stand on one foot with their eyes closed. One way to display this type of data is with a line plot. An X is used for each time.

❶ Sally's Class: Balancing Time in Seconds

32	44	27	62	4	28	19	22	16	41	46	34	19	28	30
20	7	33	17	30	41	37	32	45	60	28	7	68	41	62

0 5 10 15 20 25 30 35 40 45 50 55 60 65 70

❷ Brad's Class: Balancing Time in Seconds

27	19	12	8	31	20	16	3	35	23	17	8	4	19	9
65	4	32	65	9	16	19	8	32	5	68	27	69	65	22

❸ What is the median time for each class? ______ Sally's ______ Brad's

❹ On another sheet of paper, write a statement comparing the two classes.

Interesting Tidbit

The word *data* is the plural of *datum*.

Mixed Review and Test Prep

❺ Which multiplication fact is related to $72 \div 9 = 8$?

A. $8 \times 9 = 72$ **B.** $72 \div 8 = 9$ **C.** $7 \times 10 = 70$ **D.** $80 \div 8 = 10$

Name Date

Data: Kids, Cats, and Ads

Comparing Data With Fractions

Study the two data sets.
Then complete the statements.

Family Connection
Students have learned that fractions are particularly useful when comparing data sets of different sizes. Considering the top or bottom quarters (or thirds) of two sets can be a good way to compare them.

Joel's Class: Balancing Time in Seconds

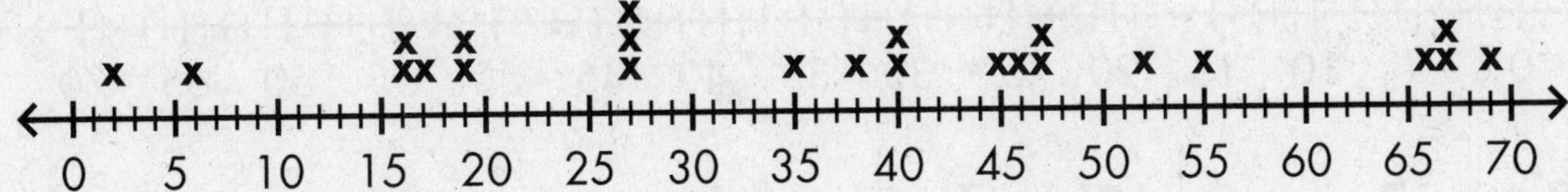

Tina's Class: Balancing Time in Seconds

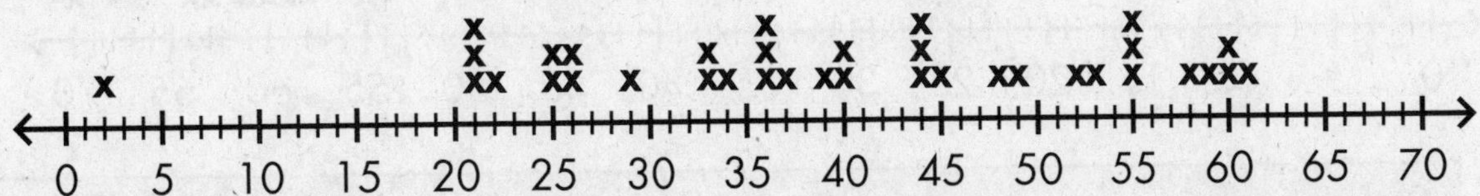

1. Half of Joel's class balanced more than ______ seconds.
2. Half of Tina's class balanced more than ______ seconds.
3. Two thirds of Joel's class balanced more than ______ seconds.
4. Two thirds of Tina's class balanced more than ______ seconds.
5. On another sheet of paper, write which class balances better. Give reasons for your opinion.

Mixed Review and Test Prep

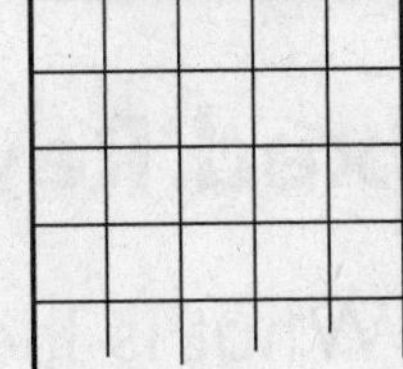

6. Arturo made an array with 100 cubes. His array had 5 columns. How many rows did it have?

A. 12 **B.** 20 **C.** 25 **D.** 500

Name Date

Data: Kids, Cats, and Ads

Comparing Data Many Ways

Study the two data sets.
Then complete the chart.

Family Connection

Students have been looking at many aspects of the data when comparing data sets. Encourage your child to support his or her conclusions with logical arguments based on data.

Girls: Balancing Time in Seconds

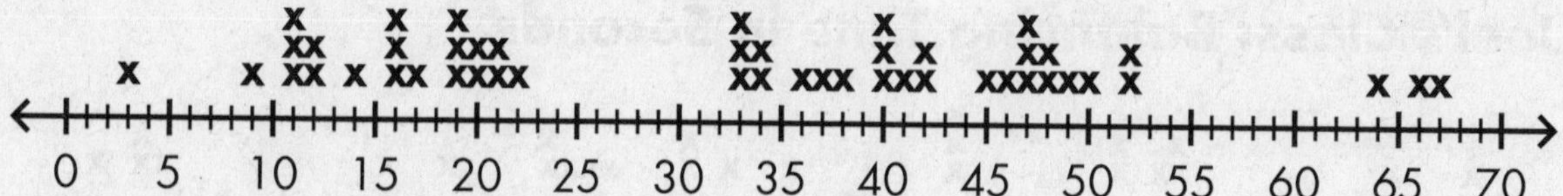

Boys: Balancing Time in Seconds

0 5 10 15 20 25 30 35 40 45 50 55 60 65 70

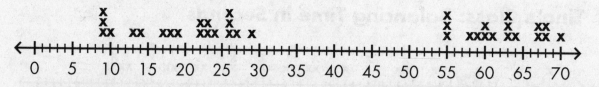

	What you are comparing?	Girls	Boys	Who's better?
1	median			
2	range			
3	highest value			
4	top $\frac{1}{2}$ above ? seconds			
5	top $\frac{1}{4}$ above ? seconds			

6. On another sheet of paper, explain which group balances better.

Mixed Review and Test Prep

7. What is the sum of 518 and 417?

A. 1045 **B.** 945 **C.** 935 **D.** 931

 Use after Investigation 1 (Balancing Act), Sessions 2 and 3.

Name Date

Volunteer Match

For these data sets, each person was asked how many hours he or she volunteered last year.

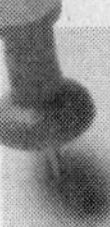

Family Connection

On this page, students apply their skills in analyzing data to guess the identities of different groups of volunteers. Talk with your child about these data sets, asking him or her to compare the data in several different ways.

Group A: Volunteer Hours Last Year

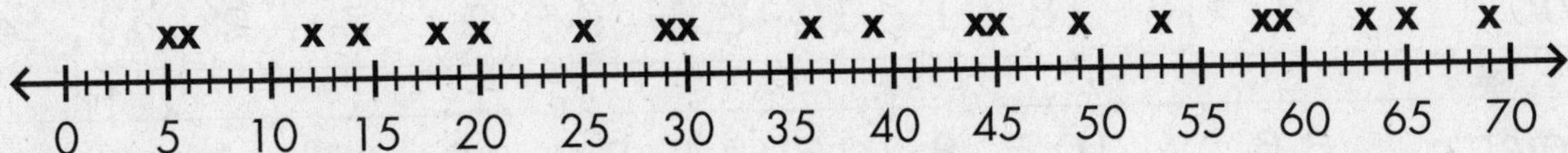

Group B: Volunteer Hours Last Year

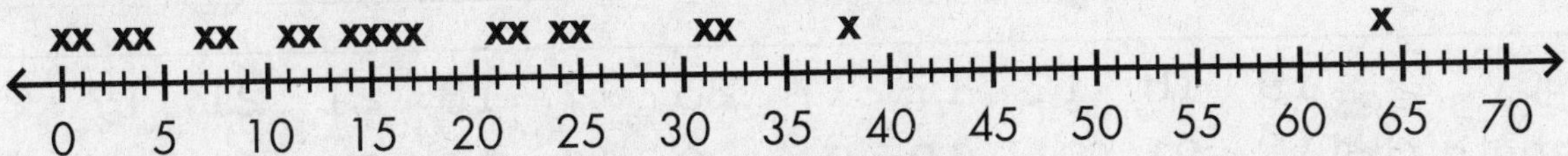

Group C: Volunteer Hours Last Year

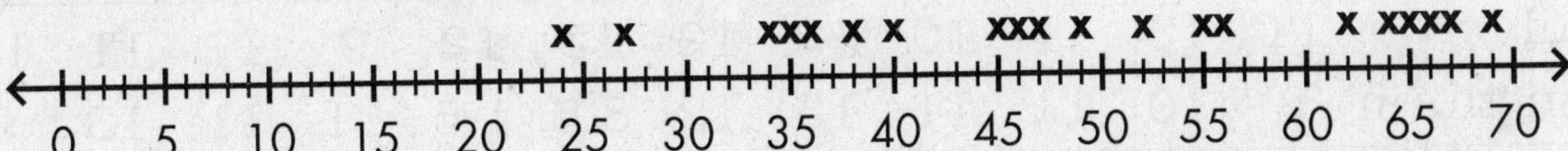

One set of data was collected from retired people, one set from teenagers, and one set from mothers of young children.

1. Match the groups to the data sets. Write the letter for each group.

   retired people _____ teenagers _____ mothers _____

2. On separate paper, explain your matches.

Mixed Review and Test Prep

3. Which cube building could have this silhouette?

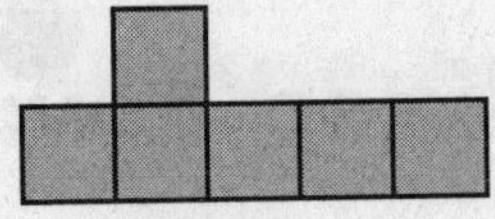

A.

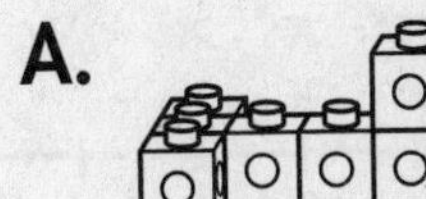

B.

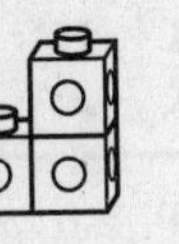

C.

D.

Name Date

Data: Kids, Cats, and Ads

Describing Cat Data

Family Connection

Students are using facts about 24 cats to practice analyzing data. **Questions you might ask your child:** "What are some ways you could organize these data?" "What is the range of each data set?"

Use the cat data to complete the statements.

Age	4	15	14	4	8	6	10	5	5	8	5	5
(yr)	2	16	18	1	12	3.5	3	1	3	2	11	4

Weight	8.5	7	10.5	8	15	14	8.5	10	18	11	9	16
(lb)	12	14.5	11	9	14.5	11	9	6.5	12	10	12	7

Body	19	16	17	17	17	23	17	18	21	21	17	24
Length (in)	17	21	21	18	21	20	15	14	24	21	21	18

Tail	11	13	11	10	12	12	13	12	9	11	11	12
Length (in)	9	10	11	11	13	12	8.5	1.5	11	11	13	9

1. A third of the cats weigh _____ pounds or less.
2. The one tail length very different from the rest is _____ inches.
3. The typical cat's tail is _____ inches long.
4. One quarter of the cats are more than _____ years old.
5. More than half the cats are _______________________.

Mixed Review and Test Prep

6. What is the median number of cavities?

A. 0 **C.** 2

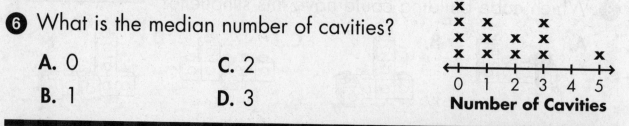

B. 1 **D.** 3

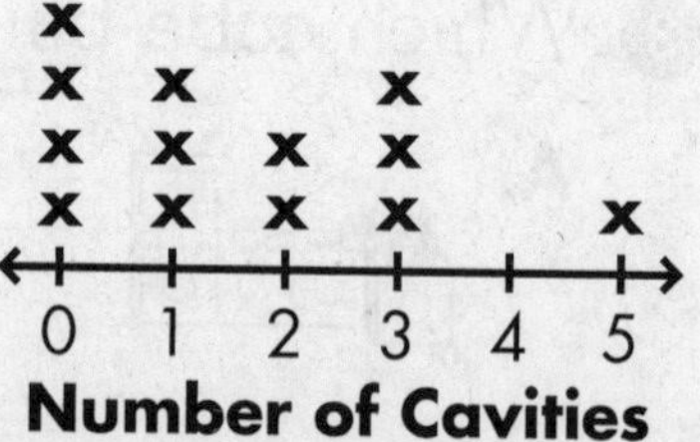

Name Date

Data: Kids, Cats, and Ads

Exploring Associations

Family Connection
Students have been using data about cats to search for associated characteristics. For example, do longer cats weigh more? Talk with your child about which characteristics might logically go together.

1 Finish the line plot to see if cat weight is related to gender. Use **M** for a male cat and **F** for a female cat.

Gender	F	F	F	F	M	F	F	M	M	F	F	M
Weight (lb)	8.5	7	10.5	8	15	14	8.5	10	18	11	9	16

Gender	M	F	M	M	M	F	F	M	M	M	M	F
Weight (lb)	12	14.5	11	9	14.5	11	9	6.5	12	10	12	7

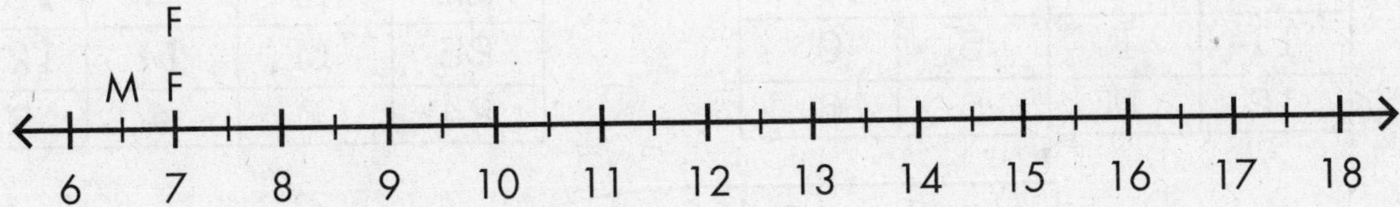

2 Is cat weight related to gender? Explain your answer.

____

____

____

Mixed Review and Test Prep

3 Which statement is true?

A. $\frac{1}{2} = \frac{1}{4}$ **B.** $\frac{1}{8} = \frac{2}{4}$ **C.** $\frac{1}{2} = \frac{2}{8}$ **D.** $\frac{1}{4} = \frac{2}{8}$

Name Date

Data: Kids, Cats, and Ads

Make a Venn Diagram

Family Connection
In the computer program **Tabletop, Sr.,** students can use Venn diagrams like this one to show the intersections of sets of data.

1 Write the number for each cat in the correct section of the Venn diagram. A few have been done for you.

Cat	Sex	Age	Weight
1	F	4	8.5
2	F	15	7
3	F	14	10.5
4	F	4	8
5	M	8	15
6	F	6	14
7	F	10	8.5
8	M	5	10
9	M	5	18
10	F	8	11
11	F	5	9
12	M	5	16

Cat	Sex	Age	Weight
13	M	2	12
14	F	16	14.5
15	M	18	11
16	M	1	9
17	M	12	14.5
18	F	3.5	11
19	F	3	9
20	M	1	6.5
21	M	3	12
22	M	2	10
23	M	11	12
24	F	4	7

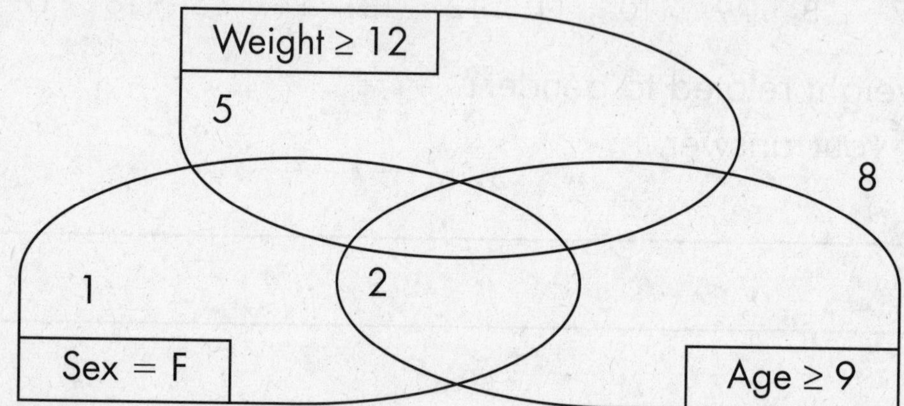

Mixed Review and Test Prep

2 Solve 42 × 8.

A. 3216 **B.** 1632 **C.** 336 **D.** 316

Name Date

Data: Kids, Cats, and Ads

Reporting Survey Results

Mark the fraction on the data strip. Then ring the closest familiar fraction on the fraction strip.

Family Connection

Students have used different ways to report the results of surveys: familiar fractions, decimals, and percents. To change a fraction to a decimal, divide the top number by the bottom number. To change a decimal to a percent, multiply by 100.

1. 6 out of 17 people like science fiction movies.

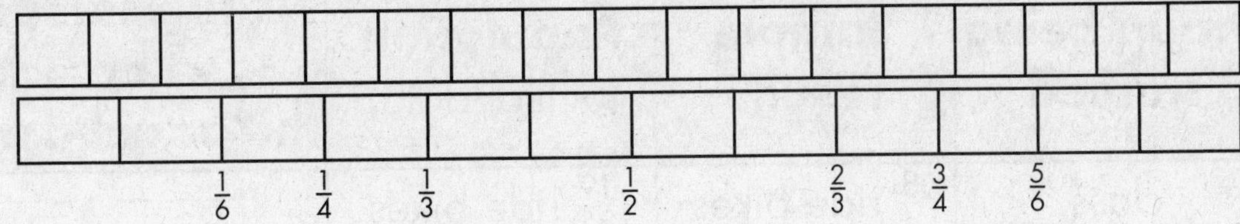

2. 23 out of 28 people use the neighborhood park.

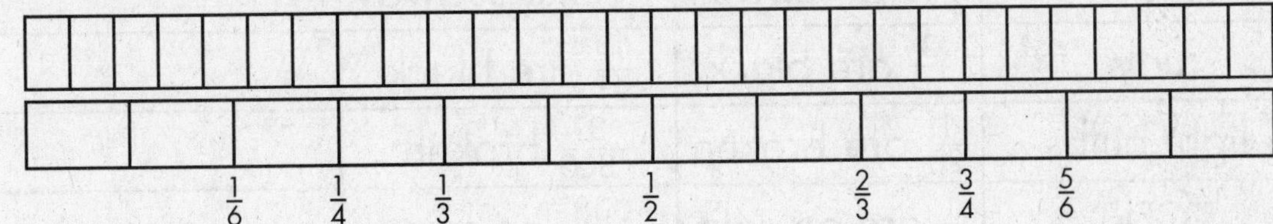

Change each fraction to a two-place decimal and then to a percent.

3. $\frac{6}{17}$ ________________

4. $\frac{23}{28}$ ________________

Mixed Review and Test Prep

5. What is the missing number in the table?

Dimes	1	2	5	10	20
Nickels	2	4	10		40

A. 5

B. 12

C. 15

D. 20

Name Date

Data: Kids, Cats, and Ads

Samples and Populations

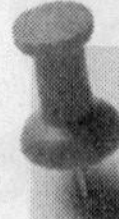

Family Connection

Students have been learning how samples are used to represent a larger group. The entire group being studied is called the "population." The population need not be people, however. It can be any type of item.

Write **>** (greater than), **<** (less than), or = to compare the sample results with the actual data.

	Group being studied	Sample results	Population (actual data)	Is the sample >, <, or = to the actual data?
1	class	$\frac{3}{4}$ ride bikes	$\frac{19}{25}$ ride bikes	
2	class	$\frac{1}{4}$ like figs	$\frac{7}{23}$ like figs	
3	class	$\frac{1}{2}$ take subway	$\frac{14}{31}$ take subway	
4	cats	$\frac{3}{10}$ are black	$\frac{12}{41}$ are black	
5	light bulbs	$\frac{1}{20}$ are broken	$\frac{37}{800}$ broken	
6	CDs	$\frac{1}{3}$ are on sale	$\frac{38}{117}$ on sale	
7	chickens	$\frac{4}{5}$ lay eggs	$\frac{97}{120}$ lay eggs	
8	customers	$\frac{1}{8}$ pay cash	$\frac{41}{350}$ pay cash	

9. Use another sheet of paper. Choose one problem and explain how you made your comparison.

Mixed Review and Test Prep

10. Which number sentence shows the following story?
Three people go out and one person returns home. Then there are four people at home.

A. $3 + 1 - 4 = ?$ **C.** $? + 3 - 1 = 4$

B. $3 + ? = 4$ **D.** $? - 3 + 1 = 4$

Name Date

Data: Kids, Cats, and Ads

How Close Is the Sample?

Family Connection
Students continue comparing samples with actual class data. In this activity, they approximate actual data to compare them with the samples.

A sample of 4 students was taken for each topic. Then the actual class data were found. Round the class data to the nearest fourth to compare them with the sample.

	Survey Topic	Sample	Class Data (actual)	Class Data (nearest fourth)
1	Have no sisters	$\frac{1}{2}$	$\frac{6}{34}$	
2	Like popcorn	$\frac{3}{4}$	$\frac{24}{26}$	
3	Can speak Spanish	$\frac{1}{2}$	$\frac{19}{26}$	
4	Went to the museum	$\frac{1}{4}$	$\frac{15}{27}$	
5	Have own room	$\frac{3}{4}$	$\frac{7}{29}$	
6	Enjoy ice skating	$\frac{1}{2}$	$\frac{16}{31}$	

7. Which sample was most like the class data? Explain your answer on another sheet of paper.

Mixed Review and Test Prep

8. Cora recorded the number of cans her family recycled each week. What does her graph show?

30	30	30	30
31	31		
32			
33	33	33	33

A. Most weeks the family recycles more than 32 cans.

B. The family recycles from 30 to 33 cans each week.

C. Next week the family will recycle 32 cans.

D. The most cans the family will ever recycle in a week is 33.

Name Date

Using Percents

Write the fraction and percent for each answer.

Family Connection

Students are learning to use percents as a way of reporting survey data. A percent is based on a ratio to 100: 1 out of 2 is the same ratio as 50 out of 100, so $\frac{1}{2}$ = 50%. Have your child tell you a couple of other examples.

	Answer	Total in Class	Fraction	Percent
1	yes: 15	25		
2	no: 10	25		
3	yes: 7	20		
4	no: 13	20		
5	yes: 10	30		
6	sometimes: 5	30		
7	no: 15	30		

Mixed Review and Test Prep

8. What are the coordinates of the circle?

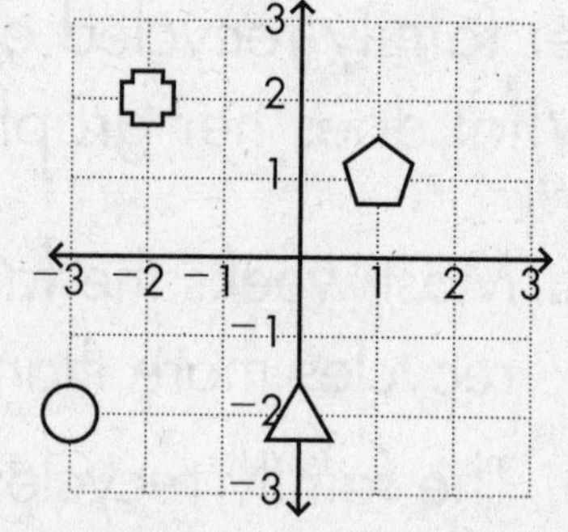

A. (3, 2) **C.** (−3, −2)

B. (−4, −2) **D.** (−2, −3)

Name Date

Data: Kids, Cats, and Ads

Fractions of Pages

What fraction of each page is gray?

Family Connection

Students have been finding the fraction of a newspaper page used for ads. They have used folding and other methods to make their estimates.

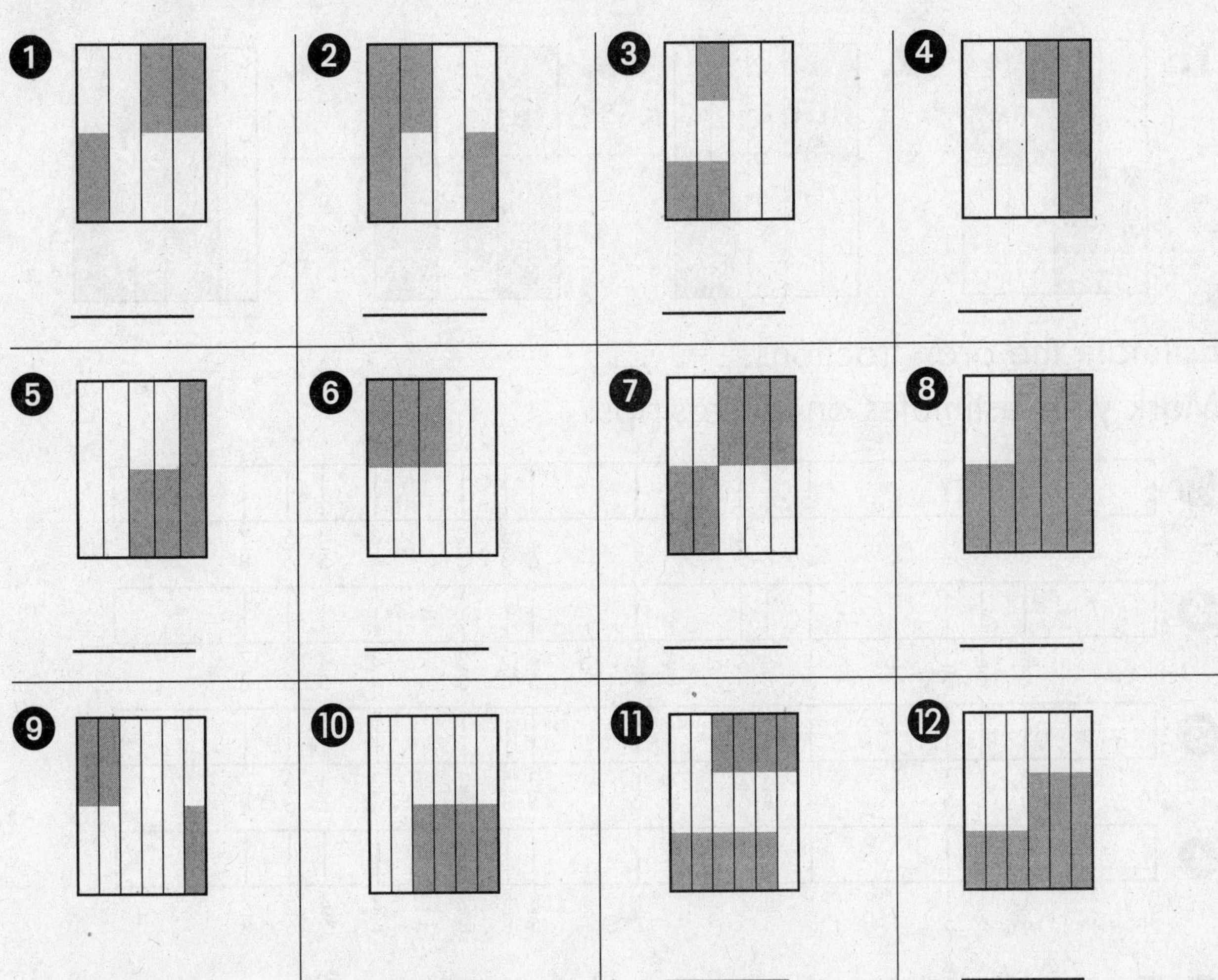

Mixed Review and Test Prep

13 Jason needs 4 wheels to make a model truck. He has 22 wheels. How many models can he make?

A. 88 **C.** 5

B. 18 **D.** 4

Name Date

Data: Kids, Cats, and Ads

Marking Fractions on Strips

A fraction of each page is shaded gray.

Family Connection
Students have estimated the fraction of a newspaper page used for ads and marked their estimates on strips. This activity relates area and length.

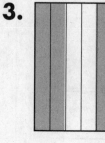

1. 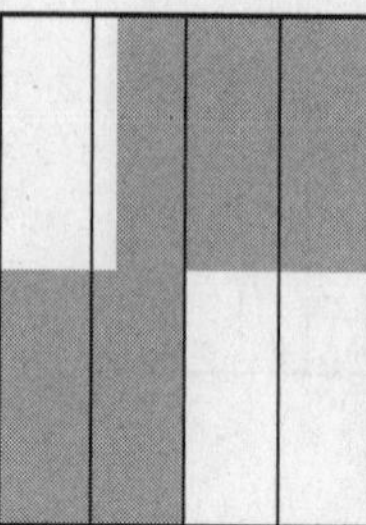 **2.** 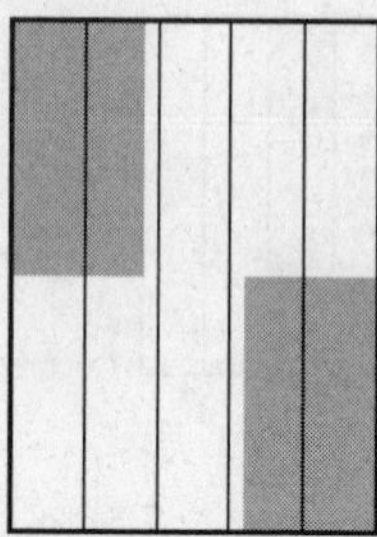 **3.**  **4.** 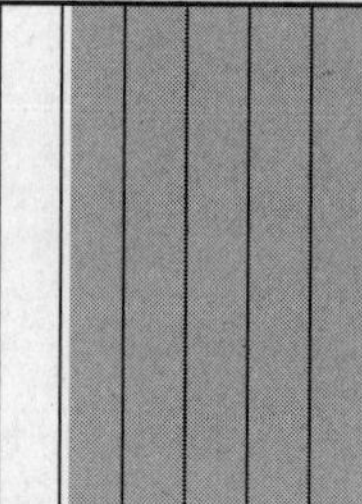

Estimate the gray fractions.
Mark your estimates on these strips.

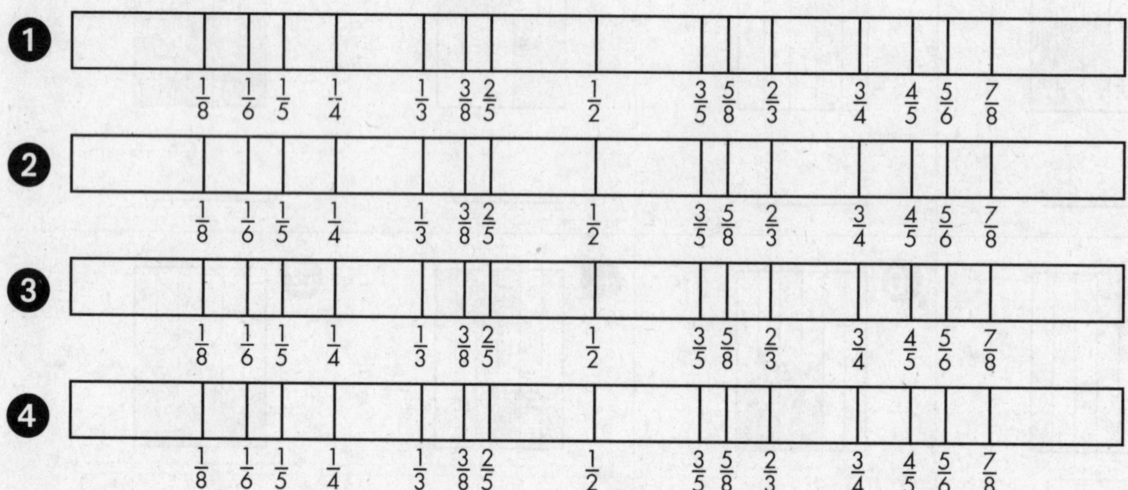

5. On another sheet of paper, explain the strategies you used to find the fractions.

Mixed Review and Test Prep

6. Suppose you have these coins.
What coin do you need to make $1?

A. a quarter **C.** a nickel

B. a dime **D.** a penny

Name Date

Data: Kids, Cats, and Ads

Familiar Fractions for Length

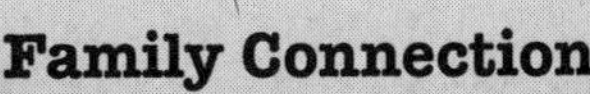

Family Connection

Students have used folding and other strategies to estimate the colored part of a long strip. Here they choose the closest familiar fraction to show a shaded length.

Ring the closest familiar fraction to show the shaded length.

1

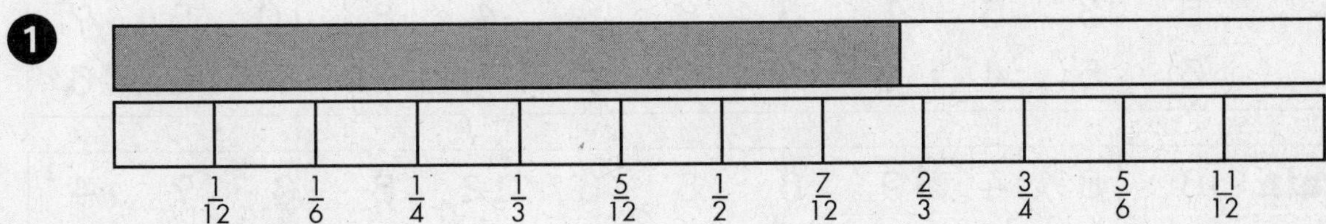

2

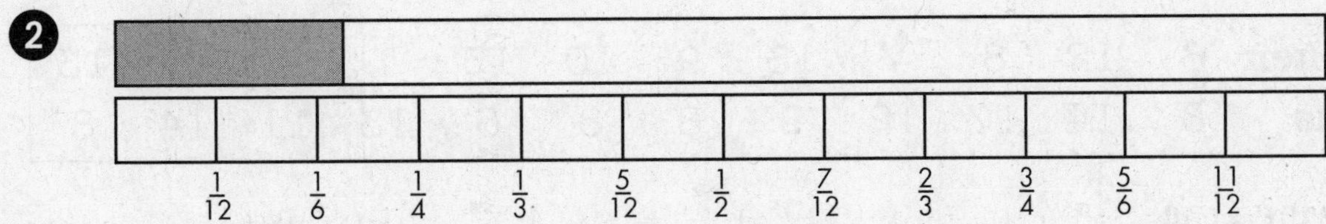

3

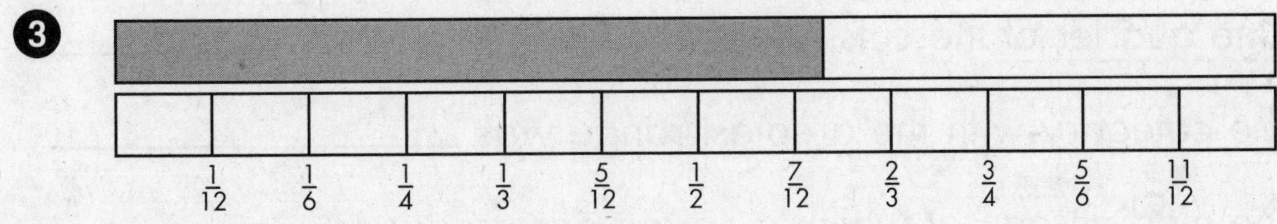

4

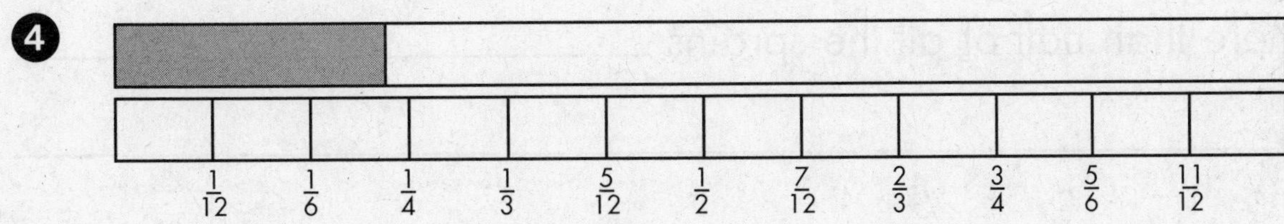

Mixed Review and Test Prep

5 Use the related problem set to find $246 - 73$.

A. 133

B. 146

C. 170

D. 173

$250 - 70 =$
$246 - 70 =$
$73 + 27 =$
$246 - 73 =$

Name Date

Data: Kids, Cats, and Ads

Comparing Data Sets

The charts show the ages at which different types of injuries first occurred. Use the data to complete the statements.

Family Connection
Students have been applying their skills in data analysis in a project about playground safety. This page shows one type of data analysis your child will be doing.

Cut	5	3	3	1	6	6	8	4	8	10	5	7
	3	5	4	4	2	6	11	5	3	5	4	6

Sprain	6	8	4	9	6	8	6	12	5	8	7	4
	8	7	5	9	6	7	5	9	11	7	8	5

Broken	6	12	8	7	13	9	10	15	7	10	9	13
Bone	8	14	17	12	9	8	8	6	13	11	14	8

1. Half of the people with a broken bone were older than _____.
2. One quarter of the cuts happened before a person was _____.
3. The category with the greatest range was ____________.
4. The median age at which a sprain occurred was _____.
5. More than half of all the sprains ______________________

____

Mixed Review and Test Prep

6. What does this shape look like from the front?

A. 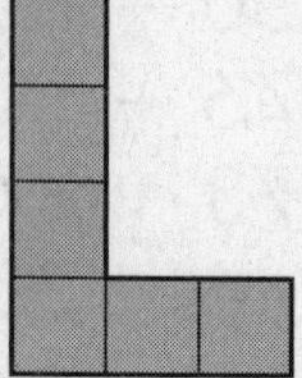 B. 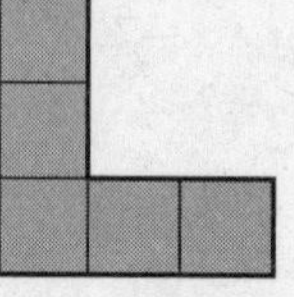 C. 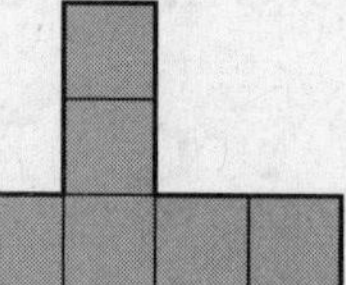 D. 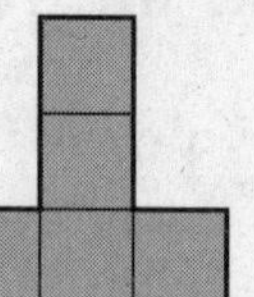

Name Date

Comparing Line Plots

Study the two data sets.
Then complete the statements.

Family Connection

Students have been taking a survey of schoolmates about playground injuries. Once the data are collected, your child might use line plots like these to analyze them.

Girls: Age at time of first injury

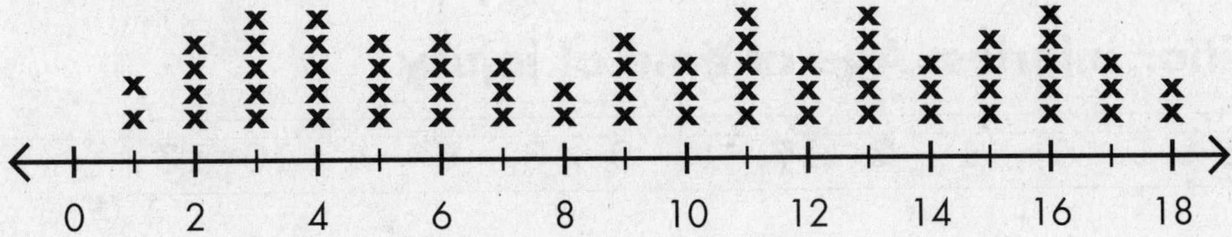

Boys: Age at time of first injury

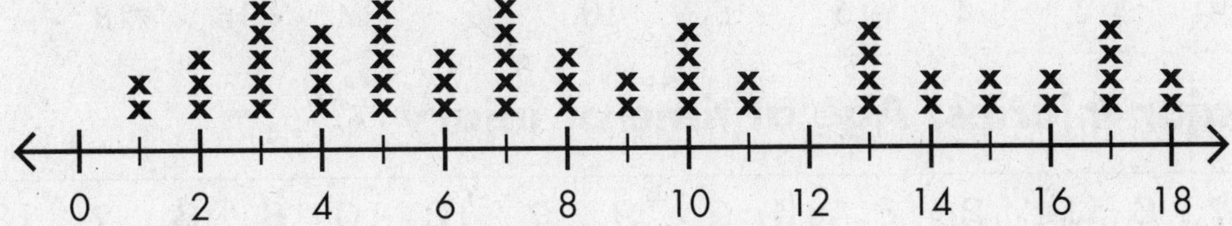

1. Half of the girls were younger than _____ years old.
2. Half of the boys were younger than _____ years old.
3. Two thirds of the girls were younger than _____ years old.
4. Two thirds of the boys were younger than _____ years old.

Mixed Review and Test Prep

5. In Andy's class, 13 out of 25 students have ice skates. Which of these familiar fractions is closest to $\frac{13}{25}$?

A. $\frac{3}{4}$ **C.** $\frac{1}{2}$

B. $\frac{2}{3}$ **D.** $\frac{1}{4}$

Name Date

Making Line Plots

Finish the line plots to see if the seriousness of an injury is related to age.

Family Connection

Students have been using the data from their injury survey to look for related variables; for example, they might investigate if injuries on the swings are associated with age. Comparing line plots is one way to look for associations between variables.

1 Minor injuries: Age at time of injury

3	1	7	4	2	17	1	9	3	5	4	10	13

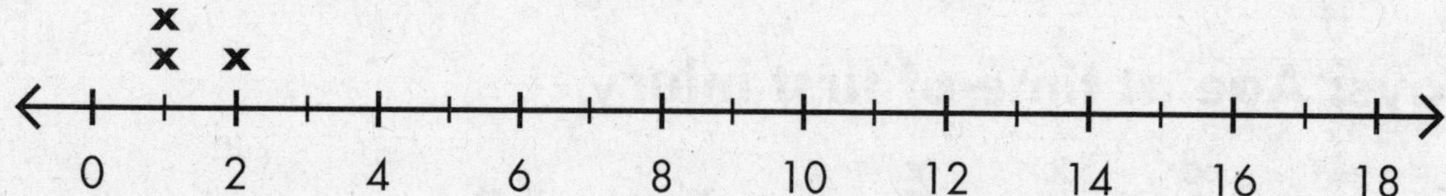

2 Major injuries: Age at time of injury

17	6	14	2	8	13	1	9	7	12	10	8	6	7	12

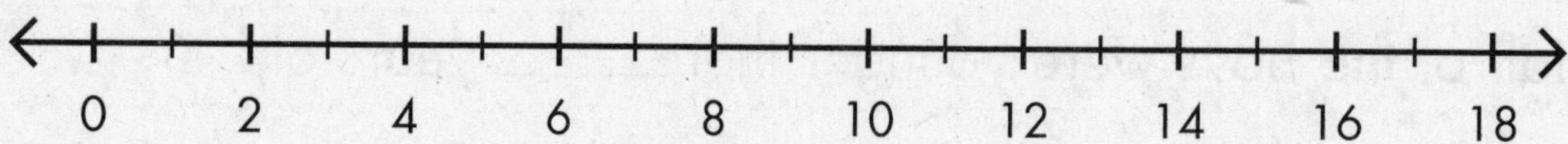

3 On another sheet of paper, compare the two data sets. Include the medians in your answer.

Mixed Review and Test Prep

4 Where is the triangle?

A. (1, 1) **C.** (3, 2)

B. (3, 1) **D.** (4, 3)

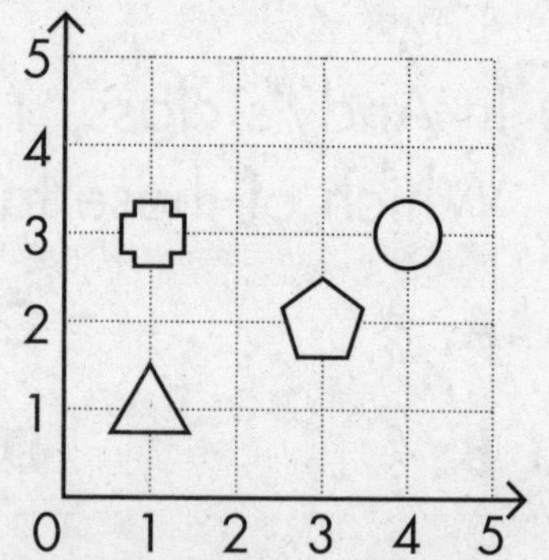

Name Date

Data: Kids, Cats, and Ads

Making Bar Graphs

Family Connection

Students have used bar graphs to analyze their playground injury data. Pairs of bar graphs such as these can point out associations between variables.

Make two graphs for each table.
Label the bars.

	Grade 1	Grade 3	Grade 5
Injuries at school	9	19	21
Injuries away from school	14	17	16

1. 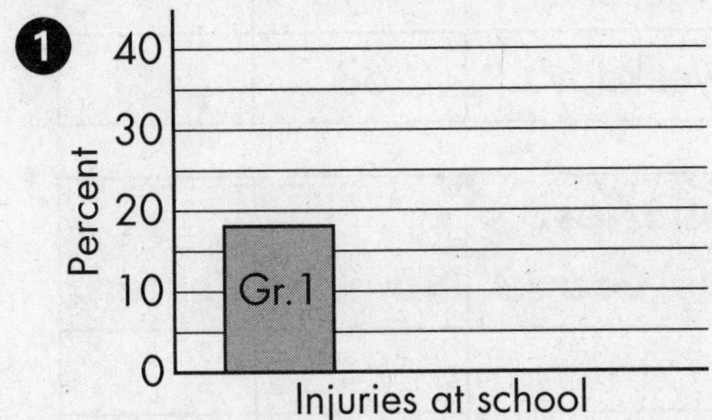

2. 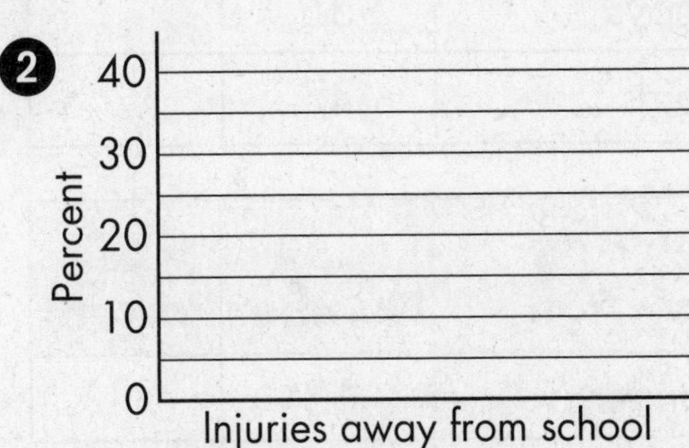

	A. Emergency	B. Serious	C. Minor	D. No injury
Under 5 years	12	17	28	9
5 and older	23	13	37	11

3. 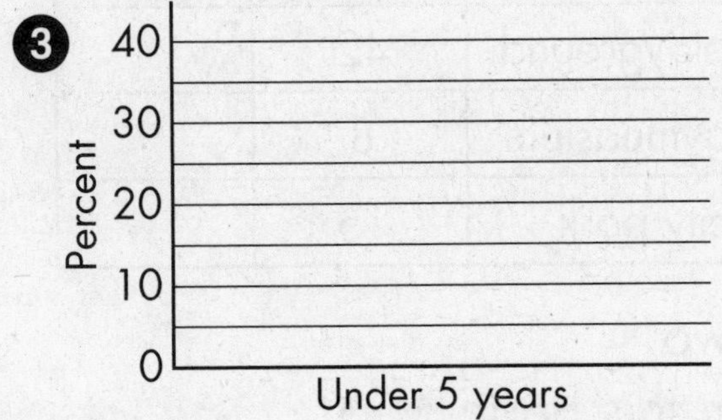

4. 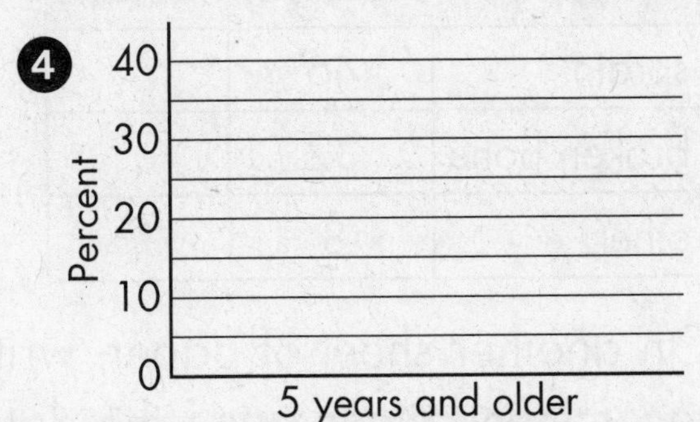

Mixed Review and Test Prep

5. Which fraction is greater than $\frac{5}{6}$?

A. $\frac{1}{2}$ **B.** $\frac{2}{3}$ **C.** $\frac{3}{4}$ **D.** $\frac{7}{8}$

Name Date

Using Percents to Report Results

Complete each chart by writing the percents. You will need to find the total in the middle column first.

Family Connection
Students have been using percents to analyze and report their playground injury data. Ask your child what conclusions were reached about safety issues in the school playground.

1

Injuries by Gender	Number	Percent
boys	35	
girls	47	

2

Injuries by Time	Number	Percent
weekend	19	
weekday	63	

3

Injuries by Age	Number	Percent
under 5	13	
5 to 10	28	
over 10	36	

4

Injuries by Grade	Number	Percent
1	24	
3	46	
5	18	

5

Injuries by Type	Number	Percent
sprain	46	
broken bone	32	
other	8	

6

Injuries by Location	Number	Percent
playground	42	
gymnasium	8	
city park	15	

7 On another sheet of paper, write two recommendations using the data on this page.

Mixed Review and Test Prep

8 Which is the next multiple of 45?
45, 90, 135, 180, 225, 270, 315, _____

A. 360 **B.** 350 **C.** 345 **D.** 305